Primary Care and Home Care Scenarios 1990-2005

Primary Health Care Scenario Committee
Chairman: Prof. E. Schadé

Primary Health Care Research Team:
Dr. H.J. Wennink, S.E. Kooiker, W.G.W. Boerma, Dr. D.H. de Bakker, Dr. P.P. Groenewegen
Netherlands Institute of Primary Health Care

Primary Care and Home Care Scenarios 1990 - 2005

Scenario report commissioned by the
Steering Committee on Future Health Scenarios

1993
Springer-Science+Business Media, B.V.

Distributors

for the United States and Canada: Kluwer Academic Publishers,
P.O. Box 358, Accord Station, Hingham, MA 02018-0358, USA
for all other countries: Kluwer Academic Publishers Group,
Distribution Center, P.O. Box 322, 3300 AH Dordrecht, The Netherlands

Steering Committee
on Future Health Scenarios
P.O. Box 5406
2280 HK Rijswijk
The Netherlands
Telephone (31-70) 3407205

Abbreviated version of the Dutch original `Toekomstscenario's voor eerstelijnszorg en thuiszorg'
by Jonathan Phillips.

ISBN 978-0-7923-2658-8   ISBN 978-94-011-0810-2 (eBook)
DOI 10.1007/978-94-011-0810-2

Contents

Foreword

CARE AT HOME - HOME CARE

Health care in the Netherlands looks to be a well structured system. Supplementing the vital level of self-care and informal care are four levels of professional care: the public health service (known in the Netherlands as basic health care) is mainly concerned with preventive work aimed at the population at large; individuals with problems can contact their general practitioner or other primary care provider, who can - depending on the problem - refer them to specialists in the cure-oriented and hospital-centred secondary sector; where necessary, patients can then be referred on to the institutions of the tertiary sector with their role in mainly long-term care.

On paper this pyramidal structure appears to work well; in practice, and in particular where complex forms of care are involved, the boundaries become blurred. Medical advances and social and economic developments may delay death to ever greater ages, but disease is not defeated; and since the risk of developing chronic conditions rises with age, more and more people become incapacitated and those who do remain so for longer. This leads to a growing demand for care and compels us to reconsider patterns of provision. The need for such reconsideration is reinforced by users' changing needs and aspirations, as patients increasingly wish to be nursed and cared for in their own surroundings if at all possible. Technological advances mean that wish can often be accommodated. Home care, in other words, is a response to quantitative and qualitative changes in the demand for care.

In complex cases the sharp divisions between the primary, secondary and tertiary sectors are no longer useful; it is probably more helpful to think in terms of care functions, ignoring in the first instance the matter of the patient's location while receiving care. Cutting across the traditional sectoral boundaries we can distinguish medical, nursing, rehabilitation and support functions.

What is needed is a reconsideration of the tasks and activities both of the different sectors and of professional practitioners who have hitherto functioned safely within their own sectoral teams. Regulatory changes, coupled with a policy of devolving responsibilities to institutions and practitioners, have opened the way to experiment. In recent years local initiatives have produced large numbers of experimental home care projects in the Netherlands; they are supported by public policy and grants from the health insurers. While this is to be applauded the choice of target groups is questionable, with some groups perhaps receiving rather too much attention and others too little. Relatively generous provision for certain categories of patient who for medical or social reasons are at the focus of interest may distract attention somewhat from groups on the boundary between health and social care: it is regrettable that interest in and provision for the mentally handicapped, chronic mental patients, the homeless, alcoholics and drug addicts falls short of that devoted to - for example - patients with respiratory disease, arthritis or cancer.

Changes in society are making people more willing to assert their rights across the board, in health care as elsewhere; patients rightly demand a greater say in their treatment and greater accountability on the part of professional practitioners, and this has implications for the structure and functioning of health care. The phenomenon is less to the fore in the case of short-term episodes and urgent cases than in that of treatment and support for patients with chronic conditions. There is a growing need for a concept of care that puts greater stress than in the past on individually tailored packages.

The shift in society towards emphasis on the individual may not help the care of chronic patients. Informal care is not always available; family, friends and others are not always willing to take on a caring role. Families are getting smaller and, owing partly to changing household structures, increasing numbers of old people live alone. The growing mobility we have seen since the early 1960s continues to reduce the number of three-generation households with their inbuilt capacity for informal care. Care at home generally means care by the female partner, at a time when women are increasingly likely to have a job or other responsibilities outside the home. The scope for expanding informal care within the family is thus limited. To what extent can society expect family and friends to step in where the professionals cannot offer appropriate care? Choices will have to be made. It may be that such trends as those outlined will make our health care system more plural in nature but perhaps also less user-friendly; new concepts of care and local initiatives are not necessarily a satisfactory replacement for the tidy tiered structure of a few years ago.

The purpose of the scenario study on primary and home care to which this report relates was to develop models which could help guide the debate on the future organization of ambulatory care. The scenarios are based on an analysis of social developments, current patterns of provision and three component studies, namely a trend study, a care study and an organizational study. The trend study charts the use of primary and outpatient care in the near future on the basis of trends in the recent past; the care study is concerned mainly with complex home care, formulating requirements for such care on the basis of various deficits in patients' functioning; and the organizational study analyses the strengths and weaknesses of the structure of health care as it is now, looking also at examples from other countries and charting the various care-innovation projects in the Netherlands.

Each scenario for primary and home care has advantages and drawbacks, strong and weak points. In this field of ambulatory care, with its varied pattern of demand and differentiated structure of provision, the scenario committee has refrained from choosing between them; we do however suggest assessment criteria and models, on the basis partly of recent developments in care and of declared government policy.

We offer this report to all concerned as a starting point for debate and a framework for local initiative. Since the purpose of this study would be defeated if it were used to justify hasty choices, we urge that small-scale experiments be conducted. It is a fundamental requirement that proposals for structural reform derive from a clear picture of the demand and need for care or of identified problems. Accurate patient-related information and careful examination of local and regional options are essential. This does justice to the concept of individualized care. We therefore hope that patients' organizations in particular will study the scenarios we have compiled.

Professor E Schadé
Chair, Scenario Committee on Primary Care

June 1991

Scenario Committee on Primary Care and Home Care

Professor F. Vorst, Emeritus Professor of Epidemiology,
Limburg State University; *Chair* (September 1988 - January 1990).
Professor E. Schadé, Professor of General Practice,
University of Amsterdam; *Chair* (From April 1990).
M. Andela, Consumer Union, The Hague.
Dr F.N.M. Bierens, General practitioner, Wehl.
Dr K.L.J. Hoefnagels, Ophthalmologist, Tilburg.
P.H. Jonkergouw, Director, Community Nursing Association,
Breda.
Dr R. Naaborg, National Public Health Council, Zoetermeer.
Professor A.J.P. Schrijvers, Professor of General Health Care,
Utrecht State University.
J.M. Timmermans, Social and Cultural Planning Office, Rijswijk.

The meetings were attended by Dr K. Schaapveld (September 1988
- June 1989) and Dr R.W. Haneveld (August 1989 onwards), acting
as project coordinators on the STG secretariat's behalf.

Research Team
Dr H.J. Wennink
S.E. Kooiker
W.G.W. Boerma
Dr D.H. de Bakker
Dr P.P. Groenewegen
Netherlands institute of primary health care (NIVEL), Utrecht

Summary

Introduction
This study is concerned with primary care and home care; the scenarios compiled relate to the future organization of this area of health care. Our focus was deliberately not limited to the primary sector as presently constituted, rather being widened to include *care provided to people living at home, together with care that could be provided, given the current state of knowledge and the technology, treatments and supervision needed, without admission to hospital.* This broader definition thus encompasses both today's primary care, outpatient specialist care and care provided from nursing and homes for the elderly to patients living in their own home.

It is essential to abstract from the existing tiered structure in this way, since scenarios for the future organization of home care will not necessarily retain the traditional divisions. This point will become all the more relevant when as a result of the reform of care insurance a basic scheme is introduced in which entitlements are defined in terms of functions rather than of provider categories. This does not mean that the scenarios generated within this project are purely a product of the imagination. Their empirical foundations comprise four parts:
- a description of the care currently available to people living independently in their own homes;
- an analysis of likely trends in care consumption if current policies continue;
- a study of the kinds of provision needed to care for patients with complex health problems living at home, and the circumstances under which this can be achieved;
- an analysis of the current care system and what will need to be changed within it to arrive at alternative organizational scenarios, supplemented with an analysis of innovative projects and foreign models.

These studies culminate in four scenarios for the organization of care for people living at home.

The main findings of the exercise are as follows.

1. Developments in society, demographic change and the changing relationship between ambulatory and institutional care make it both desirable and necessary that more care be provided at home, including in complex cases.

2. The aging of the population has implications notably for the utilization of home help and to a lesser extent community nursing. In other categories of provision the increase in consumption resulting from population aging is expected to run at around one per cent per year.

3. If past trends in the consumption of care are projected into the future in combination with demographic trends, then the expected increase in consumption is smaller in all categories than would be forecast on the basis of demography alone. This is because the expected rise in the educational level of large sections of the population and the expected improvement in people's perceptions of their own health will reduce the increase in care consumption.

4. All estimates of future care consumption show a large increase in use of care for the very elderly; this has implications for the intensity of care needs.

5. Home care for people who are at present often treated intramurally will require the deployment of a greater range of care functions and in greater amounts than is now customary; home care for patients with complex health problems is however possible.

6. A major precondition for complex home care is that informal care must be available. It is also important that the various care functions be properly coordinated through to the point of delivery. There needs to be rapid and flexible access to aids and appliances.

7. These conditions are not met in the present system of health care. Our scenarios for the future organization of primary and home care suggest solutions for the problems that exist. A requirement observed in developing the organizational scenarios was that they should retain the good points of today's primary sector as regards simplicity of organization and the nature of the care provided. The scenarios must be able to deliver simple everyday care as well as with complex or intensive care.

The implications for the future pattern of provision are as follows.

8. Coherent care systems are needed encompassing primary care, social services, specialist outpatient care, voluntary work, facilities for temporary admissions (respite care) and daycare.

9. This is given organizational shape in four scenarios:
   - the extramural network (no central control, retention of the tiered structure);
   - the extramural centre (central control, retention of the tiered structure);
   - the transmural network (central control, dismantling of the tiered structure);
   - deconstruction (no central control, dismantling of the tiered structure).

10. These scenarios are not mutually exclusive but could develop alongside one another. As plans for the reform of care insurance are implemented the interplay between providers and insurers will have a major influence on determining which models are realized where.

We now look in more detail at these findings. We begin by sketching the historical and social context of health care, and in particular that part which can be designated home care. We then outline the results of our background studies, going on finally to describe the four organizational scenarios and to assess them in the light of a number of criteria.

The historical and social context

Various social developments have combined to produce a situation in which the interest of both policy-makers and health professionals is focused on home care.

Over the long term the emphasis in care has swung between home and institutions. Before the modern hospital developed home care was the norm and care in institutions - almshouses, hospices - the exception, used mainly (and out of necessity) by the poor. Since the start of the twentieth century, however, processes of professionalization and differentiation among medical practitioners, technological advances and new thinking on treatment and care have concentrated care within the walls of hospitals; developments since the Second World War particularly have made the hospital the domain of the specialist. GPs feared that they would be left with only a residual role: as providers of non-specialized care with no specific training of their own, they seemed at risk of losing their sphere of activity and with it their identity.

Since the 1970s similar processes of professionalization and differentiation, technological advances and new thinking have helped to swing the pendulum back towards home care. This time the process was accelerated by the rapid growth in the cost of health care and by the availability of instruments for the control of planning and construction in the intramural sector. The number of hospital admissions has fallen, as has patients' average length of stay. More and more procedures and diagnostics are possible on an outpatient basis or with only a brief stay in hospital.

The primary sector has been marked by a process of emancipation. It began with the professionalization of general practice, following the classical route of the delineation of a domain (ongoing comprehensive care, life-long and family-oriented medicine), the development of a related area of scientific study and the introduction of specific training. The next area to be affected was that of community nursing, whose administration became the responsibility of new and larger organizations covered by umbrella bodies; home-help services have recently been drawn into this process. These developments are underpinned by government policies aimed at controlling the cost of intramural care; the creation of tiers of provision and the reinforcement of the primary sector were means to the same end.

In the case of the more care-oriented institutions of the tertiary sector there is a movement towards integration into the community, a smaller scale of operation and "normalization" of care. Here too, albeit under the influence of other processes, there is a trend towards extramural treatment and care. The growth in the number of elderly people needing care is bringing to light capacity problems, necessitating new approaches which chime with people's desire to continue living independently for as long as possible. New forms of housing and intermediate provision also help to meet this desire.

Demographic, social and cultural changes both fit in with and influence these long-term trends in health care. The Netherlands has an aging population, and while this may have come later than in neighbouring countries it is no less inevitable. Families shrink and the number of one-person households rises. In the Dutch society therefore there are more very elderly people living alone. This demographic individualization is reinforced by social and cultural factors in the form of growing emphases on personal independence, self-development and control over one's own life. These processes both strengthen the trend towards greater home care and put obstacles in its way. Informal care, especially within the family, must be available if people with complex health problems are to be cared for at home; it will be less available in the future. Moreover old values such as neighbourliness and the duty of care sit uneasily with the new individualism.

Reviewing these social developments we can summarize the context for the future organization of primary and home care as follows.

Growing demand for complex care will not in the first instance be met intramurally: with developments in technology and medicine making care less location-specific it can increasingly be delivered on an ambulatory basis or in the home. However, less care will be available within the family and there will be little scope for expanding informal care, implying heavy demands on professional services. The government will encourage the trend towards ambulatory care not to cut costs but to meet the wishes of an increasingly independently minded public. Patients' - consumers' - awareness of their rights and the increased power of the organizations representing their interests will help ensure that care is individualized, i.e. reflects the wishes and aspirations of each patient. Care provision will therefore become more flexible; continuity of care is essential in the case of people with long-term needs, however, and the government will underpin this with legislation and regulation.

Future trends in care consumption
Health care policy is in a state of flux, the main lines of development being a major shift towards community-based care (the substitution of extramural for intramural services), functionally defined packages of care entitlements, the reform of care insurance and the introduction of market forces into health care. To prepare for what is in store for the health care system we need at least to know how the consumption of care by people living at home will develop, aside from any policy shifts. What effect will population aging have over the next fifteen years on the use of GP or community-nursing services, for example, and will the impact be equally strong for all services? The answers to such questions make up a reference scenario for primary and home care. However care is organized in the future, a minimum requirement is that the system be capable of dealing with the increase in care use expected to result from social and demographic change and the continuation of existing consumption trends.

To answer these questions we studied past trends and estimated future shifts in the use of certain services, namely GP care, community nursing, home help, general social work, physiotherapy and specialist outpatient care; this last was included on account of its possible future role in home care.

Where possible we made three types of estimate of future care consumption, one solely reflecting demographic change, one based on past trends in care use and one relating to the pattern of supply.

The purpose of the *demographic estimate* is to chart the effects of population aging and the increasing numbers of people living alone. We assume consumption rates within groups (defined by age, sex and whether or not individuals live alone) to remain unchanged while the size of particular groups increases (as in the case of the elderly) or decreases (as in that of the young).

The *trend-based estimate* starts from past patterns in the consumption of care by various social and demographic categories; the extent to which social and demographic characteristics affect care consumption is then statistically analysed and likely trends in these characteristics are used to determine future care use. The social and demographic characteristics considered are age, sex, whether or not people live alone, level of education and subjectively perceived health. If those who perceive their health to be poor make disproportionate demands on the care system, then any increase in their number has implications for future care consumption.

The *supply-related estimate* assumes that care consumption is influenced not only by social and demographic shifts but also by patterns of availability; for practical reasons we limited this part of the exercise to GP services and physiotherapy.

Our demographic expectations are as follows. The population will continue to age and the number of people living alone to rise. Educational levels will also rise. The number of people perceiving their own health as good will increase, particularly among the "younger old" (the 55-74 age group). The disease burden appears to be shifting towards older ages.

Our demographic estimate of future care consumption over the period to 2005, given in table 1, shows population aging to have its greatest impact on the home-help service. The absence of a similar impact on community nursing may be strange at first sight, but a second demographic phenomenon is also at work here: the number of young children (the second most important target group for community nursing) is falling. In the case of the other care categories the annual increase in consumption is expected to run at around one per cent or less.

Table 1. Demographic estimate of the consumption of ambulatory care, 1990-2005 (index, 1990 = 100)

Category	1990	1995	2000	2005
GP care[1]	100	104	107	110
Specialist care[1]	100	104	108	113
Physiotherapy[1]	100	105	109	112
Community nursing[2]	100	106	111	116
Home help[2]	100	107	115	123
General social work[2]	100	106	110	114

1. Numbers of contacts
2. Numbers of clients

In the case of GP care the trend-based estimates, which reflect past trends in care use as well as social and demographic changes, show virtually the same growth as does the purely demographic estimate. This is because there has been little or no tendency for the consumption of GP services to rise: the increase in the number of Dutch GPs over the last fifteen years has tended to produce longer contacts rather than more contacts.

In the case of outpatient contacts with specialists the trend-based estimate is actually lower than the demographic estimate: past trends point to a fall as compared with 1990. This overall position conceals two contrary developments, namely a fall in contacts in the 20-54 age group and a doubling in the number among people aged 75 and over. A similar if slightly less sharp increase in the number of contacts involving the very elderly also appears in the trend-based estimate for GP care. This is highly relevant to practitioner workloads, since such contacts are very time-consuming. We also estimated the use of GP services using a mathematical model which included availability as a determinant; increasing numbers of GPs will bring about a fall in the average number of patients on each GP's list to 2000 by the year 2005. This model indicates slower growth in the number of contacts than the demographic estimate.

In the case of physiotherapy we made only demographic and supply-related estimates, since the growth in the use of physiotherapy services over the last fifteen years has been so rapid that to project past trends would produce absurd results. On the basis of a relatively modest growth in the number of physiotherapists working in extramural care from just over 9,600 now to around 11,000 in 2005, here again we expect an increase in consumption smaller than that indicated by our purely demographic estimates.

In the remaining three care categories, namely community nursing, home help and general social work, we made a trend-based estimate of client numbers (these services' "reach"); we made no allowance for the intensification of care for certain client groups, such as has been noted in community nursing on the basis of registration data. These trend-based estimates too prove to be lower than the demographic estimates, mainly owing to rising educational levels and an improvement in subjectively perceived health among adults (20-54) and the younger old (55-74).

These estimates point to the impact of population aging on certain categories of provision being less dramatic than is sometimes supposed. Other social and demographic trends also point towards a slower increase. However, these conclusions are subject to the limitations of the methods of calculation used and the data available.

Mention has already been made of the intensification of care likely to occur among the very elderly, the group for whom the number of contacts with caring services increases in all calculations. We also took no account of the problem of waiting lists; the waiting lists for places in nursing and homes for the elderly will probably lengthen, increasing the pressure on ambulatory services. Finally, we made no allowance for the implications of encouraging home care in cases involving complex health problems. A lower limit is indicated; the supply of ambulatory care will need to increase, certainly for the elderly.

Home care for patients with complex problems
We looked at likely trends in care consumption if current policies are maintained. In the public at large there is a desire, underpinned by government policy, for more home care, even for patients whose health problems are complex; moreover population trends and capacity constraints in nursing and homes for the

elderly make it vital that more care be delivered at home. We address a two-part question in the scenario study: what is the nature and scale of the care requirement for complex cases, and what conditions must be met if such care is to be delivered satisfactorily in the home situation? (What we are here concerned with is extramural care that takes the place of intramural care or makes admission to a hospital or nursing home unnecessary).

To answer the first question we need a description of care needs, starting from deficits in the caring capacity of patients and patient systems (roughly, patients and their families). Four types of deficit are distinguished, starting with the disease or disability itself (health deficits). The other three types relate to the experience and consequences of health deficits. Deficits in psychosocial competence concern the extent to which people cope with disease or disability, i.e. how health deficits are experienced. The third type relates to the patient system, generally the availability or otherwise of informal care within the family. The fourth type, finally, comprises deficits in day-to-day functioning due to the deficits of the other three types. This classification sets the framework for determining the nature and scale of future home care needs, whereby we focus on care functions and abstract from the current structure of care delivery: care functions will not necessarily be performed by the same categories of provider as at present in a new and different organization of primary and home care, particularly if the care insurance reforms go through.

We divide care functions into four principal groups:
- medical care (diagnosis, observation and monitoring; treatment, including medication; supervision and support during treatment);
- physical care (help with or assumption of activities of daily living: ADL care and support);
- domestic care (help with or assumption of household tasks);
- social care (information and advice; concrete assistance; psychosocial support; social support).

On the basis of the four categories of deficit just outlined we constructed four classes of potential home care patients; for each class we then investigated what care functions, in what quantities, needed to be delivered. We used a combination of "paper patients" and the Delphi technique. The results are summarized briefly below.

Patient class 1
The class with fewest problems. Its members, predominantly the younger old, feel healthy and generally do not live alone; they score relatively well on ADL and household-task scales.

Patient class 2
Members of this class, who are mainly elderly or very elderly, have deficits of two types. They do not feel well. They generally live with a partner. They have some problems with activities of daily living and many with household tasks.

Patient class 3
Members of this class are elderly or very elderly and have three types of deficit. They do not feel well and are more likely than those in class 2 to live alone. They still have some ADL capability but (particularly the older patients) cannot perform household tasks.

Patient class 4
People in the class with four types of deficit are very elderly and do not feel healthy; they live alone, have little ADL capability and cannot perform household tasks.

Estimates of home care needs point to heavy pressure on services; this is also the implication of the supplementary calculations of the care requirements of terminal cancer patients and the elderly mentally infirm.

Complex home care does not only have consequences for the volume of care required: organizational and regulatory changes are also needed if care is to be delivered effectively in the home situation. The Delphi study found that the conditions needing to be met were, in order of importance:
- the patient system must have the necessary carrying capacity;
- the home circumstances must be physically suitable;
- organization and coordination must be adequate;
- provision must be flexible and its volume must increase;

- more types of care must be available;
- the right aids and appliances must be available in sufficient quantity;
- regulatory structures and funding arrangements must be adapted.

The availability of informal care from patients' partners and/or children is an essential precondition for the delivery of complex home care in all scenarios. The social trends discussed at the start of this summary make it vital that informal care and voluntary work be encouraged and supported. This issue must be addressed however care is organized in the future, since otherwise the desired shift towards greater home care will be impossible and any shift forced by capacity shortfalls will result in a loss of quality.

Organization of primary and home care in the future
We enjoy high standards of health care in the Netherlands: whenever changes are proposed it is vital that we seek to retain what works well and make changes only where there are problems. An evaluation of the system as it stands must therefore be the first step in the development of organizational scenarios.

The main necessity for change relates to the requirements imposed by complex care in the home situation. For other types of care we should try to maintain the system of indirect access to specialist care, the pivotal role of the GP and open access to a plural and unbureaucratic system of care delivery. At present, however, the system is too fragmented to enable the delivery of complex home care: there are no incentives tending to bring about the kinds of coordination and cooperation needed for integrated care delivery.

These problems are not new, and a variety of solutions have been and continue to be developed and applied. Past examples include the establishment of health centres, while the "care-innovation" projects now under way display a range of possible approaches which are of great value in thinking on the future organization of the system. Analysis of the projects shows that all aim at the better deployment of different types of expertise through cooperation, harmonization and coordination; they involve in particularly the integration of nursing and other care and closer collaboration between hospitals, nursing homes and homes for the elderly. Care coordination may be achieved through the appointment of a coordinator or the establishment of a central coordinating agency. Of importance here is the extent of organizational integration: options range from merger at the one extreme (a central organization is established, making coordination an internal problem) to a federal arrangement at the other (coordination is improved but participating organizations retain their autonomy and coordination remains an inter-institutional matter).

In the areas of daycare and treatment a network of links can be built up with the secondary (hospital) and tertiary (nursing home etc.) sectors, thus blurring traditional boundaries. Respite care serving to relieve the burden on informal carers fits into this framework. Such care could be facilitated by giving the primary sector its own intramural beds, as happens e.g. in Finland and in general practitioner community hospitals in the UK. As foreign experience shows, it is important to ensure that temporary admissions are just that: if this is not done, the result is a new type of nursing-home bed whose original purpose is lost as patients fail to return home.

Mention has already been made of the two principal dimensions involved in the development of organizational scenarios, namely central *versus* dispersed control (merger *versus* federation) and the extent to which traditional sectoral boundaries and the monopoly on primary functions are abandoned. On the basis of these two dimensions we developed four organizational scenarios, and within them a number of variants (see diagram next page).

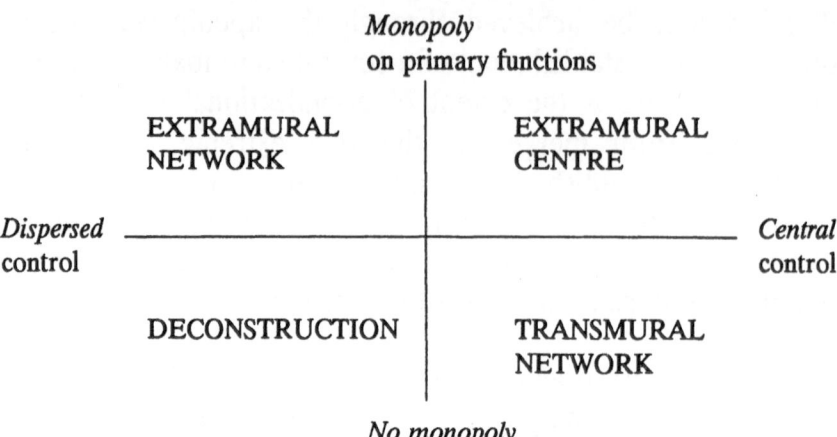

Monopoly
on primary functions

EXTRAMURAL NETWORK	EXTRAMURAL CENTRE

Dispersed control ———————————————————— *Central* control

DECONSTRUCTION	TRANSMURAL NETWORK

No monopoly

In the *extramural network* scenario cooperation and coordination are regulated by agreements and protocols covering independent practitioners and institutions providing extramural care. The coordination of care will generally be separately regulated for the medical and nursing functions. Three variants on this scenario are distinguished, one involving organization into small units providing a single category of care, one involving larger units such as group practices and merged institutions and one, to be combined with either of the other two, that adds a separate care-coordinating function.

The *extramural centre* scenario envisages an extramural structure under which all care functions are encompassed by single organizations, whose role may range from one of provider of facilities to one of employer of all practitioners. The coordination of care is regulated internally and at the level of the organization as a whole there are agreements with institutions delivering intramural care. Here the variants are that the extramural centre can be based around enlarged group general practices, home care organizations (the merged home-help and community-nursing services) or newly created organizations not tied to existing provider categories.

In the *transmural network* scenario intramural institutions are more closely involved in complex home care; indeed, the organization of primary and home care can perfectly well be entirely hospital-based. There is one central control system for the whole range of services. We distinguish three variants: integration of extramural care and nursing-home services under extramural control; a hospital-centred structure for the organization of care; and an intermediate form in which a separate structure is created between hospitals and the primary sector.

The *deconstruction* scenario, finally, envisages no monopoly in home care and no central control; care may be delivered through a great variety of collaborative arrangements and coalitions. There is little regulation and no uniform division of functions. Care coordinators are needed to ensure that complex care can be delivered in the home situation.

Assessing the scenarios
While one of the stipulations governing the scenarios was that in principle all should be capable of meeting the requirements of complex home care, this does not mean that all are equally suited to delivering the combination of complex and non-complex care.

Access for those with complex care needs is probably inadequate in the *extramural network*, particularly in its weak variant. The provision needed demands a degree of internal coherence among the different parts of the network which probably cannot be achieved in a federal structure. The construction of suitable care packages requires too much consultation and is overdependent on agreements with which compliance could not be enforced. It is questionable whether the appointment of care coordinators would be an effective solution, as their powers within such a loose structure would be limited. Nor is the infrastructure well suited to the deployment of physical resources in home care. The division into relatively autonomous units and consequent lack of any effective feedback system make it difficult to guarantee the quality of complex home care. The divisions between services may get in the way of optimizing the distribution of tasks and responsibilities. Consideration could be given to retaining a federal structure for non-complex care while organizing complex care separately; this would however create new problems of coordination.

The stronger organization of the *extramural centre*, with greater scope for quality control and a stronger position *vis à vis* the secondary sector, creates favourable conditions for complex home

15

care. The centre's size enables it to offer a full range of services while task differentiation and specialization promote the efficient delivery of care tailored to needs. Premises can include a department for the supply of aids and appliances and facilities for training users and maintaining equipment. There is however a risk of bureaucracy, rigidity and a sharp increase in overheads. Where the organization is large, service delivery is best decentralized. Growing demand for the various types of care can in part be met by support staff such as general health workers and practice nurses and by the care coordinator, though this brings with it the risk that any given patient may face many different care providers. The structure, especially in the variant involving an independent organization, lends itself to forms of patient participation and hence to the mobilization of informal care; this can lead in turn to a shift from professional to non-professional care. Good relations with the secondary sector are not guaranteed; but while the organizational division means that continuity of care and rationalization through task transfers will not happen of their own accord, the greater authority and balance of the new organization means that they are possible.

The advantage of the *transmural network* scenario is breadth of provision, with both intramural and extramural care being brought together in a single framework. The variant placing nursing homes under the control of the primary sector is at a disadvantage here, since the more specialized hospital care falls outside the framework and must be dealt with separately; in the other two variants conditions are favourable for continuity and comprehensive care. In the third variant, in which all care is hospital-based, continuity may suffer from the underdevelopment of non-complex care in the home situation. The unified organization facilitates the shift towards the primary sector, relieving the pressure on intramural services. Growing demand for primary care can be met by existing and new care functions at varying levels of expertise. The danger of the transmural network is an overemphasis on *cure*, leaving the *care* function underdeveloped and causing specialist services to be offered too readily; this risk is greater in the hospital-centred variant than in the two others. This tendency limits the potential for transferring tasks to the primary sector.

The *deconstruction* scenario, finally, while in principle offering good access, is likely in practice to involve selection of patients, especially in complex care. The independent coordinators controlling and directing care flows in this scenario are not in a position to do much about this: what does not exist cannot be bought in. The more different categories of provision have to be involved, the more difficult it becomes to assemble care packages and ensure coordination. The likelihood of gaps and overlaps is considerable. The care coordinator in this scenario is probably not a sufficient guarantee of an adequate standard of complex home care.

Our assessment of the scenarios is couched in fairly broad terms; much will depend on local circumstances and the structural approaches eventually adopted. New structures must fit in with the nature of future care provision, existing provision in the region and the needs of local institutions and practitioners; they will therefore need to be built from the bottom up. Diversity must be possible, subject to the requirements of equal access and equal rights. We shall have to wait and see to what extent such diversity can ensured if the planned health-insurance reforms go through. If the reforms create powerful insurers operating on a regional basis they are likely to use their muscle, very probably providing any cover for intensive home care through contracts with partners able to deliver a comprehensive package, as in the scenarios involving central control. If insurers engage in vigorous national competition their power will be much less; the kind of organization through which intensive home care is delivered in a given region will then depend on the relative strengths of providers. Strong single-category organizations (centring on GPs or the integrated agencies providing community-nursing and home-help services) or the hospital-based organization appear to be best equipped in this connection. If a dominant organizational form also fails to emerge on the providers' side, the deconstruction scenario is likely to triumph.

The scope for organizing and delivering complex home care in the future does not depend only on the health professionals: external developments, such as the declining availability of traditional informal care within the family or shifts in the supply of qualified nursing and other care staff, may seriously jeopardize the delivery of home care. The ability to respond to such developments is thus a precondition for a sustainable home care policy.

Introduction

The term "scenario study" is generally used to denote a form of futures research which involves describing various possible or desirable future states of affairs. Scenario studies should be clearly distinguished from forecasts: in forecasting exercises the emphasis is on quantified statements as to the most likely developments in a particular field (demography, economics etc.), while scenario studies are concerned less with quantifiable statements or likely trends than with compiling and comparing subjective expectations and visions (Postma and Eyzenga 1987, De Vries 1985, Schnaars 1987). This does not imply contenting ourselves with unstructured consultations with the notably imaginative: the fullest possible use of quantitative data and consultation with experts mean that scenario studies generate expert opinion, led by the facts (Linstone and Turoff 1975).

Scenario studies are seen as most worthwhile in situations where reliable predictions are not possible, perhaps because the time horizon is too distant for reliable forecasting (scenario studies normally extend over a period of ten to fifteen years) or because the field concerned encompasses complex and hard-to-quantify phenomena whose impact is not known with any precision. All this uncertainty explains the relatively modest focus not on *the* future but on *alternative* futures and routes leading to them. Hoogenveen and Brouwer put it like this: "A scenario describes how, starting from the present state of some part of society, some future state of affairs might be reached through a series of developments, the aim being to increase our understanding of the underlying mechanisms and of ways of influencing them" (STG 1989).

The series of scenario studies concerned with health and health care of which this report forms part dates back to 1983, when the government established an independent committee of experts known as the Steering Committee on Future Health Scenarios

(STG). For each project the STG appoints a scenario committee, also made up of independent experts, which is assisted by a team of researchers. The first STG-commissioned study focused on the implications for health and health care of an aging population; the main report appeared in 1985 (STG 1985). This was followed by studies concerned with particular conditions which place a heavy burden on the health care system (cancer, cardiovascular disease, chronic disease), and more recently by projects dealing with different care sectors (prevention and health promotion, mental health care, hospital care). The scenarios have thus fallen into two groups, one focusing on health and the other on health care.

In 1988 the STG asked the Netherlands institute of primary health care (NIVEL) to undertake research for the Scenario Committee on Primary Care. As usual this commission was preceded by a study of the feasibility of a scenario project in this field (Wijkel and Morenc 1987). The STG then appointed a scenario committee initially chaired by Professor F.A. Vorst; when Professor Vorst left to take up a position abroad he was replaced as chair by Professor E. Schadé. In consultation with the scenario committee a research proposal was drawn up focusing on the organizational aspects of primary and home care (Wijkel 1987; Wennink and Kooiker 1988, 1990).

This report, the culmination of the project, sets out alternative approaches to the organization of primary and home care. Assuming a future marked by both qualitative and quantitative change, the various scenarios cover not only the core categories of primary care as currently constituted (GP services, community nursing, home help and general social work) but also specialist outpatient care, respite care, and social services such as sheltered housing. The qualitative changes relate to the scenario committee's "ideological principles": retention of the best elements of primary care as it is now (its generalist, comprehensive, accessible and relatively unbureaucratic nature), coupled with the creation of services catering for the "emancipated patient" (customized care, flexible care packages with an emphasis on continuity). Within the overall field of health care we have limited our compilation of scenarios to ambulatory services.

1. Dutch health care in the European context

1.1. Introduction

Scenarios for the future of health care are an instrument in the formation of health care policy, their purpose being to analyse the current state of health care and to develop alternative pathways into the future. The Dutch government has made this a systematic part of policy development, initially commissioning scenario studies focusing on demography (population aging and its implications for health care) and epidemiology (possible developments in the incidence and prevalence of major categories of chronic disease and in available treatments). These studies were followed by projects on the development of the health care system, with specific projects focusing on public health and prevention, the hospital of the future and mental health. This report describes the development of scenarios for primary health care with a strong emphasis on home care.

Scenarios for the future of primary care represent a departure from the current structure of the system in a double sense: on the one hand the current structure is the point of departure for the analysis; on the other the scenarios developed depart from that structure in important respects. The first step must therefore be to describe the Dutch health care system as it is now. For an international audience we also need to place the Dutch system in a European context, thus enabling the scenarios developed here to serve as a source of inspiration for policy makers in other European health care systems.

This chapter starts with background information on the Netherlands (section 1.2) and goes on to describe the structural features of this country's current system of health care (section 1.3). By drawing attention to the differences between it and other European health care systems we place the Dutch system in its context (section 1.4). In the Netherlands, as in so many other

21

European countries, health care is in a phase of transition from what is primarily a planning-led system to one that could be described as a regulated market. These recent developments in health policy are addressed in section 1.5.

1.2. Background

The Netherlands has a population of 15,131,000 (CBS 1992); it is both densely populated (with 446 people per square kilometre) and highly urbanized (with 51 per cent living in urban and 38 per cent in suburban municipalities). The birth rate is 13.2 per 1000 population and the death rate 8.6 (in 1990); this gives a natural rate of increase of 4.6 per thousand, high by western European standards.

Immigration adds to the natural increase of the population (and indeed to its health problems). In order of arrival three groups of immigrants can be distinguished. The first comprises foreign workers from southern Europe, Turkey and northern Africa. Initially supposed to be only temporary residents, their stay in the country proved more permanent and the reuniting of their families caused an increase in immigration; 2.8 per cent of the population now consists of originally foreign migrant workers and their families, some of them born in the Netherlands and with Dutch nationality. The second group of migrants consists of people with Dutch nationality from what were once Dutch colonies in the Caribbean and South America (the largest inflow occurred when Surinam became independent in the late 1970s); they now account for 1.5 per cent of the population. The most recent arrivals are refugees from south-eastern Asia, Africa and south-eastern and eastern Europe: 21,000 people sought asylum in the Netherlands in 1990 and the number is increasing rapidly every year.

In 1991 13 per cent of the population were aged 65 or over, a low figure by western European standards. The Netherlands nevertheless ranks high in life expectancy at birth for both females and males (79.9 and 73.3 years respectively in 1989), while at 9.3 per 1000 births perinatal mortality is among the lowest in Europe.

22

The Netherlands is an affluent country. In 1990 gross domestic product stood at 33,750 guilders per head, while in 1989 national income per head was 28,400 guilders. Even so, unemployment is high at 11.2 per cent of the labour force. Health spending in 1990 totalled 8.1 per cent of GDP (OECD).

The Netherlands has three tiers of government: central, provincial (twelve authorities) and municipal (702 authorities). Both in general and in the specific field of health care central government has the greatest powers, followed by the municipalities. At central level health care is the responsibility of the Minister of Welfare, Health and Cultural Affairs; there is also a junior minister with the title State Secretary for Health. Contribution levels for public health insurance are set jointly by the Ministry of Health and the Ministry of Employment and Social Affairs, while the Ministry of Health is responsible for global planning and national policy and for setting financial targets. The provinces' main responsibility relates to the planning of hospital and nursing-home provision; that of the municipalities, which cooperate on a regional scale for this purpose, is in the field of public health and health promotion.

In theory central government has considerable scope for bringing about changes in the health care system; in practice the great influence of national interest groups means that its power is limited, since the national associations of providers (notably medical specialists, hospitals, general practitioners and insurance organizations) have little difficulty in frustrating government policies they regard as unacceptable. Such interest groups are strongly represented on national advisory bodies, which have strong links with political parties and which ministers cannot afford to ignore. Moreover the ethos of government in the Netherlands is one of compromise and negotiation. This makes the health care system resistant to rapid change.

1.3. Structural features of the Dutch health care system

Describing the structural features of Dutch health care is no easy matter. The roots of the system are in private (voluntary) initiative, often of a charitable or religious nature, and while traces of this are still visible they have largely been submerged by complex government regulations. Health care is delivered by a wide range of mainly private non-profit organizations and by independent professionals. In the insurance field there is a dual system, with compulsory public insurance for people below a certain income level and private insurance above that level. In the remainder of this section we describe the overall structure of the system, the characteristics of the main providers and the system's financial aspects.

Overall structure
The system's present structure dates back to 1974, when the government published a policy paper on the structure of health care that marked the start of more intensive state intervention. The paper was published at a time of growing concern about the health care system. Since the war the number of hospital beds, and with it the number of specialists, had grown rapidly, and the paper's aims were to contain the rise in costs due to these trends and to create a new balance between primary care on the one hand and hospital and specialist care on the other.

Figure 1. The pyramid of care

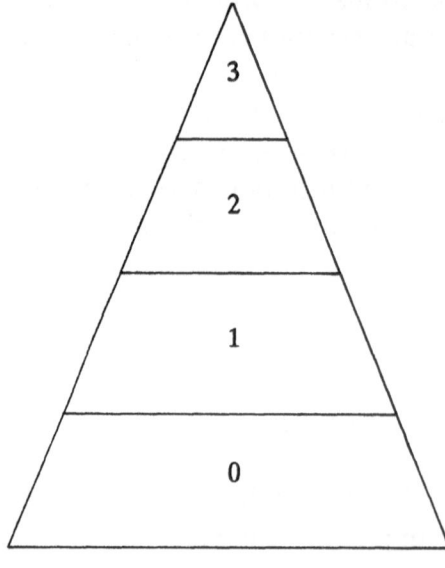

3	Specialized institutions, long-term care
2	Acute hospitals, specialist care
1	Primary care: patient-centred, generalist, directly accessible
0	Public health service: disease prevention and health promotion

The system was structured as a pyramid comprising four tiers (see figure 1); these tiers still characterize Dutch health care. At the base of the pyramid is the public health service, whose functions are disease prevention and health promotion through activities such as monitoring public health, the immunization of schoolchildren and health education; they are performed by public health authorities which operate on a regional scale and are controlled by municipalities. The second tier is primary health care, by which is meant ambulatory, directly accessible, generalist care based in the community; the providers are GPs, community nurses, physiotherapists, social workers, midwives, pharmacists and home helps. Secondary care, the third tier, comprises the hospital sector: general and teaching hospitals for acute care fall into this category, as do medical specialists, who generally work in hospitals albeit on a self-employed basis. The fourth tier is the tertiary sector, long-term care provided in specialized institutions; nursing homes and psychiatric hospitals fall into this category.

It should be noted that primary health care has a different meaning in the Netherlands than in WHO documents (de Bakker, 1989): the much broader WHO definition also includes collective prevention, ambulatory specialist care and elements of the social-welfare system as part of primary health care.

A characteristic feature of the care pyramid is that access to a higher tier is by referral; of key importance here is the GP, who acts as gatekeeper for the medical specialist. Insurers pay for hospital care and specialist treatment only after referral by a GP.

Health care in the Netherlands has no structural relationship with the social-welfare system. While links do exist - social welfare is in large part a municipal responsibility, as are the public health service and social work (part of the primary sector) - they are not of a structural nature.

The strengthening of primary care has been a major goal of government policy since 1974. This was to be achieved in two ways. The first is the transfer of tasks from the secondary to the primary sector, known in the Netherlands as substitution (involving as it does the substitution of extramural for intramural care). Aftercare following a surgical procedure in hospital is a possible candidate for such substitution, since it can as well be delivered at home by the community-based primary sector. The second way is by increasing the primary sector's capacity to deal with problems: steps towards this objective have included longer training for GPs, fewer patients on GP lists, and restructuring and enlarging the community-nursing agencies.

Coordination between the different tiers was to be brought about by "regionalization", the promotion of a coherent system of health services within clearly defined regions. Cohesion was to result from the planning of the public health service and primary care by the municipalities and of secondary and tertiary care by the provinces.

Looking back at the policy guidelines formulated in 1974 we can say that while the measures to strengthen primary care have succeeded, those aimed at containing the cost of secondary care were less successful and the regionalization policy failed altogether. This last failure was due mainly to the separation of the planning and financing of health care (Groenewegen 1992).

Funding health care
Health services in the Netherlands are funded from different sources, including public and private insurance, taxation and charges. The total cost amounted in 1990 to 22,375 million guilders (10,124 million ECUs), most of which was covered by two health-insurance schemes. Both schemes are run by health insurance funds, private non-profit organizations, working mainly on a regional scale, which cover participants' health care costs. While the funds are not part of government they function as quasi-governmental institutions; they are supervised by the Health Insurance Funds Council, on which employers, trade unions, patient organizations, health care providers and the government are represented. This independent body also advises on coverage and contribution levels. Contributions under the two schemes are set as a percentage of income and are deducted at source, with employer and employee each paying half. Funding shortfalls are covered by the state.

The first scheme, governed by the Health Insurance Funds Act, covers all the costs of medical treatment, hospitalization and drugs. Participation is compulsory for everyone whose income falls below a certain ceiling (58,000 guilders or 26,244 ECUs a year in 1992), old-age pensioners who were publicly insured before retirement and people in receipt of social benefits; as a result about 62 per cent of the population are publicly insured. The remaining 38 per cent are privately insured with one of a hundred or so insurance companies. In many cases private insurance does not cover dental treatment and those who have private cover pay part of the cost of their medical treatment; around seventy per cent have cover for GP services, and around thirty per cent choose to pay the first 250 guilders or more of any claim (KISG 1985).

The second scheme, governed by the Exceptional Medical Expenses Act, covers the whole population for outpatient mental health care, community nursing, nursing-home treatment and admission to psychiatric hospitals and institutions for the mentally handicapped. Charges are levied for some services such as nursing-home care (Schrijvers 1991).

Health care providers
Relevant features of the various providers are described below. Information on the problems presenting to them and on the nature of the care they provide is given in section 3.3.2. Chapter 4 outlines trends in the use of care.

General practitioners
The GP is the first point of contact with the system for people with health or health-related problems. At the start of 1992 there were 6,535 GPs working in the Netherlands, giving an average of 2,315 people per GP. Each GP has a fixed list of patients. About half (51.2 per cent in 1992) work in single-handed practices; of the remainder 33.1 per cent work in partnerships, 7.3 per cent in group practices and 8.1 per cent in multidisciplinary health centres in which one or more GPs work in a team with community nurses and social workers in shared premises. There is a trend towards fewer single-handed practices and more working in teams, especially in partnerships.

GPs work as independent contractors under the health insurance scheme, over ninety per cent from their own or shared private offices.

The health insurance funds were until recently obliged to offer a GP a contract when he or she set up in practice. Until 1992 the establishment of general practices was governed by statutory regulations, implemented by municipal authorities, covering list sizes, capacity planning and geographical distribution.

The profession of general practitioner is legally protected: only doctors registered with the Royal Netherlands Medical Society may practice. Registration, which is open to those completing the two-year course specifically for general practitioners, must be renewed each five years; renewal is permitted only where the doctor has actually practised as a GP.

The payment system for GPs differs as between privately and publicly insured patients. For each publicly insured patient on their list a GP receives a capitation fee at the full rate (116 guilders in 1992) for the first 1,600 and a lower rate (69 guilders) for the remainder. Privately insured patients pay their GP directly on a fee-for-service basis (33 guilders per consultation in 1992), which they can recover from their insurance company if their policy covers GP costs.

Specialists

In 1991 there were 12,477 medical specialists in the Netherlands (CBS), equivalent to one specialist per 1,200 population; the ratio of specialists to GPs is two to one. Most specialists work in a hospital setting, although the majority (about 63 per cent) are not employed by the hospital but rather work as independent contractors.

There are 163 teaching and general hospitals in the Netherlands with a total (in 1990) of almost 65,000 beds, equivalent to 4.3 beds per 1,000 population; the number of admissions per bed per year was 23.8. Between 1980 and 1990 average length of stay fell from 14.0 to 11.2 days. In addition to the teaching and general hospitals there are 80 psychiatric hospitals (24,000 beds), 122 institutions for the mentally handicapped (31,000 beds) and 326 nursing homes (52,000 beds).

Specialists are paid on a fee-for-service basis. For the outpatient treatment of publicly insured patients self-employed specialists receive a fixed amount to cover the costs of treatment over a period of up to one month. If longer treatment is needed a second month's payment is made by the health insurance fund concerned. The outpatient treatment of privately insured patients by self-employed specialists is on a fee-for-service basis.

Physiotherapy
Between 1972 and 1990 the number of physiotherapists in the Netherlands grew rapidly from about 1,500 to about 13,000, the majority (9,640 in 1990) of them working in primary care. Physiotherapy is the oldest paramedical profession in the Netherlands and has the largest number of practitioners; it is legally recognized under the Paramedical Professions Act. Qualification is via a four-year course at a college of higher vocational education. Most physiotherapists work in private practice; general and teaching hospitals account between them for twelve per cent of physiotherapy posts and nursing homes for eight per cent. Practices may be single-handed (38 per cent in 1989), partnerships (21 per cent) or group practices (41 per cent in 1989; Pool and Hingstman 1991).

Members of the public do not have direct access to physiotherapy: the Paramedical Professions Act requires a physician's referral. Physiotherapists are free to establish a practice anywhere but need a contract with a health insurance fund if they are to be paid for publicly insured patients.

Remuneration differs as between publicly (i.e. compulsory) and privately insured patients. To be paid for the treatment of publicly insured patients physiotherapists must have prior authorization from the health insurance fund concerned; they are then paid for each treatment in accordance with an agreed schedule. The number of sessions per authorization may not exceed twelve; thereafter a new authorization is required. Privately insured patients pay their physiotherapist directly, with central government setting the maximum fee; whether and to what extent they are reimbursed by their insurer depends on the cover provided by their policy (Koster *et al.* 1991).

Community nursing
In 1988 there were 6,500 nurses (full-time equivalent) and about 500 nursing supervisors employed in community nursing in the Netherlands. These nurses work for regional institutions (whose Dutch name literally means "cross associations"), of which there are about 60. Within these institutions there are teams working in defined geographical areas with an average population of around 35,000. Each team consists of one nursing supervisor, ten community nurses and two nursing auxiliaries and each individual nurse or a sub-team of two nurses and an auxiliary is assigned to a specific sub-area.

The difference between community nurses and auxiliaries lies in length of training and level of qualifications: community nurses have had either four years' training at higher vocational level (post-17/18) or three-and-a-half years' training on the job following two years of intermediate vocational (post-16) education, while community nursing auxiliaries have had either two years' training on the job in a hospital or nursing home for the elderly and a six-month course in community nursing or a three-year nursing course at intermediate vocational level (Verhey and Kerkstra 1992).

The government's policy of strengthening primary care brought a considerable growth in the number of community nurses in the 1980s: where in 1982 there was one community nurse for every 3,219 people and one auxiliary for every 15,015, by 1989 the figures had fallen to 2,903 and 11,327 respectively (CBS).

As well as nurses the "cross associations" employ dieticians, child health clinic physicians and nurse specialists. Community nurses can become nurse specialists by following an additional eighteen-month course in professional innovation, management or a clinical nursing specialty (in the care of the elderly, child health or specific chronic diseases such as cancer or rheumatoid arthritis). The associations' responsibilities include preventive as well as curative care delivered by nurses and maternity home care.

In the Netherlands, unlike most other countries, community nursing care is directly accessible; even so, half of all clients are referred by GPs, hospitals or nursing homes. The providing institutions can be contacted round the clock and care can be delivered in the evening, at night and at the weekend if necessary. Each client may receive up to two-and-a-half hours' care, spread over three visits, every day, for an unlimited period. There are also institutions providing supplementary (intensive) home care over limited periods, mainly for patients who are terminally ill or suffering from a serious chronic disorder.

The associations which provide community-nursing care are funded under the Exceptional Medical Expenses Act on the basis of the number of staff they employ; this covers about 85 per cent of their costs, the rest coming mainly from membership fees. Association membership costs 50 guilders a year.

General social work
There are about 2,000 general social workers in the Netherlands (full-time equivalent), one for every 7,700 people. Social workers have to complete a four-year course at higher vocational level before entering the profession. General social workers are salaried employees of social-work organizations (numbering about 180), which are sometimes combined with home-help agencies; their work ranges from psychosocial care to help with financial problems.

Social-work support is directly accessible to members (i.e. no referral is needed) and free of charge. In 1989 support was available from 1,250 centres, one for every 12,000 people. In the majority of cases (58 per cent) these were permanent centres; in the remainder they were locations where social workers could be contacted at particular times. Many social-work institutions can be contacted round the clock, seven days a week.

Social work is funded by the municipalities, and while the amount of funding can vary depending on local policies in practice the variations are not very large.

Home help

While home help is not a form of health care in the strict sense it does fall into the category of primary care in a broader sense, in that it enables people to continue living in their own home, thereby delaying admission to a nursing or homes for the elderly or bridging the time spent waiting for a place. Its function is to help households where the normal way of living is disrupted by the illness or disability of a family member. In practice the largest client group consists of elderly people living alone.

Home help is provided by over 200 local and regional organizations. The home helps themselves are mainly salaried employees of these organizations. For budgetary reasons, however, a growing number are paid directly by the recipients (Maessen 1989).

The work of the 35,000 or so home helps comprises housework, personal care and social support. Since 1989 the service has, like community nursing, been funded under the Exceptional Medical Expenses Act; this was the start of a process of integrating the community-nursing and home-help services aimed at enhancing their efficiency through a better allocation of care.

While home help is basically directly accessible it is often requested by GPs; moreover because of the service's limited capacity there is a system of rules and criteria of eligibility. Clients pay part of the cost themselves, the charge being based on the financial resources of the household. Since clients are mainly elderly, chronically ill or disabled people, home help is usually a form of long-term care.

Coordination

Coordination in primary care is especially important for the relatively small number of patients - such as the terminally ill who choose to die at home - receiving home care from different providers. As we have seen, each category of provider has its own organizational structure (though integration has now started in the case of community nursing and home help); moreover there is no system for ensuring coordination, providers being essentially free to cooperate, or not, as they see fit. There are different forms of coordination, ranging in intensity from *ad hoc* bilateral coordination through loosely structured primary care teams to integrated multidisciplinary health centres. In urban areas cooperation on more than an *ad hoc* basis is hampered by the fact that the target populations and catchment areas of the different providers do not coincide: community nurses, for example, cover the whole population of a defined geographical area in which there are many different general practices.

Home teams involve cooperation between at least one GP, community nurse and general social worker who consult regularly on the patients/clients they have in common (Pool 1992). In 1990 there were 460 home teams, in which 23 per cent of GPs, 17 per cent of community nurses and 35 per cent of social workers participated. They are overrepresented in rural areas, where conditions for cooperation are better thanks to closer personal relations and a closer coincidence between the target populations of the various provider categories.

Health centres involve cooperation between at least one GP, community nurse and social worker, working in shared premises. In 1991 there were 162 health centres, mainly located in new towns or districts where health care has been built from scratch; relatively few have been established by combining existing services (Boerma 1989).

Coordination between the providers of primary and secondary care is important to ensure continuity of care for the chronic sick under both GP and specialist care and for patients recovering at home after a surgical procedure in hospital. In neither case, however, is there any structural link between the primary and secondary sectors; instead it is left to the individual GP, specialist, hospital or home care organization to decide whether coordination takes place or not, with the result that there is wide variation in the degree to which coordination occurs. Coordination is especially difficult in urban areas where an individual GP or home care organization has to deal with several different hospitals (Kersten and Hackenitz, 1991).

1.4. Dissimilarities with other European health care systems

In the past European health care systems might have been classified into three broad types:
a. national health services in the context of a mixed economy in which health care is seen as a public utility;
b. plural systems in which control is shared between providers, insurers and the state;
c. state-run systems in the context of a centrally planned economy.

Recently, however, the dividing lines between the systems have become blurred as a result of the breakdown of the communist economies in the east and the introduction of market forces into the provision of health care in western European systems.

Plural systems
Together with those of e.g. Germany, Belgium and France, the Dutch health care system falls into the category of plural systems in which care is largely provided on a private but non-profit basis. GPs and specialists are usually self-employed (with the exception e.g. of hospital doctors in Germany), while hospitals may be run by public bodies, non-profit trusts or private organizations. In the Netherlands most hospitals are run by non-profit trusts, which have traditionally had a denominational basis. Community nursing and associated services are also usually provided by non-profit organizations.

Depending on the particular system, funding may come from public sources (compulsory health insurance) or a mix of public and private sources. Compulsory health insurance covers virtually the whole population in France and Belgium but a smaller proportion in the Netherlands and Germany.

In the Netherlands around 60 per cent of people are compulsory insured with health-insurance funds, which operate on a regional basis. Employees whose income falls below a certain level and certain groups of old-age pensioners and benefit recipients are compulsory insured; the remainder of the population have private cover. Private insurance accounts for a larger proportion of health care funding in the Netherlands than in any other European country.

The management of plural systems is divided between government, insurers and providers. While government is responsible for policy development to ensure accessibility, efficiency, quality of care and cost control, agreements have to be reached through national negotiations with the other parties involved and then implemented through agreements; the result is that there is no one source of power. With the growing importance of cost control health insurers have a major role in monitoring the performance of providers.

National health services
In countries with national health services - the United Kingdom, the Scandinavian countries and Italy, for example - the provision of health care is mainly public. With the exception of a few private establishments (in the UK and Scandinavia still a marginal phenomenon, but more common in Italy) hospitals are publicly run and hospital doctors are salaried employees. Depending on the system GPs may be self-employed independent contractors with the national health service, as in the UK and Denmark, or salaried employees, as in Sweden and Finland; a mixture of the two, as in Norway and Italy, is also possible. Community nursing is publicly funded and usually organized at municipal level.

National health services are funded from taxation, whether national, local or both. There is usually also a small but growing private sector.

In contrast with plural systems, the state plays a major role in national health services at various levels of government, depending on the particular system.

State systems
The health care systems of the former communist countries were closely tied up with the organization of economic activity, with an emphasis as much on occupational as on general health care. Large factories had their own internal health centres to provide health care for their workers; large multi-specialty centres were responsible for primary health care for the remainder of the

population. Health care providers, like everybody else, were salaried employees.

Health care was funded either directly by the state or indirectly through employers under a centralized planning system. There was a black market in private care of unknown but considerable size. While it is difficult to say anything definite at the moment, the tendency in reforms is towards decentralization, the introduction of an insurance system, independence for health facilities and providers and, for the patient, freedom of choice of provider. The trend is towards a plural system of health care rather than a national health service.

Of important in the present context is the position of GPs and community nurses in European health care systems. Since they play central roles in primary and home care and in relation to specialist medical care and hospital nursing the position of these two professions is considered separately below.

The general practitioner
Important aspects of the GP's position are the system of remuneration, the degree of competition between GPs as indicated by ratios of GPs to population, the profile of GP services and the mode of access to specialist care.

The three basic systems of GP remuneration, all of which operate somewhere in Europe, are:
- salaried employment, as in some Scandinavian countries;
- fee-for-service payments, as in Belgium, France and Germany;
- capitation payments, with a fixed sum being paid for each patient on a GP's list irrespective of the number of consultations etc., as in Italy; capitation payments may also form part of a mixed system, as in the UK and Denmark.

The Netherlands has a mixed system of remuneration: for publicly insured patients GPs receive a fixed yearly capitation fee while privately insured patients pay their GP for each consultation.

The system of remuneration is closely related to another aspect of the GP's position (Groenewegen *et al.* 1991). A capitation system, whether on its own or as part of a mixed system, requires GPs to have fixed patient lists, with the result that patients are tied to a particular GP or practice. This promotes continuity of care, since patients' histories, including their social and family circumstances, are known to the GP. In list systems, as used in the UK, Denmark, Italy and the Netherlands, access to specialist and hospital care requires referral by a GP, so that the referral system sets the boundary between primary and secondary care. In the German system the boundary is between directly accessible GPs and ambulatory specialists on the one hand and hospital care on the other, however, while in e.g. the French, Belgian and Swedish systems specialist and hospital care are directly accessible without referral (parallel access).

In systems with parallel access GPs usually provide a narrower range of services than in those involving referral; some sections of the population, mainly the more highly educated, tend to consult a specialist directly for certain problems (particularly in the fields of gynaecology and paediatrics, but also in that of general internal medicine). In Italy children up to the age of fourteen are formally on the list not of a GP but of a paediatrician. The large health centres typical of eastern Europe are all multi-specialty institutions, so that the range of services provided specifically by general practitioners is clearly restricted.

A final aspect of the GP's position concerns relative numbers. At one for every 2,300 head of population the Netherlands has the lowest density of GPs in Europe; Belgium has the highest, at one for every 650.

Community nursing
By and large community nurses in European health care systems are salaried employees of non-profit organizations; of the countries surveyed in a recent study (Verheij and Kerkstra 1992) only Belgium and France had significant numbers of independent self-employed nurses working in the community. The organizations providing community-nursing support may be private (voluntary) bodies, as in the plural systems (where they usually have a denominational background) or public agencies, as in the national health services. Community-nursing organizations in the

Netherlands fall into the former group, although the original denominational organizations have by now all merged.

Community-nursing organizations may be funded either through formula-based fixed budgets or in relation to the number of services, visits or patient-days. Formula budgets, usually historically based, are used in the national health services and in the Netherlands; in other plural systems payment is on a fee-for-service basis.

Community nursing has two target client groups: young children and their mothers, and the elderly. In some systems (e.g. in the Netherlands, Scandinavia and the UK) care for both groups is the responsibility of the same agencies; in others it is delivered through separate organizations. In the Netherlands both target groups have historically been served by the same nurses; the position is however now changing rapidly. Community nursing for the elderly is home care in a literal sense: in all the European countries in Verheij and Kerkstra's study a comprehensive range of care was provided and a large percentage of care consisted of home visits.

Round-the-clock access was introduced in the Netherlands in the 1980s; it also exists in Belgium and Finland and in large municipalities in Norway, but not everywhere in the UK, Germany and France. France and Germany are not yet fully covered by community nursing services for the elderly. In Scandinavia, the UK and Germany patients do not pay for community-nursing care; in Belgium and France charges depend on the insurance status of the patient, while in the Netherlands a yearly membership fee is levied (this is a leftover from the time when community nursing was provided by purely voluntary organizations). In some countries, the Netherlands among them, there is a limit on the amount of care that may be provided per day; home care for terminally ill patients may have to be organized separately in those countries as a result. In Scandinavia, the UK and Belgium there are no such limits.

1.5. Recent developments in Dutch health policy

The last ten years have seen a dramatic shift in health care policy in the Netherlands away from reliance on planning and towards reliance on market forces and self-regulation. Underlying this shift have been two factors: the identification of a number of persistent problems, mainly at the point of transition between primary and secondary care, and evidence of inadequacies in the planning approach emerging from an evaluation of the working of planning procedures in a small number of regions.

These two factors came into play at a time of more general change in attitudes towards government influence in major sectors of society. In line with policy changes elsewhere in Europe there was an emphasis on "rolling back the frontiers of the state", self-regulation and the introduction of market forces into health care. Such reforms aim at increasing freedom of choice for the consumers of health care and at promoting competition both among health insurers and among health care providers.

In the mid 1980s an external committee was appointed to advise government on the structure and funding of health care; its report, published in 1987, recommended a new system of health insurance together with the introduction of regulated competition both among providers and among insurers (Dekker Committee). The recommendations have been broadly accepted by the government.

The committee's main recommendation was that the health care system be funded under a single basic care insurance scheme encompassing the whole population and covering about 85 per cent of all health care costs. To cover the remaining 15 per cent (e.g. for physiotherapy and medication) the committee advocated optional supplementary insurance. The care insurance plan would be funded from general taxation. The providers of funding for health care (health insurance funds and private insurance companies) would be financed from this general taxation at so much per person enrolled, the amount being based on such determinants of care consumption as age, sex and region.

For those who are currently publicly insured the Dekker proposals meant greater freedom of choice as regards supplementary insurance cover and the possibility of paying some part of medical costs in return for reduced contributions; for the privately insured they implied a greater appeal to solidarity between the healthy and the sick and free access to services under the care insurance scheme.

For the providers of health care funding the Dekker proposals meant the disappearance of the distinction between private and public insurers. The health insurance funds, which receive subsidies under the present system, would run greater financial risks; formerly regionally based, they anticipated the new situation with a series of amalgamations, a process which could lead to there being only a few, national, health insurance funds in the near future.

Two major changes have been made or planned in the relationship between the providers of funding and the providers of health care. Health insurance funds were formerly required to offer contracts to legally established or recognized care providers; this requirement has now been abolished, giving the funds the countervailing power needed to negotiate effectively with care providers regarding the price and quality of care. A second major change involves defining the scheme's coverage in terms not of provider categories but of functions. Hitherto people needing home nursing, for example, have been entitled to the services of a nurse employed by a legally recognized community-nursing institution. Under the Dekker proposals there is no recognized provider, simply an entitlement to nursing care on the part of those concerned; different providers may then compete to provide that care. These could be community-nursing organizations as in the past, but also hospitals providing outreach services or nursing agencies working on a private basis. The expectation underlying the Dekker proposals was that insurers would seek to conclude contracts under which the cost to them was minimized and the standard of care maximized.

Initial criticisms of the Dekker proposals focused on two main issues.

The first was the question whether the proposals would indeed cut costs. In a market where the elasticity of demand is high, as is the case in health care, the introduction of greater competition among suppliers could lead them to generate new demand, causing aggregate costs to rise; the high cost in terms of percentage of gross domestic product of market-based health care systems like that of the United States is cited as evidence for this view. Moreover the market mechanism could be distorted by cartel agreements between health insurers. To avoid this and to prevent risk selection detailed anti-cartel regulations would be needed, together with the bureaucracy to enforce them.

The other issue raised concerned the 15 per cent of costs not covered by basic insurance. One of the assumptions made in the Dekker proposals was that almost everyone would take out supplementary cover, but critics argued that the lower paid in particular would not do so: faced with high costs they would turn to the safety net offered by the social-welfare system.

The Dekker report was published in a period when the government was a coalition of Christian Democrats and market-minded liberals, including a liberal State Secretary for Health. When in 1990 a government of Christian Democrats and social democrats took office the new social democratic state secretary for health modified the Dekker proposals to allow a substantially larger part of medical costs to be covered by the national system of health insurance.

The first small steps towards implementation of the system in January 1992 (which included bringing the cost of prescribed drugs under the social-insurance system) triggered a new national debate on the structure and funding of health care. The effect on the premiums paid by the privately insured was considerable and employers feared that this would produce demands for higher wages. Opponents also argued that with such generous cover health care costs would rise.

The result of this debate was that implementation of the new funding structure for health care was postponed; further changes would be made step by step, with careful evaluation after each one.

The original plans were also modified in the direction of greater state involvement. At regional level the provinces and large city authorities were to be given greater powers in respect of access and coordination: together with the providers of health care and the insurers, the provinces and large cities would develop "regional visions", i.e global strategic plans for the development of the regional health care system. These plans would set the framework for contracts between the providers of finance and of health care.

1.6. Conclusion

This section highlights a number points to be borne in mind while reading this report.

First, the Netherlands has a plural health care system in which power and responsibility are divided between government, providers and insurers. In this situation it is no easy matter to construct scenarios, still less implement blueprints, for the organization of health care.

Second, the structure of health care in the Netherlands incorporates sharp boundaries between primary care on the one hand and specialist and hospital care on the other. This creates problems in the areas of continuity of care for the chronic sick and of aftercare for patients discharged from hospital.

Third, within the primary sector there is considerable variation in the organizational basis of different providers and provider categories, which range from self-employed professionals without defined catchment areas to organizations with salaried employees covering geographically defined areas. This causes problems of coordination within the sector.

Fourth, the delivery of care in people's homes is gaining in importance owing to the limited capacity of intramural provision and the deliberate policy of shifting care out of institutions and into the community. Home care is also becoming increasingly complex.

A final and important dimension of the process of reorganizing Dutch health care is that it opens up opportunities for new structures which have hitherto been impossible.

2.   Social trends and home care

2.1.   Introduction

It is not always obvious why a particular topic becomes a focus of attention and interest. At first sight this is the case with home care: don't we all know that Dutch health care is a decent and humane system? why should it have to change? It is only on closer inspection that the links with a range of social trends become clear, showing the concern with home care to be more than a chance matter. In this chapter we outline the social context of the scenario study.

2.2.   From home to intramural care - and back

Until modern times the sick, the elderly and the handicapped were cared for within the family: care was a private matter, taken over by professionals only for lack of an alternative. Care at home was the rule, care in hospital the exception. From the end of the last century onwards, however, care was increasingly professionalized, with the result that hospital care became the rule and home care the exception. The last decade has brought a shift in the other direction, with home care returning in new forms.

A striking illustration is provided by the rise and transformation of intramural health care. The history of intramural care, which can be seen as a process driven by advances in medical technology and developing views on treatment and care, falls into three phases: that of provision for the poor in hospices and almshouses; the phase when the hospital took on its familiar form, with an emphasis on care for people with chronic degenerative diseases and cancer; and the current phase in which hospitals are "withdrawing" into short-term specialist care (STG 1987a). Since the development of ambulatory and tertiary care appears to have mirrored that of hospital care, we now look briefly at the historical background.

Hospitals as we know them today grew out of the medieval system of hospices and almshouses, institutions intended not so much for the sick as for cripples, the poor, the old and travellers. Querido writes: "In the middle ages it would not have occurred to anyone that a sick person would benefit from admission to an institution in order to cure them of their disease. People entered institutions because they were crippled, old and poor, because they needed food, warmth, light, somewhere to rest" (Querido, quoted in: Stevens 1990). Medical care was normally given at home, by surgeons and doctors. Institutions began to be differentiated as towns started to provide separate facilities for travellers and to distinguish between provision for the poor who were capable of work and provision for those who were sick. Doctors did not become involved until late in the history of intramural care, roughly at the time their occupation was professionalized. In the Netherlands legislation introduced from the middle of the nineteenth century onwards tidied up the practice of medicine: the doctor became the central figure, the pharmacist was bound by the doctor's prescriptions, the midwife's role was tightly circumscribed. Two processes thus contributed to the development of the modern hospital: on the one hand the growth of institutions concerned with the care of the sick, on the other the professionalization of medicine.

With the rapid growth of medical knowledge and technology in the early part of this century treatments were developed which could only by offered in hospital. The growth of medical knowledge also led to increasingly narrow specialization. As Querido says, "The hospital thus gradually became a medical centre, a concentration of facilities for investigation, treatment and surgery, of expert staff, and at the same time the centre where both future doctors and future nurses were trained. All this made it seem steadily more natural that the treatment should not be taken to the patient but that the patient should go to seek treatment" (Querido 1974). In this view the concentration of health care in hospitals reflects the concentration of medical technologies (STG 1987).

Given the shift towards specialization and hospital care the general practitioner developed into a physician providing general care. Stevens (1990) draws attention to the almost exclusive relationship between the intramural setting on the one hand and specialist treatment and intensive care on the other. Medical care outside the hospital evolved into the opposite of intramural care, i.e. non-specialist and non-intensive. In the middle ages the opposition between home and hospital was also an opposition between rich and poor; this may no longer be true of the opposition between home and general hospital, but for a significant proportion of intramural nursing and care the old opposition is still valid: the long-term residents of institutions such as mental-handicap homes, psychiatric hospitals, nursing homes and homes for the elderly come predominantly from the lower socio-economic groups. In the area of acute care the development of medical technology and the professionalization of medicine replaced the rich/poor opposition with an opposition between intensive and non-intensive care, while for the less affluent chronically sick or disabled there developed what was almost a separate set of institutions. There thus grew up three sectors of health care: the hospitals, providing specialist, intensive, short-term care; a set of institutions caring for long-term care-dependent and generally less affluent patients; and home care for non-intensive care.

The changing fate of the general practitioner, as revealed in this brief historical outline, is noteworthy. The rise of the hospital and advances in technology resulted in the general practitioner giving more and more ground to the specialist: "the domain of the general practitioner was unclear, his tasks were ill-defined, and there was no clear boundary between his domain and the specialist's" (Schadé 1989). The tide began to turn in the mid 1950s, however, when the Dutch College of General Practitioners was set up, and in the following decade the development of general practice as an area of study in its own right was pursued with vigour; this culminated in the establishment of university courses for aspiring GPs (Runia and Van Herk 1991). Goudriaan (1988) refers in this connection to a real revival, a movement of rehabilitation, in which "normal care", the care that as it were remains after specialist and hospital care, is upgraded as "continuing, comprehensive and personal care" which only the GP is adequately equipped to provide. The division of health care into tiers, as favoured in the government policy paper of 1974 (Structuurnota) gave the GP a specific role as gatekeeper, ensuring that patients did not come under specialist care or enter hospital unnecessarily.

The GP has thus developed into a specialist, but a specialist in non-specialized care. Working alongside the GP are the core services of community nursing, home help and general social work, whose origins, professionalization and position in the system are also closely tied up with the history of intramural care. In many cases the professional groups and institutions involved with the GP in home care, have followed their own route from charity through voluntary initiative to mainstream institutions of community nursing, home help and general social work under the aegis of the state. What matters particularly in this context is that in response to the development of hospital care, extramural care became the domain of less intensive care.

Professionalization and technology explain not only the growth of the general hospital but also the changing position of institutions for the care of the chronic sick and care-dependent, known in the Netherlands as the third tier or tertiary sector. Here the medical profession made its entrance at a still later stage than in the hospices. Until late in the last century such institutions were little more than asylums, refuges for the homeless, the insane or the elderly, overseen by trustees and run by housefathers and housemothers. The arrival of the medical profession was accompanied by the introduction of the associated medical model, with the result that the institutions gradually came to be modelled on the general hospital (Oetomo 1970, Huismans et al. 1973). In other words, through the application of the medical model the third tier has come to offer something more like hospital care. Here the driving force is not so much medical technology in a narrow sense; rather is it the growth of drug therapies and new views on care and treatment that have turned what was once an asylum or refuge into a sort of specialized hospital. In these cases there seems to have been a shift of objectives and methods, with the provision of shelter making way for a form of care patterned rather on the medical model. De Vries considers that the Dutch

48

tend to have confidence in this type of institutional care, a confidence that has to a large extent been induced by professional care providers, citing in this connection the historian Schama: "The Dutch seek sustainable and democratic solutions for the problems confronting them. The core of Dutch solutions comprises reliability and accountability, conditions best realized in institutions" (De Vries 1988).

In recent years the trend of increasing emphasis on intramural care appears to have been reversed: thanks to population aging, the individualization of society and advances in medical technology (NZR 1989) hospital care and the third tier (long term institutional care) find themselves on the brink of radical change. The growing demand for complex care reflects population aging; the new emphasis on the individual and on choice mean that hospitalization is now less likely to be accepted as a matter of course. Psychiatric hospitals and nursing homes are dispersing their residential function, creating small housing schemes across their regions. Technological advances are influencing the organization of hospital care.

There seems no end to the spectacular progress in medical technology achieved in recent years. Dunning sums up in one sentence the potential of medical science: "Biotechnology will produce new drugs using recombinant DNA techniques, medical physics will develop new applications of laser technology and ultrasound, immunology will improve transplant surgery and increase demand for donors, molecular biology will chart the human genome" (Dunning 1990). Less spectacular but no less important is the process of miniaturization, thanks to which equipment is no longer tied to particular locations. As Schrijvers notes, "After the Second World War the growing dependence on laboratory facilities and diagnostic and therapeutic equipment meant that the work of medical specialists was concentrated in hospitals. Modern equipment is more compact and more mobile and can be remote-controlled; it can therefore serve patients in their own home" (Schrijvers 1990a). Technological advances are prompting processes of dispersal and organizational change in hospital care.

The scenario study dealing with hospital care in the twenty-first century (STG 1990a) discussed these various developments at length. They concern in the first place diagnostic technologies such as ultrasound, computer tomography, magnetic resonance and PET scanning, computerized imaging techniques that make diagnosis easier, cheaper, more mobile and above all usable on the spot, including outside hospital. Then there are the developing curative technologies, mainly in the area of "half way" technology: non-invasive techniques, medication using implants, biosensors and remote monitoring. Advances like these make it increasingly possible to continue nursing and care outside hospital. Finally there are the developments in communications and information technology, the remote access to relevant medical data offered by personal computers and data networks. How all this might affect care in the future is shown in this personal vision: further growth in the size of hospitals to 500-700 beds; reduction in the number of hospitals to around one hundred, each serving a population of 200,000-300,000; an average length of stay of seven days; GPs attached to hospitals; specialists working extramurally; close links with the primary sector; on-line access to specialist information for GPs; a comprehensive care package, including home care, with the hospital as organizer, and aftercare provided in nursing homes (Greve, interviewed in Het Ziekenhuis 1988).

Technological advances and changing views on care seem likely to erode the *raison d'être* of intramural care. The need to concentrate patients in institutions is diminishing. For a number of years the growing replacement of inpatient treatment with outpatient and day treatment has meant that average length of stay and occupancy rates have fallen; Van Velde and Van der Zee (1990a, 1990b) report an increase in day treatment from zero in 1975 to 270,000 days in 1988. The hospital scenario refers to an increase of 24 per cent in day treatment over seven years and a fall in average length of stay from 17.9 days in 1969 to 11.5 days in 1987; allowing for population aging this represents a fall of 44 per cent. The 1990 Social and Cultural Report noted a fall in occupancy rates, to the point that in 1988 a little over a quarter of the country's 73,150 hospital beds were unoccupied. There is no doubt that a shift is under way in the intramural sector from inpatient care to ambulatory care, day treatment and short-stay admissions.

Trends in the organization of intramural care include both centralization and dispersal, at first sight contradictory processes. On the one hand there is an increase in the scale of activity, with small hospitals disappearing (the number of hospitals fell from 200 in 1971 to 146 in 1986); on the other there is a trend towards dispersal, with the development of multi-site hospitals. Organizational expansionism is thus accompanied by a drive towards larger numbers of smaller-scale establishments (STG 1990). This trend affects general and psychiatric hospitals and nursing homes. Also noteworthy are the calls for the dismantling of the tiered system and the creation of networks in which hospitals cooperate harmoniously with their extramural partners and the nursing homes (NZR 1989; HZH 1987, 1990; LSV 1988).

The care provided is also undergoing change. With its post office, coffee shop, magazine racks and hairdresser's the modern hospital has opened itself up to society; but while this is a significant change, of greater importance is the increased emphasis on gearing care to individual patients' needs, the transition from "care management" to "managed care": flexible support, customized services, user-friendly transitions from one care form to another, the elimination of waiting times and a choice between hospital care and home care. The clear objective is to give patients a more central role in the care process.

These trends imply an expansion of home care and the development of residential provision on the one hand and a slimming-down of intramural facilities to small-scale specialized centres on the other. If this process continues the relationship between home and hospital care will again be reversed, with home care becoming the rule and admission the exception - as urged in the Basic Paper accompanying the Draft Key Paper on Health Policy: "The situation that intensive or supplementary home care is provided where admission to hospital is indicated must change: home care must become the norm, intramural care the exception" (Ministry of Welfare, Health and Cultural Affairs 1989). Where admission is required, this should be on the basis of a positive indication: residential admission where the patient is unable to look after him- or herself, clinical admission where treatment can only be provided in hospital (Stevens 1990). Publications from the

51

world of general practice point in the same direction. Under the title "From hospital care to home care" Schadé (1990) analyses recent developments, referring to financial constraints, technological advances and what he sees as patients' changing feelings towards hospital care: growing specialization and obtrusive technology mean that patients now feel less at ease in hospital and are therefore more inclined to favour home-based care.

How far is a shift towards home care possible? In the nursing-home and mental-hospital sectors the development of new forms of dispersed residential provision is in full swing, and since the delivery of care is not tied to specific technical facilities there is no reason why it should not be home-based. While this possibility is less obvious in the case of the seriously ill, here too there appear to be no insuperable technical obstacles. The scenario study on this topic (STG 1988) referred to developments in home-care technology - electronics, alarm systems, diagnostic kits, new drugs, new methods of administration (implants, controlled-release techniques, etc.), developments in pain control and parenteral nutrition, light but strong prostheses - but concluded that, while the means might be available their introduction could be expected to present problems. These problems related to the inappropriate organization of primary care, unsuitable funding arrangements, care providers unfamiliar with the use of the new technologies and, last but not least, the lack of expertise on the part of both patient and care provider. The trend could be said to be one of "extramuralization", with hospital care giving way to home care. This shift is moreover reinforced by demographic and cultural trends and fits in with government policy.

2.3. Population aging and individualization

The composition and structure of the country's population are changing; two aspects of this change of direct relevance to our subject are population aging and individualization.

The 1990 population forecast (CBS 1990) indicates both a declining growth rate and a change in composition. The low variant envisages the population peaking at 15.6 million in 2005, falling back thereafter to 12.6 million in 2050; in the middle variant the peak of 16.5 million is reached in 2025, followed by a decline to 15.3 million in 2050; the high variant, finally, sees the population rising to 18.4 million in 2040 and falling back to 18.3 million in 2050. As a result of this process the breakdown of the Netherlands' population will come to resemble more closely that of other European countries, i.e. average age will rise. The number of young people (aged 0-19) will fall from 3.8 million in 1990 to 2.9 million in 2020 (low variant), remain fairly constant until 2000 and then decline to 3.4 million in 2020 (middle variant), or rise to 4.3 million in 2010 and then fall back to four million in 2020 (high variant). We can of course be more precise about trends in the elderly population than about future numbers of young people. The number of people aged 65 and over will rise from 1.9 million in 1990 to 2.9 million (low variant), 3.0 million (middle variant) or 3.2 million (high variant) in 2020, while the proportion of people aged 65 and over in the population as a whole will rise from 12.8 per cent in 1990 to 18.5 per cent in 2020. Moreover among the elderly there will be an increase in the proportion of the very old ("double population aging"). In 1990 people aged 75 and over made up 5.4 per cent of the total population; the figure is expected to increase to around 7.4 per cent by 2020, when the very old will comprise some 40 per cent of the 65+ age group.

The implications of these demographic trends for the demand for health care and the supply of services required have been considered in various scenario studies, among them those concerned with population aging (STG 1985), cardiovascular disease (STG 1986), cancer (STG 1987b) and chronic disease (STG 1990d, 1990e). These are summarized by Schrijvers (1990b), who expects the demand for care to increase by one per cent per year as a result of population aging; the rise in the number of chronic sick associated with the aging of the population will add a further 1.5 per cent per year. Other factors taken into account include technological progress (e.g. in the transplant field) and an element of catching up (as waiting lists and certain other problems are alleviated), giving an additional annual rate of increase of 0.4 per cent. Overall, Schrijvers thus sees the demand for care increasing by some three per cent per year.

Capacity shortfalls mean that this increased demand is unlikely to be met without special measures. The 1985 scenario report on population aging (STG 1985) noted that if current policies were maintained there would be a shortfall of 50,000 places in homes for the elderly and of 5,000 beds in nursing homes; an increase of 85,000 units was also required in the area of adapted residential provision. The growth in demand can therefore not be accommodated within the current stock of 51,000 nursing-home places and 137,900 places in homes for the elderly. According to the 1990 Social and Cultural Report (SCP 1990) provision in these areas is currently marked by waiting lists and rising occupancy rates and no great increase in capacity is possible in the short term. This leaves the further expansion of home care, professional care and informal care as the only means of meeting increasing demand. The expansion of informal care will be no easy matter, partly on account of demographic trends, as the following discussion of the process we may call individualization makes clear.

The Welfare Policy Harmonization Council distinguishes definitions of individualization at four levels, the personal, the organizational, the cultural and the political: at the personal level it is concerned with feelings, attitudes and perceptions; at the level of social organization it is the process whereby increasing emphasis is placed on the smallest unit in society, the individual; at the cultural level relevant concepts are those of autonomy, freedom, self-development and dignity; and at the level of politics and government, finally, the issue is whether the relevant unit for purposes of welfare benefits and income should be the individual or the household (Koot and Stegerhoek 1986).

Individualization thus has two aspects: on the one hand are demographic processes - households shrink, more and more people live alone - which increase the number of one-person households; on the other are social and cultural factors such as the growing stress on self-development, personal freedom and autonomy. Both have a direct impact on the developing relationship between supply and demand in the field of health care and both mean that the new interest in home care is not merely a matter of chance. This section covers the demographic aspect; the social and cultural dimension is the subject of the next section.

Individualization can be seen as the last stage of a process of radical change in traditional patterns of interpersonal and social relations. Industrialization and the growth of the nation state brought with them the urbanization of society and in its train the replacement of the extended family - usually living close together, often under one roof - with the nuclear family; now we seem to have entered a phase in which the nuclear family itself is losing ground as a social structure. Addressing the question "Is there still hope for the family?" Roussel (Pineau 1990) draws attention to its steady shrinkage as one or two children become the norm, the family circle narrows, people have fewer uncles, aunts and cousins, and geographical mobility makes contacts less frequent. There is also a trend towards later marriage and less marriage, more frequent marital breakdown and less frequent remarriage (Ministry of Education and Science 1990; STG 1990b).

The result is a rapid growth in single living, especially among the elderly. According to the 1990 population forecast of the Central Bureau of Statistics the number of divorced elderly women will increase from four per cent of the population in 1990 to twelve per cent in 2010 and the number of divorced elderly men from 3.3 per cent to ten per cent. Schrijvers (1990a) estimates that the proportion of unmarried, widowed and divorced persons will rise from 53.4 per cent of the population in 1990 to 57.8 per cent in 2010.

The combination of demographic individualization and the shift towards home care that we can expect in view of technological, demographic and ideological trends generates an obvious problem, one moreover which could be greatly aggravated by increasingly demanding attitudes on the part of consumers: "The more people become aware of their own personality and the more the individual is seen as the main unit in society, the greater will be the weight attached to autonomy, self-development, dignity and the like, and the more strongly people will demand their realization in the material and non-material foundations of life" (Koot and Stegerhoek 1986). It is to this social and cultural dimension of individualization that we now turn.

2.4. Freedom, equality and choice

The 1960s were a decade of protest, of the questioning of authority, of revolt against the then dominant norms and values notably in the cultural sphere. Groups became increasingly unwilling to accept second-class status, with e.g. women, students, soldiers and homosexuals leading the way in demands for equal rights. Looking back it is striking how easily such rights were conceded in the Netherlands: the cultural revolts of the 1960s led with little opposition to legislation enshrining new rights and freedoms as (for example) the universities were reformed and women were given a statutory entitlement to equal treatment and equal pay with men. The various liberation movements' success was undoubtedly due to the fact that they reflected underlying social shifts. The demographic or structural changes described in the preceding section were the cause of a new relationship between the individual and society.

The role of the family has altered, people have become more mobile and as a result participation in social life has changed. Better education and greater affluence have also played a major part in the ongoing process of individualization. Not only are there more people living alone, it also seems that the citizen increasingly manifests himself/herself as an individual and takes his/her cue from and participates in a variety of social networks. According to the "lifestyles scenario" (STG 1990b) social networks, with their powerful role in regulating individual behaviour, have fragmented: we have neighbours to keep an eye on our home, friends to discuss emotional problems with, other friends to go out or take part in sport with. Adriaansens sees this as a paradoxical process: on the one hand people are increasingly solitary while on the other they enter into an ever greater and more global collective order; there is less neighbourliness, more support for Amnesty International (Adriaansens 1990). The lifestyles scenario refers to individuals' growing need to decide their own fate, a growing emphasis on individual development and young people's increasingly early independence (STG 1990).

De Swaan has described what is happening as a shift in the pattern of people's dealings with one another from one based on authority and obedience to one based on negotiation, as hierarchical relations - vertical differentiation between man and woman, teacher and pupil, father and son, master and servant, mother and daughter, professor and student - have made way for more horizontal structures: "In some spheres of life a wider range of conduct and expression is now acceptable and the injunctions of society and conscience have weakened. But this relaxation is subject to new limitations laying down not so much what relations may or may not exist between people as how they are to regulate their relations" (De Swaan 1982). In other words, while more things are possible they have to be negotiated. This requirement appears to cover everyone, including providers of care and patients.

Such changes in the pattern of interpersonal relations are manifested e.g. in the area of production and consumption. Schrijvers summarizes the position thus: "Rising affluence has accustomed people to courteous treatment in other service sectors such as tourism, retailing and banking, and they are likely to expect similar courtesy in hospitals and nursing homes: the patient-as-customer is sovereign, while the care provider's role increasingly has elements of the waiter's or shop assistant's. The growing diversity of lifestyles made possible by rising affluence, weakening pressures to conform and closer contacts with those who 'do different' is producing a growing demand for care and information tailored to individual requirements" (Schrijvers 1990a). This passage forms part of a line of reasoning in which home care is seen as an adjustment not only to technological and demographic change but also to an emancipatory movement - "patients' lib" - whereby patients have been transformed into clients (Schadé 1989; Knapen 1988).

Greater equality in the doctor/patient relationship is manifest in the disappearance of the traditional white coat, the replacement of authoritarian attitudes with methodical procedures, listening to the patient and taking time over consultations. Community nurses are also dispensing with their uniforms and making their entry into clients' lives in altogether less formal fashion. De Swaan too notes the changed relationship between patient and care provider: "More recent studies present the patient as someone who, while in the more dependent position, nevertheless has an active role in the relationship, choosing and ranking their problems, engaging implicitly or explicitly in negotiations regarding diagnosis and treatment, obeying or disobeying 'doctor's orders', demanding or ignoring information, shopping around, or playing medical staff off one against the other" (De Swaan 1982).

The role of a client differs from that of a patient: it brings with it no automatic right to weakness or to the suspension of social obligations. With the rise of alternative views of sickness and the appreciation of its psychosocial aspects, the new emphasis on prevention and the media's growing concern with health-promoting behaviour and risk factors, the sick are themselves taking on, consciously or· unconsciously, greater responsibility for their situation. This is manifested e.g. in a trend towards healthier lifestyles and what the Social and Cultural Planning Office identifies as an ever greater priority accorded to health (Laeyendecker 1990). De Haes draws attention to the interest in physical fitness reflected in the decline in smoking and drinking, reduced consumption of fatty and sugary foods and increased participation in sport and physical exercise (De Haes 1990; SCP 1990); people want to be and stay healthy and strive for slimness, beauty and fitness. De Haes would class under the same heading the trend towards self-care using home treatments, not consulting the general practitioner for minor complaints and increased interest in alternative remedies. In De Haes's words, these are all signs that "for the authority of the doctor people have substituted the desire to discover for themselves what suits them" (De Haes 1990).

The parallel with the process of secularization which marked the 1950s and 1960s is striking. When Sartre proclaimed the "death of God" he meant that humanity had left its childhood behind, that right and wrong, human destiny, could no longer be made comprehensible by reference to some supra-human divine being; with this came freedom, but also responsibility. The shift from the patient role to the client role is analogous: as patients we were helpless and blameless; as clients, in contrast, we must stand on our own feet, take responsibility for our situation. Where illness was once, as Laeyendecker puts it, "the incapacity to perform roles and tasks" (Laeyendecker 1990), the interpretation has shifted to "the absence of wellbeing" (SCP 1990). Stevens (1990) describes how the earlier, negative, view of health as "the absence of illness or handicap" gave way to definitions such as that given in the government's 1966 statement on health policy: "It has increasingly become clear that health is not the absence of disease, the state which follows physical or mental recovery, but rather a state of physical and mental wellbeing which is to a considerable extent socially determined" (SZV 1966). Koster-Dreese's description of illness from the patient's viewpoint is illustrative here: "In my view illness is not the inability to perform roles and tasks. On the contrary, in most cases an illness enables people to perform their roles and tasks better in the long run and to determine their content for themselves. Illness is not simply a physiological process but also one which has the effect of purifying, clarifying, prioritizing, and enhancing awareness" (Koster-Dreese 1990). In this formulation illness is not a form of deviance; illness does not exist, there is only variation which society makes worth the effort.

Against this background it is noteworthy that formal ratification of the individual's emancipated role and position is taking longer in health care than in other sectors: someone who qualifies for help receives it in kind and has only a limited say in its timing, quantity and nature, and where the change from charity to entitlement has been made in the field of social security, in health care the move remains controversial. For many the very word "care" suggests charitable activity rather than established rights. Dahrendorf puts it as follows: "The term 'caring' is misleading. Its paternalistic overtones divert attention from the fact that we are here concerned with rights. Pensions and health care, accident insurance, even education and perhaps the minimum wage: these are all civil rights, not forms of charity" (Dahrendorf 1988). The Dutch patients'/consumers' association LPCP accordingly rejects the term "care", consistently referring to "health services": "The use of the word 'care' detracts from the legal nature of the entitlement to service". The LPCP's alternative formulation of the objective of health services is "assistance with the maintenance or reestablishment, as far as possible, of personal autonomy" (Van der Wilk 1988).

That health care should lag behind other welfare sectors in this way undoubtedly reflects the medical profession's powerful independent position between system and client, which results in matters which would elsewhere be decided by the client being reserved in health care to the doctor. The aim of the patient/consumer movement is to take over that privileged position: "The requirement is that all groups in the health services and related fields unambiguously recognize the legitimacy and importance of the patient's viewpoint and act accordingly... in a word, a service in which the patient's viewpoint is the guiding principle" (Van der Wijk 1988). The implications of this position are vast: health care does not exist; there is only the delivery of services in connection with the maintenance of personal autonomy. The demand could not be clearer: it is that the patient should be treated "as a client, not as a child incapable of making his or her own decisions" (Koster-Dreese 1990). In Van der Wilk's words, "the patient is the care coordinator, the patient manages the budget".

Does this mean that individual patients in fact seek and obtain a greater say *vis à vis* the care provider? Sickness, fear, pain and personal attitudes all have a powerful effect on assertiveness, and in such situations people often prefer to subordinate themselves to a doctor's authority. However, there are also forms of "liberation by proxy", with pressure groups or ombudsman-style organizations promoting the interests of those they represent. As Schnabel notes, "The patients' movement has come to be dominated to a significant extent by what Kobben has called 'public advocates', non-patients and ex-patients who, legitimated by the moral moment of the 'case', act as spokespersons for and in the name of patients" (Schnabel 1985).

These changes are not necessarily all be for the better. "Liberated" patients demand care tailored to their requirements and, some believe, in increasing quantities. Dunning (1990) fears that patients' growing awareness of and insistence on their rights may provoke a flight into "defensive medicine", with testing and treatment taking place not because they are strictly speaking indicated but because patients' demands must be met. In De Kam's view (1990) developing technology will inevitably generate growing demand: where the means exist the patient, spurred by the publicity given to medical matters, will insist on their use. The impact of the media should not be overstated, however; to the extent that it has been explicitly investigated, no direct effect on consumption has been found (Huisman and Schadé 1987).

What is clear is how far everyday life has been medicalized. People have increasingly become subject to rules of behaviour set by the medical profession, and an aging population and early diagnosis of health problems will mean that people are under medical supervision for ever longer periods (Laeyendecker 1990). In this connection De Swaan uses the term "medical regime", by which he means that questions of dependence and need are subordinated to "the totality of injunctions issued by doctors in respect of their fellow humans, their dominant influence over people's information, perceptions and conduct in matters relating to the maintenance and restoration of functions" (De Swaan 1982). He goes on to say that "The establishment of this medical regime means that in society as a whole people have increasingly come to be guided by medical instructions in many phases and aspects of life and have thus become more dependent on the medical profession." In their daily lives too people increasingly take their cue from general medical guidance: "Over the last half century that medical involvement has extended widely over fields where doctors' expertise does not offer adequate answers and where other approaches are perfectly conceivable."

This may not matter much in relatively trivial cases where people have some measure of choice, but the position is different where there is a prolonged need for care. The need for care implies dependence on institutions and on other people and hence a loss of freedom. The new interest in home care appears to be related to this point. Patients' ongoing "liberation" has been associated with a loss of faith in intramural care. The demand for home care is thus a demand for deinstitutionalization and a reflection of a "declining confidence in all types of intramural institution for people with social problems" (Lerman 1985). The suggestion is that home care should form part of the client's daily life in such a way that it is by definition subordinate to their particular life situation (Schrijvers and Van Londen 1990a, b, c; Philipsen 1988). The home situation differs sharply from the situation in the hospital, where the patient is bound by the rules of the institution. Associated with home care, therefore, is the wish to replace the medical regime with a "social regime" comprising the unwritten rules that arise in the client's own sphere of life (Philipsen 1988).

As we have seen, the emancipatory processes that have marked other areas of society are also making themselves felt in health care. Patients' new self-confidence, associated with the formal recognition of patients' rights, will promote the development of home care and may produce a sharp increase in demand. Against the background of this observation it is interesting to consider the development of government policy in recent years.

2.5. Government policy

Official health policy in the Netherlands is closely bound up with the features and fortunes of the welfare state, whose operation is largely in the hands of quasi-public non-governmental organizations - mediating institutions - which grew out of voluntary initiative. These institutions, with their religious or ideological roots, play a major and characteristic role in Dutch society: "In the Netherlands the state has traditionally been modest in scale. One of the most stubborn myths about this country is that the state performs very many - too many - functions and has control of everything. Compared with the position in neighbouring countries, the state does very little here. The *collective* sector may be very large, but within it the state is certainly not dominant and indeed in some areas it is virtually absent" (Aquina 1990). Government has only limited influence on health care, mainly because, as Aquina notes, health services are still largely run by mediating institutions, by what the Dutch call the "social midfield". This does not mean government has no influence: of course it has, through legislation, regulation and funding, but its influence is largely exercised by creating frameworks and setting conditions. The state's influence on the actual delivery of services is much smaller, and policy in that area is mainly reactive. Policy is generally developed and implemented through negotiation and is never revolutionary in nature. As Aquina notes, "The government paper on the structure of health care was written as if the state had power in this field, even though policy formation in respect of health care in the Netherlands was still virtually entirely in the hands of voluntary bodies and independent contractors" (Aquina 1990).

De Swaan has described how the state has gradually taken on responsibility for people's welfare and wellbeing in many areas of life. The rise of the welfare state meant a shift from individually to collectively borne risks in respect of illness, death, accident and unemployment (De Swaan 1989), with government underwriting the citizenry's collective welfare. This involves action of two kinds, with the welfare state both undertaking the redistribution of material goods and guaranteeing equal access for all to certain material and non-material or social goods (Koot and Stegerhoek 1986). Through a set of collectively funded statutory schemes the state ensures the availability of welfare services, among them health care. "A basic feature of our health care system is its egalitarian nature," Fortuyn writes (1990). While the construction of the welfare state was begun after the Second World War, the growth of health care occurred relatively late, following the expansion of the coverage of the Health Insurance Act and the introduction of the Exceptional Medical Expenses Act in 1968 (Greve, interviewed in *Het Ziekenhuis*, 1988).

It is an irony of history that just as the welfare state approaches completion the system is beginning to look inappropriate. We have seen the growth of what has been called the post-industrial economy as new technologies, particularly in the information field, have shifted the centre of gravity within the manufacturing sector and as the latter has been overtaken by a much larger service sector (Adriaansens 1990). At the same time the traditional patterns of social and family life have been eroded. In the Netherlands these developments prompted the various reform plans of the 1980s - social-security changes, the simplification of the tax system, health care reforms - as solutions were sought to stubborn problems in the areas of cost and control. The cost of health care, for example, rose from 3.3 per cent of GNP in 1950 to 8.8 per cent in 1983 (Schrijvers 1990b); according to Fortuyn the figure is now over nine per cent, even though the recent past has brought a stabilization or slight fall.

The combination of high cost and poor control is reflected in the strong wording of the Dekker Report: "The current system is rigid from regulation, its costs are out of control and unsustainable and it fails to match supply and demand" (Dekker Committee). The government hopes to alleviate the problem by substituting expensive forms of care with cheaper (while of course safeguarding access), increasing cost-consciousness, cutting taxes and public borrowing and, remarkably, further strengthening the "social midfield" of mediating institutions.

As this indicates, the official strategy is now deregulation. Following a period in which the main themes were the maintenance of access and democratic safeguards for quality the current emphasis is clearly on rolling back the frontiers of the state: efficiency improvements and cost reductions are to be achieved by entrusting tasks to mediating institutions and by manipulating demand with the help of market forces (Fortuyn 1990). The picture that emerges is one of a more or less "powerless" state, as witness the comment in the most recent Social and Cultural Report to the effect that government is guilty of overproducing policy. What this means is that a failure to achieve objectives leads not to their abandonment but rather their refinement: there is an omnipresent impulse to continuous policy development with little regard to feasibility, and the Report concludes that "The problems encountered in implementing policy on education and the caring services are partly the result of overestimating the rate at which and extent to which change can be achieved in complex organizations" (SCP 1990).

A constant theme of government policy in recent years has been that of rolling back the frontiers of the state. This is of course no easy matter. Such major policy changes have to be legitimated, and it is here in part that the source of official interest in home care, informal care and the "emancipation of the citizen" is to be found. Policies prompted by a recalcitrant combination of high costs and ineffective controls are given a political and ideological underpinning in terms of what Adriaansen (1990) refers to as a revival of "civic culture", the notion of the "caring or responsible community". The reasoning runs as follows. People are no longer used to taking responsibility for one another: expecting the state to provide, they feel ever less concern for the fate of the weak in society. In this view the process of individualization has gone too far, eroding people's natural solidarity. The relationship between the state and mediating institutions, and between the state and individual citizens, has become lopsided, with too much being done by the state and not enough by the citizens themselves. This puts a heavy strain on collective resources and, in the area of health care, leads to underuse of self-care and of informal care within the family. The state must therefore encourage people to take greater responsibility for themselves and each other by pursuing policies of "social activation". The policy statement issued when Mr Ruud Lubbers' first government took office at the start of the 1980s looked forward to a "transition from a welfare state which threatens to become unaffordable and oppressive to a caring society in which people stand by one another. Culture and civilization imply mutual protection from neglect, despair and loneliness" (in: Koot and Stegerhoek 1986).

The wording used in such contexts includes such phrases as "care tailored to individual needs" and "substitution of care", key notions in thinking on home care developed in the 1986 Budgetary Statement on Interdepartmental Welfare Policy. The Welfare Policy Harmonization Council summarizes the thought process thus: "The characteristic concept developed for the broad field of care provision is that of 'customized care', whereby the government seeks to foster personal responsibility and to counter excessive professionalization. This 'customized care', which is generally simpler and less expensive than traditional approaches, implies tailoring services more closely to individual requirements by not providing an all-in package (as happens by definition in institutions) and by offering flexible services close to home, supplementing care within the family and voluntary work, and improving horizontal and vertical coordination. It also implies developing a wide range of intermediate care forms tailored more closely to the requirements of specific groups and individuals" (Koot and Stegerhoek 1986).

Analysis of the relevant policy documents issued by successive governments in the 1980s reveals the development, always underpinned with references to the concept of 'customized care', of proposals for major shifts in the pattern of care: from intramural to extramural care, from extramural care to voluntary work, from voluntary work to care within the family, and from family care to self-care. According to the *Nota 2000* policy paper a shift of emphasis is needed from professional care to voluntary work and informal care and to self-care. In its comments the Welfare Policy Harmonization Council did not mince words: "We cannot escape the impression that the minister and state secretary are in difficulty with the notion of the 'caring society'. They find themselves in a paradoxical situation, in that they regard self-care and informal care as vitally important but recognize that it is very hard for government to foster them. And since the government sees informal care as offering scope for constraining the growth of formal provision and perhaps even for cutting it back, it thus has wishes that it is powerless to realize" (Koot and Stegerhoek 1986).

The conclusion may be drawn that the government's allocation of a central role to home care was directly linked to the need to cut costs and the desire to deregulate. This policy shift was legitimated by reference to the notion of the 'caring society'. In concrete terms this political philosophy was manifested in two policy goals, the development of customized care and the strengthening of informal care. In the next section we consider how realistic the hope for a shift from formal to informal care is.

2.6.   The shift towards informal care

Formal and informal care can be defined thus: "Formal care is care that is delivered (or whose delivery is secured) by the state on a public basis; it is governed by the requirements of statutory and administrative accountability. Informal care concerns the private interests of citizens accountable only to one another" (Koot and Stegerhoek 1986). Formal care is delivered by professionals who possess a systematic body of knowledge and/or specific skills. Informal care, the care devoted to one's own health or that of family, friends etc., is independent of, or supplementary to, professional care; it may be classified under the headings of self-care (individuals meeting their own care needs), care within the family or among friends, group self-help (people working to resolve their own and each other's problems, usually in some specific area), and voluntary work done without obligation or financial reward for the benefit of other members of society (Koot and Stegerhoek 1986). The question to which we now turn is this: can the growing need for home care by met by informal carers?

The first point to recognize is that the growing demand for care is due in large part to population aging: even aside from health problems old people are more likely to have difficulty in looking after themselves, and any deficits in self-care will normally be met within the individual's immediate social circle of family and friends. The availability of such care implies the existence of a social network extending beyond the individual's partner or children. Research has shown, however, that the main recipients are carers' own parents or parents-in-law, that the carers are mainly women (one in three women aged 30-60 looks after elderly relatives) and that of the three-and-a-half hours of care provided on average every week most (more than three hours) is provided by women (Tjadens and Woldringh 1989). The same research showed the numbers involved to be large: Tjadens and Woldringh estimate that ten per cent of the population of the Netherlands have some difficulty in looking after themselves and that of these only 62 per cent receive the informal care they need.

The demographic, social and cultural changes of recent decades have had a direct impact on the availability of informal care. The *Nota 2000* policy paper drew attention to an interplay of factors: a decline in the practice of aged parents living with their children, a greater desire for privacy on the part of both parents and children, the smaller homes built since the war, the housing shortage and people's increasing mobility. Philipsen points out that households have been shrinking for over a hundred years, that people today have fewer children and other relatives, that children tend to live further away from their parents than in the past, that the traditional carers - daughters and daughters-in-law - are now more likely to have paid jobs and that "People expect less from one another and are prepared to do less for one another" (Philipsen 1989a). Bensing cautions against excessive expectations of informal care: "The disintegration of the extended family and of community life, particularly in the cities and commuter suburbs, an increasingly mobile population (so that children no longer necessarily live close to their parents - and indeed may not live anywhere long enough to build up social networks), the abolition of children's statutory duty to provide for their parents (when the National Assistance Act was introduced in 1965): all these factors make heavy reliance on informal care a precarious matter" (Bensing 1983). The effect is to narrow theoretically available social networks to those individuals who by their direct proximity and emotional ties are effectively condemned to take on the caring role: partners, daughters, daughters-in-law. If these commentators are right, younger women are likely to have less time, energy and willingness to act as informal carers, leaving a "care network" consisting solely of elderly women looking after their elderly partners.

If family and friends cannot provide the necessary care network, could volunteers conceivably fill the gap? Having investigated the potential contribution of voluntary work Langeveld is not optimistic: while volunteers do in practice replace informal rather than professional carers, the scale on which this happens is so small that no real solution is likely along these lines. Heerdink and Knapen's estimates (1986) of the volume of informal care within the family and voluntary work - 150,000 and 5,000 person-years per year respectively - make clear that voluntary work represents no more than a drop in the ocean. Langeveld also draws attention to various obstacles to the use of voluntary work: there is no obvious way of increasing the number of volunteers; the scale of voluntary activity is always small; it tends to involve specific individual tasks rather than complex care; and the types of help on offer depend on the types of helper that happen to be available (Langeveld 1985).

Moreover social and cultural individualization perhaps make it improbable that growing numbers of people will feel called to do voluntary work. Where lifestyles increasingly stress youth and health people are less and less likely to come into contact with sickness and death in their daily lives. In such a culture it is by no means certain that the young and healthy will wish to help the old and sick, or indeed that those who need help will not opt strongly for professional rather than informal care. With regard to the factors limiting people's willingness to do voluntary work Jonker

(1976) notes that "a policy aimed at promoting and improving informal networks must pay greater attention to the costs, material and non-material, incurred by informal carers". The material costs include both actual outgoings and opportunity costs (incurred because the time spent is not available for other activities), while the non-material costs cast a clear light on the sometimes thankless reality of voluntary work: the work is often hard and exhausting, making heavy demands on volunteers' emotional resources; it is frequently taken for granted (and thus unappreciated) by recipients; little support is available from professionals; and informal carers feel that they are pushed aside the moment the professionals make their appearance. Considerations such as these led the Welfare Policy Harmonization Council to conclude that the potential contribution of informal care was very limited: "We are not optimistic as to the extent to which informal care can stand in for formal care. There is little ground for believing that substitution can occur on any scale" (Koot and Stegerhoek 1986). This pessimism is echoed in more recent statements of government policy such as the Core Statement on Health Policy and the paper Working on Care Renewal (Ministry of Welfare, Health and Cultural Affairs 1989, 1990).

Since no great expansion of informal care can be expected the further "extramuralizing" of health care must imply in the first instance the expansion of professional care. As we shall see in the chapter on complex home care, however, while informal care may not be the answer on its own it is an essential part of the answer. Professional home care, certainly in complex cases, is by definition supplementary to care by family and friends; in the absence of such informal care it is very probably unworkable (STG 1988). Informal care is vital but not enough is available, and this perhaps indicates the limits to home care: home care for care-dependent persons living alone is not feasible in the absence of informal care.

2.7. Conclusion

This chapter has discussed various trends and developments - in medical technology, demography, cultural and social factors, government policy - which together will put a considerable strain on extramural services (cf. also the summary in Schrijvers 1990). The government's policy of containing intramural care while strengthening informal, primary and home care appears to be in line with the wishes of both consumers and producers: it is what the "liberated consumer" wants, and it is made possible by the technological and organizational changes taking place in health and social care. The rallying cry of "customized care" has undergone a shift of meaning, with the emphasis moving from the "caring society" to "individualized care". The conclusion is that the care professionals have taken up the philosophy and then given it a specific content. "Customized care" now stands for liberation and patients' rights, with notions of substitution (whether of extramural for intramural care or of informal for professional care) being pushed into the background. Together these various developments set the social and cultural background for the organizational scenarios, which may be summarized thus:

The growing demand for complex care will not in the first instance be met intramurally. As developments in technology and medicine make care less location-specific it can increasingly be delivered on an ambulatory basis or in the home. However, less care will be available within the family and there will be little scope for expanding informal care, implying heavy demands on professional services. The government will encourage the trend towards ambulatory care not to cut costs but to meet the wishes of an increasingly independently minded public. Patients' - consumers' - awareness of their rights and the increased power of the organizations representing their interests will help ensure that care is individualized, i.e. reflects the wishes and aspirations of each patient. Care provision will therefore become flexible; continuity of care is essential in the case of people with long-term care needs, however, and the government will underpin this with legislation and regulation.

Before introducing the building blocks of the scenarios we look at the subject of the scenario study: the next chapter is devoted to a consideration of primary care and home care and the boundaries of our subject are set.

3. Caring for people at home

3.1. Introduction

In this chapter we define the boundaries of the area with which the scenario study is concerned, looking first at the relationship between primary care and home care. In part this is a definitional matter. In the last chapter the terms were used as if they were unproblematic: this is not the case, however, and as an examination of the literature shows, home care is by no means a well-defined concept. It is essential to the success of this study that we are quite clear as to its subject; it is also important in exploring possible futures that we stand back from the current organization of care. To prevent our discussions from becoming purely theoretical, however, we present a picture of the care currently available to "people at home". We then focus on the central issue, namely the scope for a radical extramuralization of care. Our analysis continues with a consideration of the question of coordination, and we end with a look at the organizational context of primary and home care (ambulatory care).

3.2. Primary care and home care: definitional questions

Home care, despite what the term suggests, does not only mean "care in the home", and without some terminological clarification it will therefore not be possible to mark off the field with which we are concerned. Two questions are addressed:
- what is the relationship between primary care and home care: are they the same thing?
- how worthwhile are distinctions between primary care and home care, between "normal" home care and supplementary or intensive care in the home situation, between primary care and certain forms of specialist care, between primary care and daycare, and so on.

As we shall see, the concepts of home care and primary care are not easily defined, tied up as they are with the goals, interests or ideologies of government, providers and consumers.

Official goals have remained unchanged since the 1974 policy statement on the structure of health care: they are to contain and reverse the growth of intramural services, to reduce the use of specialist care and to hold down costs, notably those of intramural care. Since progress towards these goals has not been rapid new policy statements have appeared with some regularity containing variations on these themes.

The 1974 paper emphasized regionalization, decentralization, tiered provision and the strengthening of the primary sector; its focus was very much on structures and services. The term "primary care" fits into this kind of thinking, relating as it does to the system of tiers based on the type of care provided. Primary care is generalist and comprehensive; not specialized, it is concerned with both body and mind, "the whole person in his or her social environment"; it is directly accessible, without referral; and it is delivered in the context of patients' normal life. As the National Council for Public Health puts it, "The primary sector is the care subsystem made up of non-specialized services and characterized by its comprehensive approach to the patient/client in care delivery, extending to aspects of his or her social and physical environment" (NRV 1987).

In the Netherlands the term "home care" was introduced in the policy statement "Health policy in circumstances of limited resources" (Ministry of Welfare, Health and Cultural Affairs 1983): "The term home care was chosen to emphasize how this model gives priority to those forms of care which allow patients to keep the largest possible measure of independence and to remain in their normal surroundings, so that the order is: self-care and informal care, home care, specialist care and finally residential care." Home care implies a certain philosophy as to the patient's role: when Spreeuwenberg, for example, writes that "Home care comprises all the services aimed at enabling the 'patient' to remain safely in his or her own surroundings for as long as possible and with maximum independence" (Spreeuwenberg 1988a), there is clearly an underlying notion that staying at home and retaining one's independence are a good thing. Use of the term thus relates to the desire to gear provision to maintaining patients' independence, with a new set of tiers based on a locational criterion: the patient receives care either at home or intramurally.

In recent years the term "home care" has become symbolic of services providing care and support at home, thus emphasizing the client's independence. Despite the difference of emphasis the 1983 policy statement regarded primary services and home care as synonymous. With regard to the relationship between the two the statement noted that "The term 'home care' is imprecise, to the extent that the reference is not just to the help that people receive in their home but also to that which is available in neighbourhood facilities. We can thus also (...) speak of primary health care, albeit this term relates to the system of tiers, which is based on more criteria than just the degree of independence retained by the patient" (Ministry of Welfare, Health and Cultural Affairs 1983).

The terminology invites confusion, with two different terms being used for roughly but not quite the same thing: on the one hand primary care with references to organizational structures and the philosophy of comprehensive generalist care, on the other home care underpinned by the same philosophy but with a focus on patients' preferences. It is not surprising that the terms are used interchangeably, since there are no fundamental differences of purpose: primary care is comprehensive and generalist care delivered close to home, in the local community; home care is also comprehensive and generalist but is delivered even closer by, actually at home.

Turning from purpose to practice, however, there is a difference: home care is a specific area of care, namely long-term complex care for the chronically ill, the handicapped, the dependent elderly and so on. Behind the discussions of home care there seems to be a fear that the tiered system impedes effective care for the more dependent patient: as Heydelberg puts it, "The tiered model is increasingly an obstacle to the efficient bringing together of the necessary expertise, capacity and facilities at the level where the problem exists, i.e. in the home situation"; "Between the different levels of specialization that mark the tiered model 'partitions' have developed that (...) make it difficult to align supply and demand" (Heydelberg 1988).

Such thinking can only begin to bear fruit if home care is seen not simply as a rough synonym for primary care but rather as something more or better. Hattinga Verschure emphasizes the importance of informal care, using the term "care mix" to point out the fact that home care must involve a combination of formal and informal care (Hattinga Verschure 1982). On the professional side there is a need for networks of services and institutions, "a range of professional providers, institutional and individual, operating both intramurally and extramurally and thus able to deliver a broad and varied set of professional services to the patients concerned" (Stevens 1991). Such a definition, which brings ambulatory specialist care and daycare under the heading of home care, implies that in the present situation the necessary cooperation between provider categories is impossible. This side of the home-care philosophy runs roughly as follows: complex care in the home situation is set to increase but the primary sector as currently constituted is incapable of delivering it, since cooperation and coordination within the primary sector are inadequate and moreover specialist and intramural services also need to be involved. In this connection government papers refer to the need to create "care networks" (Ministry of Welfare, Health and Cultural Affairs 1989, 1990) to help ensure the availability of flexible and continuing care. For the most part the Dutch health-insurance system entitles patients to benefits in kind from designated providers, and one of the ways in which the government has sought to promote the creation of such networks is through the uncoupling of individual patients' needs from the existing pattern of providers.

While we may therefore conclude in principle that home care and primary care are not the same thing, in practice confusion is inevitable. Since the main providers of home care are community nurses, home helps and GPs, the greater part of home care *is* primary care. Where a patient's care needs increase and/or diversify to the point that the normal care package no longer suffices, then under current arrangements the normal entitlement to service is replaced with a supplementary service, linked to an admission indication. A proportion of home care is thus not freely accessible but rather available only to patients for whom admission to hospital or nursing home is indicated, i.e. the terminology is tied up in part with the funding channel. On the one hand we have the normal entitlement to provision in kind, mainly funded under the Health Insurance Act and the Exceptional Medical Expenses Act; on the other there is supplementary care in the home situation, separately funded from supplementary resources, which is *not* an entitlement. While such supplementary care need not be intensive in nature (e.g. sitter and sleep-in services), it does mean more care or care at other times than is normally possible. Extra confusion results here from the use in the Netherlands of the term "intensive", since all that is meant is that the care so designated is not funded from the usual sources. Confusion is inevitable if the same kinds of care are funded sometimes as primary care and sometimes as home care; no doubt it is felt that different labels are appropriate if different funding channels are used.

What is most confusing, however, is the attributive use of "home", since "home care" can also include the care provided by GPs at their surgeries, daycare provided at nursing homes, hospital outpatient services and the support provided for the residents of flats attached to nursing homes and other forms of sheltered accommodation. This last form of "home care" squares with the notion that for many elderly people, people with disabilities and mental patients the generally small-scale institution-based residential units in which they live should be as much like normal homes as possible: the primary function of the institution is not therapeutic but residential. In the development of thinking on long-term institutional patients the notion has gained ground that general health care should also play a part (Schrijvers and Van Londen 1990; Ministry of Welfare, Health and Cultural Affairs 1989). "Home care" thus often covers any form of care provided to people who have not been admitted to a hospital or nursing home. Perhaps it is safest to interpret "home care" in terms of its ultimate goal, which is to avoid or postpone admission to an institution.

The definitions given in the literature seldom relate purely to theory or principle; rather do they often refer to some form of right or title, perhaps because authority over the delivery of care is being claimed or because some aspect of funding needs to be settled. Home care is thus variously defined because it is new and because market shares have yet to crystallize out. Under the heading "Problems in home care" Spreeuwenberg draws attention to the jostling among potential providers: "Home care is an area in which private nursing agencies, insurers, the home-help organizations, the community-nursing service, hospitals and nursing homes and GP organizations are all jostling for a place. In its experimental home-care projects the Council of Health Insurance Funds made up to 200 guilders per client per day available for community-nursing and home-help services: large sums of money and major interests are at stake, and it is easy to see why everyone is trying to make sure of their share" (Spreeuwenberg 1988).

In the literature (see Wennink and Goudriaan 1990a, b, c) home care is sometimes defined as care delivered actually in the client's home. Such a limited definition encompasses only some elements of primary care, mainly community nursing and home help. Van de Zandt, for example, understands by home care "All services delivered in the home situation" (Van de Zandt 1987), thereby excluding the substantial proportion of GPs' work that takes place in their surgeries. Schadé, in contrast, stresses the role of the GP: "[We cannot] ignore, for the sake of convenience, the fact that GPs have traditionally provided medical home care, sometimes general but often very specific and intensive in nature. I would happily give them the title of 'masters of home care'" (Schadé 1989). The GPs' national association has made its position clear in two papers: regular home care is nothing new - it has always been part of the GP's role (LHV 1988, 1990).

Philipsen takes a different tack, defining home care as all the services delivered by the four core groups of professional providers (GPs, community nurses, home helps and general social workers) "to support, supplement or replace self-care and the informal care given by family and friends" where "the patient/client lives at home and needs care" (Philipsen 1988). The providers are limited to the four core groups; the starting point is self-care and informal care, and no distinction is made between care delivered at home and care accessible from home. A similar claim is made in a joint paper issued by the four primary provider groups, in which they

76

define home care as "personal, comprehensive, continuing, directly accessible, generalist rather than specialist, complementing self-care and informal care, and concerned with patients' general circumstances as well as their medical condition" (LBO 1987). Giving home care the substantive characteristics of primary care in this way excludes specialist and intramural care.

There is another group of definitions that do not limit home care to care given at home but include all services aimed at helping recipients remain in their own home. According to the National Public Health Council, for example, "Home care comprises all nursing, treatment and other help and support provided in the home situation, whether in the form of self-care, informal care by family and friends, voluntary work or professional services, which have the specific purpose of enabling recipients to go on living in their own home" (NRV 1989c). Here the emphasis is on the collective role of all possible providers, the assumption being that home care as currently organized is excessively compartmentalized and that services are needed that cut across existing patterns of provision. Such definitions encompass care delivered in the home and in consulting rooms and indeed specialist care of a temporary nature; they include not only many elements of primary care but also daycare, outpatient services and temporary admissions, thus extending beyond primary care and probably also beyond simple specialist support.

Some authors seek to push all complexities to one side: "Home care is all care provided to people living in their own home; it includes the four core services, together with welfare services, ambulatory mental health care, specialist outpatient services and day treatment for many patient groups" (Schrijvers 1987). This represents an attempt to bypass the existing structure and to think in terms of functions. Heydelberg's definition has the same characteristic: "Home care refers to facilitatory and support services for people who find it difficult or impossible to cope independently in one or more areas of life. This does not alter the fact that, increasingly, rehabilitation, diagnosis and certain curative areas of health care too are or can be organized extramurally, in or close to the home situation" (Heydelberg 1988). Insurers are eager to embrace the functional approach. The health insurers' national organization (KLOZ), for example, would like to see an end to the situation in which care is regulated jointly by government and providers; this is seen as a supplier monopoly, reducing consumer influence. KLOZ defines home care as a "cluster of functions which do not necessarily have to be performed within the recognized institutions", going on to say that "in the primary sector in any event, no provider can be certain that insurers will be buying services from them in a few years' time" (KLOZ 1989). Similar noises have come from the health insurance funds, which emphasize the financial interests involved in home care and would prefer the coordination of care to be in the hands of the insurers.

The fullest definition is probably that of Van Londen, who brings in notions of care quality and patient satisfaction as well as of care functions: "with the care and care needs of the patient and his/her social environment as its starting point, [home care is] a combination of functions tailored to those needs, delivered in or accessible from the patient's home and jointly chosen by the patient and health care and social-service professionals, such that the likelihood of the help provided being effective and efficient and giving satisfaction to the patient/client is maximized" (Van Londen 1990). Reiterating this definition, Schrijvers and Van Londen (1990) emphasize the preservation as far as possible of the patient's normal life circumstances, the necessary combination of formal and informal care and its explicit purpose, namely to enable people to cope in their own home. As Van der Zee notes, this definition strictly speaking implies that home care cannot exist if the patient is not satisfied (Van der Zee 1989). So wide a definition of course brings with it the problem that virtually nothing is excluded, but that may well be the intention.

Van der Zee (1989) finds home care a "somewhat unreal concept": "Taking the notion quite literally, a life-saving emergency operation in hospital would also constitute home care, since were the operation not to take place the patient would never return to home at all." One solution might be to follow Schrijvers in treating all care "received at home or accessible from home" as home care or alternatively as primary care; the latter course would so cut across established terminology, however, that the result would merely be new confusion.

3.3. Caring for people at home

3.3.1. Demarcation

As our discussion of the term has demonstrated, there is no clear and unambiguous definition of "home care". It is worth noting that this is also true of "primary care": open access has always been seen as a characteristic of the primary sector, for example, even though in the Netherlands access to physiotherapy requires referral by a GP. A clear demarcation of the field to which this scenario project relates is nevertheless necessary.

A common element in the various definitions is the emphasis on the demand side of the care process, in particular the demands of those living in their own homes. The use of the term implies a drive to find more ways of meeting the care needs of people living at home, with even relatively complex forms of care being delivered in the home situation. The care would not necessarily have to be generalist in nature but would be geared to the patient's needs. Moves in this direction are prompted by cost and ideological considerations and are made possible in part by technological progress. Home care could be simply defined as *care given to people living at home*, but this does not mark off the field with which our study is concerned. If the limits were set by the care now available to people living at home, then we should fail to consider currently unmet needs which could be met, now or in the future, thanks to developing technology. With this in mind we define our field as follows:

This scenario project on primary and home care is concerned with care given to people living at home, together with care that could be provided, given the current state of knowledge and the technology, treatment and supervision needed, without admitting people to hospital or nursing home.

Schrijvers (1987) refers in this connection to a "network of care" for people living at home; Michels arrives at a similar notion, suggesting replacement of the current care tiers with the two-way division "primary care at home, secondary care in hospital" (Michels 1987).

This broadly defines the field with which we are concerned. It would however be beyond the scope of a single study to deal in detail with all its aspects: limits are needed on practical grounds. First, our considerations are limited to the services of *GPs, physiotherapists, community nurses, home helps* and *general social workers*, together with ambulant care provided by *medical specialists*. While these categories provide the bulk of care for people living at home this does not mean that other services are not also relevant, now or in the future, to the delivery of home care (exercise therapy can be of great help to people with musculoskeletal problems, for example, but is provided on only a limited scale at present). Other, virtually autonomous, care networks serving people living at home can also be distinguished (e.g. midwifery: many Dutch babies are born at home), but they are large enough in themselves to serve as a subject for a separate scenario study.

A second restriction relates to the type of care offered. This study is concerned only with the care of individual patients/clients or patient/client systems; we do not consider collective prevention, even though various groups of primary providers undertake preventive work. On this point reference may be made to the scenario report on the public health service, with its role in prevention and health promotion.

Having marked off the field with which this study is concerned, we look in the next section at the health problems of people living at home and at the services available to them from GPs, specialists, physiotherapists, the community-nursing and home-help services and general social workers.

3.3.2. Patients and providers in home care

The care needs of people living at home can be charted using information from a random sample of the patient populations of a number of general practices (Foets *et al.* 1991); virtually everyone in the Netherlands is registered with a GP. The great majority of people living at home consider themselves to be healthy: when asked if they feel well around 85 per cent say they enjoy good health, despite the fact that most have frequent minor health problems such as colds, headaches, coughs, tiredness or "nerves" (see figure 3.1). Half of the home-living population have chronic problems, generally of a relatively minor nature, such as backache or headaches; a relatively small proportion suffer from more serious chronic conditions, most commonly respiratory and cardiac disorders (table 3.1). Eighteen per cent of over-15s have difficulty with one or more activities of daily living (eating, drinking, getting into and out of bed, and so on) or household tasks (such as shopping and preparing food); eight per cent are unable to perform one or more such activities without help. The need for help increases with age, with almost half of all over-75s needing assistance with one or more activities. A significant section of the population also have problems of a psychosocial nature.

These various health problems do not generally lead to contact with health services; where contacts do occur, in the first instance they are generally with the general practitioner. The picture is shown in figure 3.1, which sets the ten conditions occurring most commonly in the population at large against the ten most frequently presenting to general practitioners. The commonest acute conditions found in the population reappear in part among the problems presenting to GPs; they include infections of the upper respiratory tract, "nerves", sleep disorders and acute bronchitis. It is also clear that people contact their GP in connection with only a very limited proportion of their health problems. The position is different in the case of the more serious chronic conditions (table 3.1), where patterns in the population at large and among patients contacting GPs coincide more closely. Chronic patients in general practice typically suffer from more than one chronic condition (Van der Velden 1990); another feature of the problems presenting in general practice is that in the view of

81

GPs mental or psychosocial factors often play a part, even where the patient presents with physical problems.

Figure 3.1. The ten commonest health conditions in the population at large and among patients contacting their GP

Acute problems most frequently reported in the preceding 14 days by the population at large

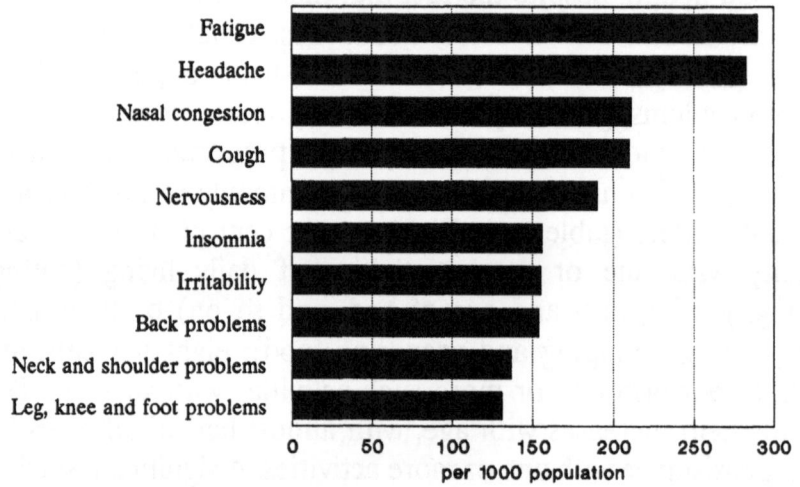

Commonest causes of contacts with GPs (GPs' diagnoses)

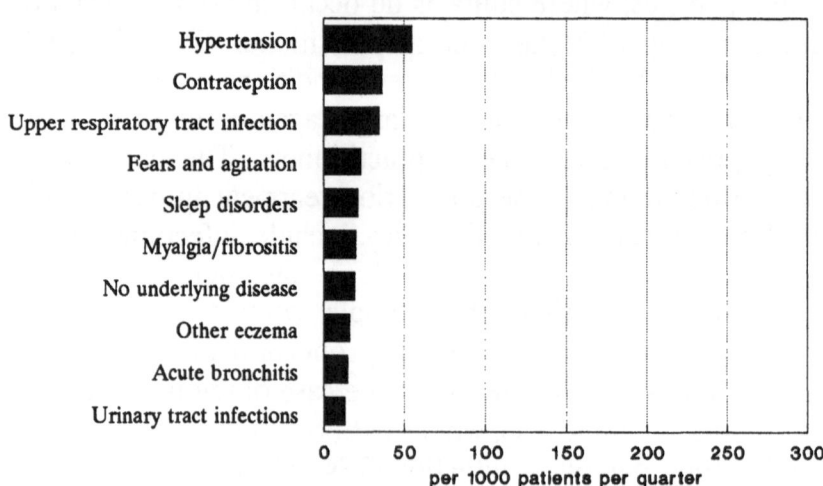

Source: Van der Velden et al. 1991.

Table 3.1. Serious chronic conditions in the population at large (survey figures) and among patients consulting their GP (three-month periods)

Condition	Per 1000 population	patients
COPD (chronic bronchitis/asthma)	81	24
Heart conditions/pulmonary oedema	55	32
Rheumatism, arthritis, arthrosis	32	13
Serious sequelae of accident	24	2
Diabetes	18	3
Chronic kidney disease/kidney stones	14	3
Diseases of the nervous system (Parkinsonism, multiple sclerosis, epilepsy)	12	11
Neoplasms (benign/malignant), cancer, leukaemia	8	10
Arteriosclerosis	7	4
Handicap due to hereditary disorder	5	6

Source: Foets and Sixma 1991; Van der Velden et al. 1991.

From the problems presenting to GPs we turn now to the latter's responses. Talking is an important part of GPs' work - they tell patients about their condition, give reassurance, counsel patience, and so on - reflecting the fact that most of the conditions presenting are relatively minor and transient. Another important task is the prescribing of medicines, with over 900 prescriptions being written per thousand patients in each three-month period (more than half are repeat prescriptions, often dealt with by practice receptionists); medicines are prescribed in almost half of all contacts. Compared with talking to patients and writing prescriptions, laboratory tests and specifically medical procedures are much less common. The proportion of problems brought to GPs requiring referral to a specialist is even smaller: in over 90 per cent of consultations the GP himself or herself can offer a solution, while in the remaining ten per cent patients are referred to specialists (two thirds of cases) or other primary providers (mainly physiotherapists). General practitioners thus encounter a broad range of often relatively minor health problems, the vast majority of which they can deal with themselves. This clearly illustrates the GP's selection function.

Where as little as fifteen years ago referral by a GP generally led to admission to hospital, nowadays more and more of the diagnostic and curative work of *medical specialists* is done on an outpatient basis; specialist care has thus joined the range of services available to people living at home. The conditions presenting at specialists' outpatient clinics are largely determined by GP referrals, since the first contact following referral is almost always on an outpatient basis and since in the Netherlands people rarely consult a specialist without having been referred by their GP. When they do, this happens mainly in hospital accident and emergency departments: while the GP's consulting rooms should normally be the first port of call following minor injuries, with hospitals being used only in more serious cases, in urban areas in particular people often go straight to their local hospital. Local research has shown that in the opinion of the medical staff on duty most of the injuries with which people present to hospital could perfectly well have been treated by a GP.

Table 3.2. GPs' three commonest diagnoses in connection with referrals to specialists

Specialty	Three commonest GP diagnoses		
Ophthalmology	Refractive disorder	Disorders NEC	Cataract
Otolaryngology	Acute otitis media/ myringitis	Non-serous otitis media (inc. glue ear)	Sinusitis
General surgery	Cartilage/ligament damage	Tendinitis/synovitis	Inguinal hernia
Internal medicine	Angina pectoris	Diabetes mellitus	COPD NEC*
Obstetrics/ gynaecology	Pregnancy confirmed	Prolapse of uterus/ vagina	Subfertility/infertility
Dermatology	Eczema NEC*	Warts	Varicose veins
Paediatrics	Asthma/asthmatic bronchitis	Acute bronchitis/ bronchiolitis	General malaise
Neurology	Herniated disk	Epilepsy, all forms	Conditions of the peripheral nervous system NEC*

* Not elsewhere classifiable
Source: Gloerich and Van der Zee 1991.

The problems presenting to each medical specialty are summarized in table 3.2, which gives the three commonest diagnoses reached by GPs prior to referral; subspecialties are included in the case of general surgery and internal medicine. There is considerable variation in the extent to which GPs deal with problems themselves or refer them on. Among patients with refractive disorders, for example, referral is very frequent: of the 1000 cases presenting in general practice over 900 result in referrals, while in addition many people probably go direct to an ophthalmologist. In other cases referral is much less frequent.

Research into variation in referral rates (Gloerich and Van der Zee 1991) has shown GPs to have a measure of discretion as regards referral in particular cases. In the grey area between what are clearly their respective provinces there is scope for closer cooperation between GPs and specialists to ensure that the level of specialization is appropriate to the problem concerned. One field in which this has happened (albeit not to everyone's satisfaction; see Riteco and Hingstman 1991) is that of obstetrics: the new list of obstetric indications includes guidance for the inputs from the primary and secondary sectors.

Another service which has grown considerably in importance in the care of people living at home is *physiotherapy*: in 1989 almost 13 per cent of the population - the figure has risen sharply in recent years - consulted a physiotherapist (see section 5.3). In the Netherlands physiotherapy, like specialist outpatient care, is available only on referral, in this case by a GP or specialist. GPs account for the bulk of referrals, providing physiotherapists with 80 per cent of their patients (Kerssens *et al.* 1986).

As might be expected, most GP referrals are for musculoskeletal disorders: 85 per cent of patients referred by their GP for physiotherapy have problems relating to the musculoskeletal system. The ten commonest GP diagnoses, listed in table 3.3, account between them for more than half of all referrals; muscle pain (myalgia/fibrositis) and backache are by far the commonest. The conditions with which patients are referred for physiotherapy are not generally life-threatening; they make it difficult to perform normal day-to-day activities, however, largely through the pain they involve, and the relief of pain is the commonest treatment goal (Kerssens *et al.* 1987). The purpose of physiotherapy could be said to be to improve the quality of life. In the case of patients with chronic conditions physiotherapy is by way of being "maintenance work". Patients with lung disorders, arthritis and cardiovascular problems often receive very long-term treatment, in many cases in

their own home or at the homes for the elderly where they live
(Groenewegen *et al.* 1986).

Table 3.3. New physiotherapy patients: GPs' ten commonest diagnoses on referral

Provisional diagnosis	Percentage of all referrals	Cumulative percentage
Myalgia/fibrositis	13.3	13.3
Lower-back pain	10.7	24.1
Disorders of the shoulder	5.9	30.0
Tendinitis/synovitis	4.2	34.3
Lateral epicondylitis	3.3	37.6
Problems affecting several muscles NEC*	3.2	40.9
Disorders of the cervical vertebrae	3.2	44.1
Back symptoms/problems	3.1	47.2
Herniated disk	2.6	49.8
Ischialgia	2.2	52.1

* Not elsewhere classifiable
Source: Uunk et al. 1991.

Community nursing plays an important role in the care of people living at home. The service's generalist nature is evident from the wide range of tasks performed, from nursing procedures in the strict sense to group-oriented preventive work and from psychosocial support to the supervision of medication. The main client groups are young children and the elderly, and in the latter case in particular the service provided is literally care at home. Patients receiving community-nursing support at home have a deficit in their ability to care for themselves, generally due to chronic disease or its consequences (Vorst-Thijssen *et al.* 1990). Table 3.4 shows the commonest underlying diseases of community-nursing patients, chief among them conditions of the musculoskeletal system (mainly arthritis), cardiovascular conditions other than CVA, and diabetes. Among community-nursing as well as among GP patients chronic diseases often do not come singly: almost 30 per cent of community-nursing patients suffer from more than one chronic condition.

Table 3.4. The underlying disease(s) of community-nursing patients, as percentages of all patients receiving care (N = 3315)

Underlying disease*	Percentage
Musculoskeletal disorders	20.4
Cardiovascular disease (other than CVA)	17.2
Diabetes	14.9
Cancer	12.6
Neurological conditions	12.2
Cerebrovascular accident (CVA)	9.6
Physical handicap	6.7
Dementia (including Alzheimer's disease)	6.6
Chronic obstructive pulmonary disease (COPD)	6.1

* More than one may be present in a given patient
Source: Vorst-Thijssen et al. 1990.

The tasks performed by community nurses and nursing auxiliaries are very diverse, the commonest categories being in the areas of physical hygiene (washing, dressing etc.), nursing (applying powder/ointment, prevention/relief of pressure sores, etc.) and social and administrative support (conversation, making appointments, etc.); the interplay with informal care is also important (see chapter 6).

Home help, which has been included among the core primary care services since 1983, is geared not so much to disease as to its consequences for families. Where a family member is incapacitated, wholly or partly, certain household tasks may be neglected; these can then be taken over by the home-help service. The incapacity may result from acute illness (whether or not the person concerned is hospitalized), chronic disease or, most commonly, the frailties of old age. In the case particularly of the chronic sick and the frail elderly, home help can enable people to continue living independently by postponing the need for admission or bridging the time spent waiting for a place in a home for the elderly.

The reasons why people seek home-help support are summarized in table 3.5; they mainly involve frailty, handicap or chronic illness.

Table 3.5. Grounds for receiving home-help support, as percentages of all recipients

Ground	Percentage
Old age	63
Chronic illness	40
Physical handicap	24
Psychiatric problems	12
Acute illness	6
Divorce/desertion/bereavement	5
Other	3
Pregnancy/childbirth	1

Source: CBS 1985.

Home helps mainly provide assistance with domestic and personal tasks, together with social support and guidance. In virtually all cases (99 per cent in the CBS's 1980 client survey) domestic assistance is indicated; domestic assistance alone is indicated in just over 40 per cent of cases (CBS 1985). Home help may be provided over extended periods, particularly in the case of elderly people living alone. There is a clear correlation between the receipt of support and the absence of informal help, with home help being chiefly provided where informal help is unavailable (Kwekkeboom 1990); a combination of professional home-help support and informal care is rare.

The last service which plays an important part in the care of people at home is *general social work*, which helps to meet deficits in people's ability to cope at the social level by providing "support in difficult times". Such deficits may result from illness, family or personal problems, traumatic events, ignorance of official regulations and procedures or a lack of basic requirements.

In most cases (56 per cent) social-work contacts are initiated by the client (VIVAM 1990); elsewhere an important role is played by GPs. More than half of all clients have previously had some contact with the mental-health services (Friele and Verhaak 1991); social-work clients tend to score very low on indicators of mental health, at a level comparable with that of clients of the Regional Institutes for Ambulatory Mental Health Care (RIAGGs). In socio-economic terms, however, there is a clear difference, with the recipients of social-work support considerably more likely to belong to lower income groups (Friele and Verhaak 1991).

Table 3.6. Long-term recipients of general social-work support: main problem categories

Problem category	Percentage of long-term clients
Family or personal problems	35
Psychiatric problems	35
Income, housing, work	16
Other, including physical problems	14

Source: Friele and Verhaak 1991.

Family, personal and psychiatric problems account for the major part of the support needs of social-work clients (table 3.6); problems of a material nature form a markedly smaller category, at least among long-term clients. Social workers provide help of many kinds, ranging from concrete activities such as form-filling to long-term support for people with psychiatric problems and assistance in dealings with official agencies. The main type of help given is psychosocial support and counselling, followed some way behind by information, advice and advocacy. Support may extend over long periods, in more than half of all cases more than three months (VIVAM 1990).

The nature of the tasks involved in general social work means that it occupies a position intermediate between health care and welfare services, and the degree of orientation towards one side or the other is a subject of debate. The fact that general social work is funded from municipal resources could lead to a growing orientation towards the welfare services, which are also a municipal responsibility.

This completes our survey of the health problems of people living at home, the problems they present to care providers and the latter's response. Both the problems arising and the services offered range very widely. The general practitioner has a central role, since he or she is often the first point of contact with the support services and the problems presenting to the other provider categories are in many instances channelled via the general practitioner; this is true particularly of physiotherapy and ambulatory specialist care, which in the Netherlands are accessible only following referral by a GP, but in the case of the other providers too many patients or clients make contact at their GP's instigation.

As soon as more than one category of care provider needs to be involved in a particular case the issue of coordination comes to the fore. It is to this that we now turn.

3.4. Coordination

The current system, in which the categories of provision are separated into tiers and each has its own organizational structure, is not conducive to the establishment of coordinated care networks. Health care, especially in the primary sector, is often said to lack coordination (Boerma 1989; Duyn 1989; STG 1988; Schrijvers and Van Londen 1990). Mur-Veeman and Tyssen (1990) characterize the present situation as one of structural imbalance, noting the lack of a common culture and, particularly, of any coordinating authority. The different institutions and professions have different target groups and catchment areas, funding arrangements, care cultures, indication criteria and procedures, and conditions of access and availability. In the primary sector this absence of system has advantages (limited bureaucracy, direct access, short waiting times, low overheads) as well as drawbacks (variations in access and availability, gaps and overlaps, continuity of care not guaranteed). The drawbacks are aggravated at the point of transfer between care sectors (admission/discharge, pre-admission and post-discharge care, blocked beds, waiting lists) and where different services are used within the primary sector.

The question we now address is that of the volume of care needs where more than one category of care is involved and coordination may therefore be required. Two approaches are used, one based on utilization and other on needs.

Table 3.7 gives an indication of the extent to which different categories of care are received over the same period. The relatively small number of people using more than one category in a given year (11 per cent) can be taken to include patients who require well coordinated care. The GP is by far the most important provider of care to those who have used only one category of care, with almost half of those who have consulted a GP having no contact with another category of provider; this clearly demonstrates the GP's selection function. Among those receiving specialist care the great majority are users of two services, the common combination being GP/specialist. In the case of the remaining provider categories the majority of clients are helped by more than two services, with multiple use tending to increase as we move through a list running from physiotherapy, community nursing and general social work to home help.

Table 3.7. Service users, by the number of services used in the preceding year

| | Number of services used | | | | | | |
	0	1	2	3	4+	Total	N
Population	21	39	29	9	2	100%	12846
Contact with:							
GP	-	46	38	13	3	100%	9547
specialist	-	9	60	25	6	100%	4516
physiotherapist	-	3	37	48	12	100%	1641
community nurse	-	8	37	37	18	100%	894
home help	-	8	21	30	41	100%	252
general social worker	-	5	30	40	25	100%	286

Source: NIVEL, Dutch National Survey of General Practice 1991.

The need for coordinated care is not equally great for all users of three or more services. The figures are for people using several different services in the course of a year, and it could be that they are used in connection with different problems. To determine the extent to which coordination is required we must look at patterns of need. There is a clear correlation between the number of services used and indicators of care need (table 3.8): the greater the number of services used, the more likely the user is to be old, to live alone, to perceive his or her health as "less than good", to suffer from more than one chronic condition and to need help with activities of daily living. There is also a greater likelihood of a low score on an indicator of mental wellbeing (GHQ, Goldberg 1972) and of experiencing more "life problems" (BIOPRO score, McWhinney 1979). Even so, the majority of those who use more than two services perceive their own health to be good, are not chronically ill, do not need help with activities of daily living and on average do not register extreme scores on indicators of mental health. The majority of this group can therefore reasonably be supposed not to require greater care coordination.

Table 3.8. Service users' health characteristics, by the number of services used in the preceding year

	Number of services used			
	0	1	2	3+
% aged 75+	1.5	2.4	4.4	5.5
% living alone	6.9	8.2	10.9	14.4
% in "less than good" health	6.8	9.2	21.4	32.3
% with one serious chronic condition	6.8	10.3	20.0	23.8
% with more than one serious chronic condition	0.9	2.5	7.0	10.0
% needing help with ADL	3.0	4.8	10.5	22.1
Average GHQ score*	1.0	1.6	2.2	3.4
Average BIOPRO score*	1.0	1.3	1.6	2.1

* Excluding persons aged under 20
Source: NIVEL, Dutch National Survey of General Practice 1991.

Another needs-based approach to the question of care coordination is possible on the basis of chapter 6 of this report. In chapter 6 experts assess the ideal care requirements of several categories of chronic patient, with four classes being defined in terms of ascending care needs. In the experts' view members of all four classes require care from all categories of provider. Table 3.9 shows actual service utilization by patients in the different classes. As is to be expected, patients in all four show above-average service utilization, with higher levels in the classes with the greater care needs. Nevertheless, even in the latter classes only a minority make use of community nursing, home help, social work and physiotherapy. The GP is the only care provider used generally by people in all four classes.

Table 3.9. Contacts with care providers in the preceding year, by need class

	Need class 1 (n = 605)	2 (n = 220)	3 (n = 195)	4 (n = 78)
GP	88%	91%	93%	95%
Specialist	65%	71%	72%	72%
Physiotherapy	25%	31%	35%	39%
Community nursing	8%	9%	17%	27%
Home help	5%	11%	16%	27%
General social work	4%	6%	6%	9%

Source: NIVEL, Dutch National Survey of General Practice 1991.

The class of patients needing coordinated care is hard to demarcate but in any event probably very small. It may be that high-dependency patients fall outside the scope of surveys of the type used here; if this is the case, we may be underestimating the size of the class most affected by problems of coordination within the primary sector and at the primary/secondary interface.

The relatively small number of patients needing coordinated care may explain why multidisciplinary structures are not widespread in Dutch health care. The development of multidisciplinary services can be seen as an attempt to enhance the primary sector's capacity for dealing with problems in respect of categories of patient for whom cooperation is necessary. In organizational terms the tightest form of cooperation is exemplified in the health centres, whose numbers have steadily grown. In 1990 there were almost 160 such centres, and eight per cent of GPs worked in them. Home teams are more widely spread but as new ones appear old ones tend to disappear. The trend of recent years seems to be towards bidisciplinary cooperation; of particular significance in this regard are cooperation between GPs and specialists and between the community-nursing and home-help services.

The care system will have to change if the requirements associated with home care are to be met. Schrijvers and Van Londen summarize the lack of coordination under two headings as "lack of unity of organization and lack of unity of funding" (Schrijvers and Van Londen 1990). They believe that basically two strategies are available to bring about improvements, on the one hand the creation of home care centres and on the other case management. This points to a twofold requirement which will play an important part in the development of organizational scenarios: given the need for home care, better coordination must be established not only among the various institutions and professionals but also in the care delivered to individual patients.

3.5. The problem of coordination

The process of regulating and harmonizing the services of separate institutions is generally known as coordination while regulation of the care delivered to individual patients is known as case management (see also Wennink and Goudriaan 1991); often no explicit distinction is made between the two activities, however, and since they are in a sense variations on the same theme - the organization of "a package of different types of care and service tailored to the needs of the individual client" (Willems 1988) - the term "care coordination" is sometimes used to cover both. There are differences even so. Regulation of the care delivered to an individual patient is possible in all scenarios, though it will not be necessary to coordinate the care provided by different institutions to the same degree in every case. The activities can take shape as separate strategies: on the one hand those aimed at improving the care system by coordinating institutions, on the other those designed to improve care delivery itself, i.e. case management (see also Philipsen 1989a; Brouns and Dassen 1988; Spreeuwenberg 1988a; Austin 1983; Intagliata 1982; Henselmans 1990).

What is case management? Heydelberg and Van de Meydenberg (1988) define it as "acting as the patient's agent", necessary because - the list of shortcomings is by now familiar - care is fragmented, continuity is lacking, there are access problems and when something goes wrong no-one in particular is answerable. Tackling these shortcomings will be no small challenge, which is why Philipsen dubs whoever takes it up Caseman, the Batman of health care. A useful definition is given by Zawadski and Eng (1988): "Case management is any method of combining, regulating and coordinating services in order to meet clients' needs and comprises by definition the determination of care requirements, coordination of the response, and follow-up (see also Stikker 1989). Case management is virtually always a complement to informal care. Philipsen notes that the focus of case management is not the individual patient or client but rather the system formed by patient and chief carer, i.e. partner, daughter or other informal carer. Analogously, the care requirement reflects deficits not in the client but rather in the client system. If the burden of these deficits exceeds the capacity of the client system but care at home is nevertheless preferred then home care is indicated, and its complexity demands case management. There is widespread agreement in the literature as to the tasks involved; following Bachrach (1989), four are generally mentioned: the assessment of care needs, the linking of care to needs in a care plan, progress monitoring and finally advocacy. Where different carers are involved in these diverse tasks, the removal of linguistic and cultural barriers would go a long way towards solving the problems of coordination.

The introduction of case management as a health care function in its own right would give rise to predictable problems. It would erode the autonomy of individual professionals and institutions and could increase bureaucracy, reasons enough for Philipsen to reject the recognition of case management as a separate function: "As I have outlined, one of the problems with care is the ineradicable tendency towards bilateral contacts. The addition of a further partner will probably resolve nothing unless you have a central position in the communication system. The chances of this for newcomers are minimal" (Philipsen 1989b). Lamb (1980) too rejects the separation of care from case management. Criticism of the complexity of the care system and the growth of bureaucracy comes as a cry from the heart: "We are in danger of inserting a new structure between the existing organizations. The formalization of coordination, of powers, rights and duties, will produce new bureaucracy, with the risk of diminished efficiency and a greater likelihood of unwanted interference" (Schadé 1989). Seidl and Applebaum believe that case management would be most effective if there were one funding scheme and central operation; they also believe, however, that the already complex structure of health care would become even more complex as a result (Seidl and Applebaum 1983).

There seems to be an inconsistency in discussions of case management: on the one hand persuasive arguments are advanced as to the danger of increased bureaucracy, while on the other there is a strong suggestion in the literature that case management is only likely to work if care is centrally managed, institutions are centrally funded and managers are given their own budgets (Seidl and Applebaum 1983; Van Lieshout and Heydelberg 1990). On this point Schrijvers is forthright: "... without powers or cash to share out, case managers are no more than interfering busybodies who moan about cooperation and the need for care plans" (in: Hesterman 1988). This is the dilemma: for case management to succeed the health care system must become more coherent, while at the same time case management is seen as a means to the end of greater coherence. The coordination of institutions appears to come before the coordination of care.

Excessive structuring must in any event be avoided. It would be imprudent simply to brush aside worries about the erosion of professional autonomy and the growth of bureaucracy. Moreover the search for better ways of organizing complex home care must not be to the detriment of non-complex care: the introduction of new structures must not be at the expense of the delivery of relatively unproblematic forms of care, especially since, as is argued, the volume of non-complex care delivered far exceeds that of complex care. The challenge is thus to find ways of building on the good points of the current tiered system while improving coordination. In Philipsen's words we need to opt for an "optimizing strategy". He believes that professional providers favour minimal coordination ("Regulate as little as possible - if anything happens we'll hear") while policy-makers incline towards the opposite ("Everything covered by regulations"). Philipsen goes on: "We have yet to engage in a well-considered search for an optimizing strategy: how do we decide the minimum regulations needed to avoid making a mess?" (Philipsen 1989b). The drawbacks of increased administration could be offset by ensuring that clients with different care needs are guided through the system along different paths; De Waal (1988) calls this "routing".

3.6. Conclusion

In constructing scenarios for the future we need to abstract from the present. As has been indicated, the exercise must not extend to elaborating new structures for areas of care whose operation is currently relatively problem-free. It is from the foregoing that the framework for our thinking on the future organization of primary care and home care must be crystallized.

For the purposes of ambulatory care the relevant institutions and practitioners need to form care networks, also encompassing informal care, beds for temporary admissions (respite care) and specialist care, which will enable patients with complex needs to be cared for in their own homes for as long as possible. The emphasis must be on care of a primary, i.e. comprehensive and generalist, nature. The purpose of network formation is to improve coordination among institutions and practitioners, with provision for case management alongside the actual delivery of care. An optimizing approach is needed to institutional coordination, with the good features of the present system (short waiting lists, direct access, little bureaucracy, minimum overheads) being retained and patients with different care needs taking different routes through the network.

Several building blocks are still needed and will be supplied in subsequent chapters. The first is an estimate of future care utilization, and chapter 5 describes past patterns in the use of ambulatory care and gives estimates of future trends to 2005 on the assumption of unchanged policy, i.e. with care continuing to be organized as at present. Chapter 6 looks in more qualitative terms at the make-up of care required by patients with complex needs and at the conditions that must be met if it is to be delivered in the home situation. Chapter 7 briefly outlines how the scenarios were developed. Once all these various elements are in place, in chapter 8 we bring them together and compare the organizational scenarios from various angles. First, though, chapter 4 looks at the design of the scenario study and gives an account of the methods used.

4. Study design and methodology

4.1. Introduction

In this chapter we describe the design of the scenario study and explain the underlying methodology.

Earlier STG studies were mainly concerned with specific disease categories, while more recently studies have been commissioned on care sectors, such as the hospital sector, mental health care, prevention and health promotion, and primary care; the studies thus fall into two groups, one focusing on health and the other on health care. When the scenario project on primary and home care was launched a number of health studies had been completed, but as yet no sectoral studies. In section 4.2 we discuss the main differences between care sector and health scenarios, raising certain important methodological problems; the solutions adopted in the present study are described later on in the chapter (section 4.4). We first look briefly at the sectoral studies that have previously been published, on mental health and its care and on hospitals in the twenty-first century (STG 1990c and 1990a); a comparison of the approach adopted in these two projects sets in perspective the choices made in this report.

The model that guided the scenario project's design and development is described in section 4.5. It comprises three parts, covered in three separate studies:
- an analysis of past and likely future trends in the use of primary care and outpatient specialist care (the *trend study*);
- an analysis of the services needed in complex home care and of the conditions that must be met (the *care study*);
- an analysis of the organization of primary care and home care and of possible reforms (the *organizational study*).

An account of the design of these three studies is given in sections 4.6, 4.7 and 4.8. The chapter ends by describing how the different parts of the scenario study are combined with a view to assessing the different scenarios' relative merits.

4.2. Scenario studies on health and on care sectors

The difference between the two types of scenario derives from the difference in their subject matter. Health scenarios focus on a particular aspect of public health and the questions with which they are concerned are epidemiological in nature, i.e. relate to mortality, risk levels, the incidence and prevalence of disease and the consequences of disease for the quality of life; futures research in this field involves estimating incidence and prevalence rates and considering developments in therapy. Sectoral scenarios are concerned on one side with the whole range of care needs in a particular sector and on the other with the services available from the various practitioners and institutions. The supply side of a care sector comprises professional groups and institutions, each organized in its own way, while on the demand side we find both healthy and sick people with care requirements which vary widely in nature and intensity. Both sides are thus heterogeneous by definition, and we touch now on a number of the problems that this creates.

Since a sectoral scenario is not limited to one type of client or service, the demarcation of the research field presents a major problem at the outset. As our consideration of the various definitions of primary care and home care in chapter 3 showed, the boundaries are in some degree arbitrary.

Given the range and diversity of the care needs relevant to any one sector, an approach based on developments in the nature and volume of needs across the sector is not feasible. A specific problem in the case of primary and home care is that needs cannot be simply defined in terms of conditions with a more or less established course: they arise from health and health-related problems and their consequences for people's functioning rather than from well defined disease syndromes.

In each sector there is by definition a mix of care - formal and informal, medical and non-medical - delivered by a variety of carers and institutions; moreover similar care functions are in some cases performed by different categories of provider. There is therefore a greater need than in care scenarios to take account of trends in the use of care. There are two related problems. First, comparable data on the utilization of different care types are often unavailable; even where records of care use exist, their structure differs from one category of care to another and they rarely include long-term figures. Second, analysis of the utilization of different categories of care is by definition shaped by the existing organizational framework of the sector concerned, while the development of organizational scenarios requires us precisely to abstract in some degree from that framework.

Finally, a major difference between health and sectoral scenarios is that it is harder to conceptualize and determine autonomous developments in organizational structure than in the incidence and prevalence of disease: policy on aspects of health care can change over relatively short periods, moving in different (and unpredictable) directions.

The design of a sectoral scenario thus presents problems which differ from those arising in the case of health scenarios and for which no ready-made solution exists.

4.3. The design of other sectoral scenarios

To set the choices made as part of this project in perspective we now look briefly at the scenario projects on mental health and its care and on the hospital system, each of which solved in its own way the problems just discussed.

Within the broad field of mental health and its care the scenario project on that subject opted to focus on four themes - dementia, schizophrenia, occupational incapacity due to mental disorders, emotional and behavioural problems in children and young people - which between them reflected the field's diversity. The main point on which they differ is the extent to which the problems and care in question are socially and culturally determined. The basic model for the analysis of the four themes centres on trends in the condition in the population at large and in the consumption of care. With the present position regarding the occurrence of mental-health problems and the consumption of care as the baseline, three types of scenario were developed: reference scenarios (comprising the developments deemed most likely), alternative exploratory scenarios (based on alternative expectations as to autonomous developments affecting the occurrence of problems and the consumption of care), and target scenarios (detailing the measures needed to achieve a target level of occurrence or consumption). The approach adopted was thus relatively close to that used in health scenarios, with the difference that the themes were less tightly defined than has thus far been the case in health scenarios, that extensive attention was devoted to the utilization of services and that policy variations were introduced with a view to achieving certain goals in the future. No attempt was made to describe and analyse supply and demand in the sector as a whole or models for its organization.

In the scenario project on hospitals in the twenty-first century, in contrast, a comprehensive approach was adopted with the aim of designing alternative scenarios for the organization of the sector as a whole. Two opposing scenarios were constructed on the basis of a wide-ranging background study covering a multitude of general social and sector-specific trends and developments.

In subsequent sections we describe how we have sought to combine elements from the approach adopted in these two studies into one appropriate for a sectoral scenario for primary care and home care.

4.4. Methodology for a sectoral scenario

One way of reducing the complexity of a scenario for a care sector is to split the project into separate studies of particular sets of health problems, care types or providers; this produces a series of separate health scenarios and has the drawback that pronouncements covering the sector as a whole are thereby made difficult. However, since it would not be practicable to take the sector as a whole and in all its aspects as the field of study, some other way must be found of dealing with complexity

In this study it was decided that the scenarios' central focus should be on the future organizational framework. This meant that we could not limit ourselves to analysing and calculating the nature and volume of future care consumption in terms of the existing framework: while such analysis and calculation are a central element in this study, if there were nothing else we would not be able to say anything useful about likely developments under different organizational arrangements.

Our topic must therefore be defined in such a way as to allow us to abstract from the current organizational framework and the groups of practitioners operating within it. In chapter 3 we defined our subject as, briefly, the care of people living at home. We have opted for an approach in which the criterion of specialization (on which the current tiered structure of health care in the Netherlands is largely based) is replaced with one relating to where services are delivered rather than who delivers them. The use of a location criterion implies abstracting from the current organizational framework, leaving to a later stage the determination of who delivers care, where it is delivered and in what organizational arrangement.

By defining our field of study without reference to the current structure we can cut across the conventional tiers. Even so there are several care sectors, with varying degrees of autonomy, which we do not consider, despite overlaps or points of contact with primary and home care; they are prevention and health promotion, psychiatric care, dentistry, and obstetrics and midwifery, and all are in any event the subject of STG scenario projects under way or completed as we go to press.

The care of people living at home can be described independently of its current distribution across the groups delivering it by starting from a description of care needs in terms of functions. Care profiles can then be compiled for patient and client categories showing what types of care, described functionally, are needed in the home situation and under what organizational conditions they can be delivered. An indication can then be given as the organizational scenarios are developed of how the needs detailed in the care profiles can be met.

This sectoral scenario makes use of information of various kinds: utilization data (e.g. numbers of consultations per year with different categories of provider) taken from surveys, qualitative information on the care of specific target groups with a view to charting future changes in the pattern of care, and finally descriptions of organizational developments in order to be able to formulate appropriate scenarios.

4.5. A model for the scenario project on primary care and home care

The various considerations regarding the methodological problems involved in a sectoral scenario led us to the following model for our project.

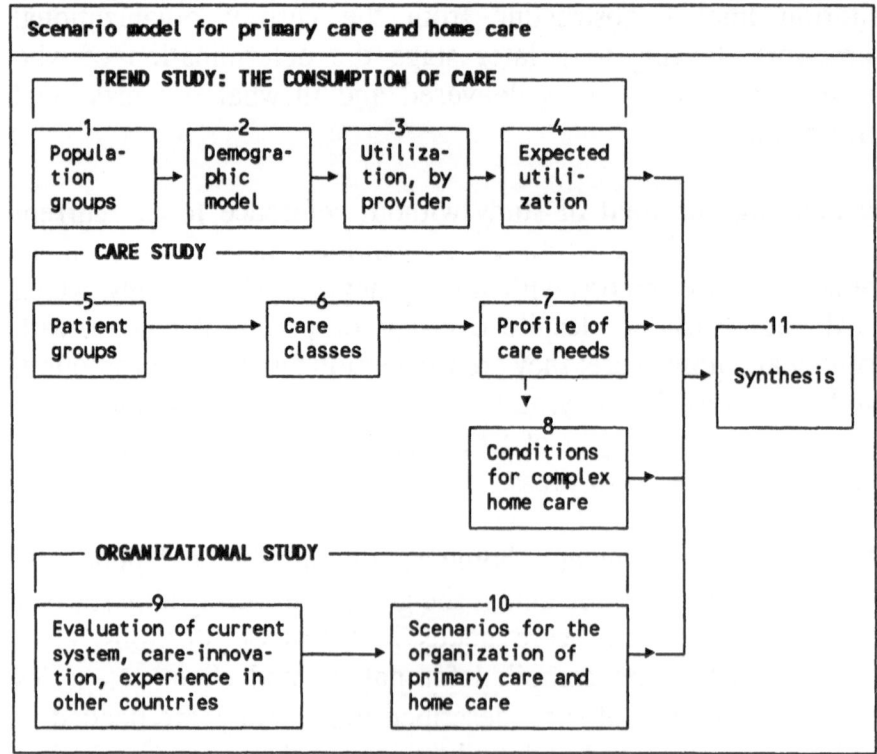

Box 1: Population groups
User groups in the population at large, defined by sex, age, educational level, subjective health and household type. The estimates relate to the population as a whole.

Box 2: Demography
Estimates of the future size of population groups.

Box 3: Utilization, by provider category
Current levels of utilization in each population group of ambulatory care delivered by community nurses, home helps, social workers, physiotherapists and specialists (outpatient care).

Box 4: Expected utilization
Based on observed trends an estimate is made of future utilization levels, assuming no changes in the nature or intensity of care needs or in legislation and regulation.

These four boxes form the trend study.

Box 5: Patient groups
Specific target groups for complex home care, defined by condition (heart failure, non-insulin-dependent diabetes mellitus, chronic obstructive pulmonary disease, rheumatoid arthritis, stomach/intestinal cancer, lung cancer, breast cancer and moderate dementia), sex, age, subjective health, household type and dependence on help with activities of daily living and household tasks).

Box 6: Care classes
The patient groups are generalized into classes ranked by complexity of care needs.

Box 7: Care profile
The care needs of the different care classes, expressed in terms of functions.

Box 8: Conditions for complex home care
The conditions under which the needs making up the care profile can be met in the home situation.

These four boxes make up the care study.

Box 9: Evaluation of current system, care-innovation, experience in other countries
We drew on three sources of inspiration for the development of organizational scenarios: an evaluation of the present system's strengths and weaknesses; an analysis of care-innovation projects in the Netherlands; and differing organizational approaches found in other countries' care systems.

Box 10: Scenarios for the organization of primary care and home care
The different organizational scenarios and their variants are described.

Box 11: Synthesis
The results of the three studies are brought together, providing a basis for assessing the scenarios' relative merits.

The three studies are summarized in sections 4.6, 4.7 and 4.8.

4.6. The trend study

To estimate trends in the use of a number of categories of care by the population as whole we made use of population groups defined by sex and age, combined with an indicator of socio-economic status, subjective health and the availability of informal care.

The data we used, taken from surveys carried out by the Central Bureau of Statistics (CBS), the Social and Cultural Planning Office (SCP) and the Netherlands Institute of Primary Health Care (NIVEL), give global information on the number of times that respondents saw their GP, attended a specialist outpatient clinic, etc. in each time period. We calculated the number of people having contact with practitioners (GPs, community nurses, home helps, social workers, physiotherapists and specialists providing outpatient care) and the number of contacts in ambulatory care as currently constituted.

For those years in respect of which the necessary information exists we calculated the annual volume of consumption for each population group and provider category.

These data are used for the analysis of time series for the various population groups, i.e. groups of users defined on the basis of attributes which are both regarded in the literature as determinants of care use and reasonably homogeneous as regards care use. Observed use trends are thus not explained directly by shifts within the user groups.

There are several reasons for gearing the analysis of long-term trends in care use to population groups. While it would no doubt have been simpler to look at trends in the population as a whole, it is clear from the literature that care use varies widely from one group to another (cf. for GP services, Van der Zee 1982, Mootz 1981, Sluijs 1985; for community nursing, CBS 1984, Van den Bos et al. 1988; for home help, SCP 1988, CBS 1985, Gerritsen et al. 1988; for general social work, CBS 1988; for physiotherapy, Van den Brekel 1985, Crebolder 1983, Van den Bos 1989).

To define the population groups we used the determinants of consumption most frequently mentioned in connection with all categories of care, namely age, sex, subjective health (feeling well/less than well), household type (living alone/with others) and educational level (high/low). Defining characteristics like these commonly form part of models seeking to explain the consumption of care such as that developed by Andersen and Newman (1973). With the help of data from the Dutch National Survey of General Practice (Foets and Van der Velden 1990, Bensing et al. 1991) the large number of categories was reduced using cluster analysis to twenty population groups which are homogeneous in respect of care consumption.

We extrapolated from past patterns in each group's care use in a two-stage process. The first step was to make demographic estimates, i.e. estimates based purely on demographic factors;

average care consumption within each population group was assumed constant, so that total care consumption varied with the size of the groups. We also made trend-based estimates, extrapolations from past trends, and looked at the possible influence of changes in numbers of providers on the consumption of care.

4.7. The care study

Estimates of future care consumption expressed as numbers of contacts per service clearly give no information on what the care comprises or on any necessary or desirable changes. Our second study, the care study, is therefore concerned with the changes needed in the care of specific target groups for home care. Serious or chronic problems requiring complex care loom large here; given the particular relevance to chronic patients of the home-care philosophy a focus on chronic conditions is appropriate in a project on primary care and home care (cf. chapter 2).

Since the care study is also concerned with non-medical care, we opted to consider chronic health problems of low incidence and high prevalence which have a major impact on people's daily lives and require a mix of care from several sources. Conditions meeting these criteria are: diabetes, cardiovascular disease, CNSLD (chronic non-specific lung disease), cancer, disorders affecting mobility, and geriatric syndromes.

Greater specificity was needed, however, and within each diagnostic group we chose reasonably common conditions whose trend in the population is well established (so that experts can indicate, on the basis of epidemiological information, the likelihood of functional limitations arising), making the forecasting of future care requirements a straightforward matter. The approach coincides with that used in clinical epidemiology to assess individuals' risk of illness (cf. Vandenbroucke and Hofman 1988). Following consultation with experts in the various conditions the following were selected: heart failure, non-insulin-dependent diabetes mellitus, COPD, rheumatoid arthritis, stomach/intestinal cancer, lung cancer, breast cancer and moderate dementia.

108

Care was described without reference to its current distribution across the various services. For each user category a profile was compiled of the types and amounts of care - treatment, nursing, personal care, support and counselling, rehabilitation - needed in the home situation. The care profiles are thus couched in functional terms.

Specialists in each field were presented with "paper patients", with details of diagnosis, sex, age group, educational level, subjective health and availability of informal care, and were asked to indicate deficits in their capacity to perform listed activities of daily living and household tasks. The paper patients were divided into two groups, with low and high probabilities of displaying such deficits; the high-probability group became the potential target group for home care, and their care needs were listed using standardized task descriptions (the LIER system, CRG 1986; the WAS system, NK 1980; the Joint/general social work data system, Joint 1988; the form of application for physiotherapy; for GP services, the consultation form of the Dutch National Survey of General Practice, Foets and Van der Velden 1990; various protocols for specialist care). The various tasks were combined into care functions and any care overlap for any patient type was eliminated.

This approach produced care profiles for several categories of chronic patient. To abstract from the specific diagnoses the patient categories were generalized into care classes on the basis of deficits in the patients. In a Delphi study the profiles for each class were submitted to a panel of experts who considered the care needs and the conditions for meeting them in the home situation.

4.8. The organizational study

The purpose of this study was to develop organizational scenarios for the future of primary care and home care, subject to the general requirement that the models be able to deliver "normal", generally simple, primary care as well as complex home care. Broad quality requirements, expressed as desirable features of the care provided and the care system, also had to be met.

The current care system falls short in a number of respects and alternative scenarios for the future had to offer improvements. Possible improvements were generated from three sources: an analysis of the strengths and weaknesses of the current system; new organizational arrangements identified in an analysis of renewal projects in health care; and organizational arrangements in other countries' health systems. Four organizational scenarios were developed, each with a number of variants.

4.9. Synthesis: the scenarios assessed and compared

The next stage in the scenario section of the project was the evaluation of the scenarios. While the scenarios deliberately incorporated desirable features of care content and delivery, the extent to which such features could be realized might differ from one scenario or variant to another. The first element in the evaluation process was therefore a comparison in respect of the various desirable features.

The second element was the comparison of the scenarios in respect of the extent to which they met the conditions emerging from the care study.

The third element was formed by likely trends in care consumption (the results of the trend study), the desired intensification of care, and intended and unintended changes which would result from the implementation of the various scenarios.

Finally we looked at the likely feasibility of each scenario in the light of social trends and developments in government policy.

5.   Care consumption: trends and estimates

5.1.   Introduction

Scenario studies are a form of futures research aimed at underpinning long-term (notably government) policy. In this study we sketch out the future of ambulatory care, focusing particularly on home care. Chapter 2 discussed the social trends which have fostered interest in home care, while chapter 3 looked at health problems in the population and at the responses of the various primary providers to the problems presented to them. In this chapter we chart the use of ambulatory care over the period 1990-2005 on the basis of trends in care consumption over the last ten or fifteen years. In identifying and extrapolating from these trends we opted for a *quantitative* approach: data on past care consumption were subjected to statistical analysis and the results used in extrapolation.

Quantitative analysis of past trends assumes the availability of adequate *data* on care consumption over the period concerned, but assembling sufficient data proved no easy task. In today's computer age any self-respecting business or other institution can provide a quantitative picture of its "product", but this emphasis on product and the use of computers are of recent date and we were unable to obtain from non-computerized records the details we needed to chart trends in ambulatory care over the last ten or fifteen years. Information was however available from national surveys conducted by the Central Bureau of Statistics (CBS) and the Social and Cultural Planning Office (SCP), and in the absence of data from other sources this survey material was used in the trend study. The CBS's Life Situation Survey (LSO) and the SCP's Supplementary Survey of Service Use (AVO) are general surveys involving interviews on a wide range of topics with a random sample of the non-institutional population. They are not specifically designed to measure the use of ambulatory care; when the matter does arise it is treated very briefly, and moreover the questions asked may vary from one survey to another. These surveys have been conducted since 1974; of more recent date is the CBS's health survey, which covers the use made of ambulatory care. By combining the results of these surveys, supplemented with information from the NIVEL survey, we can create a database covering the period 1974-1988; it is on this database that our analysis of trends in the use of ambulatory care is founded.

Survey data tell us about two aspects of care consumption at most: whether or not there has been contact with a practitioner over a period of three or twelve months and, in some cases, how many contacts there have been. The substantive aspects of care are thus not covered in the trend study; nor is it possible, on the basis of the survey data, to describe the care provided in terms of functions. The content of care was discussed in chapter 3, while a functional description of primary care and home care is given in chapter 6.

Patterns in the use of care do not exist in isolation but are closely related to the make-up of the care-using population. This point was made in chapter 2, where mention was also made of the discussion of population aging. That wide variations exist in the use of care by different groups was noted in chapter 3, which looked at the different patterns of care use associated with age, sex and functional deficits.

To be able to relate trends in care use to the populations of care-users we distinguished several population groups for which we analysed use trends over the period 1974-88, extrapolating from them through to 2005. To complete our picture of future care use we estimated the future size of each group. Care use by the population as a whole was then estimated by summing across the various groups. Except in the case of GPs, who also visit patients in homes for the elderly, the use data in the trend study relate only to people living in their own home.

In the next section this division into population groups is amplified and an estimate made of the make-up of the population in 1990-2005. Section 5.3 is concerned with trends in the utilization of different services, and section 5.4 gives estimates of future care consumption.

5.2. Trends in and estimates of the size of population groups

The kinds and quantities of ambulatory care delivered, in the past, present or future, can to a large extent be explained by reference to the size and composition of the population. The trend study takes account of this through a subdivision into population groups defined by *age, sex, household size, educational level* and *perceived health*. This choice of defining attributes mainly reflects the application of certain criteria in a search of the literature on the use of ambulatory care: these were that the characteristics had to occur in all the databases used, correlate statistically with care consumption, show trends and provide a sound basis for extrapolation into the future. In what follows we briefly review trends in these attributes.

In the Netherlands the number of births fell sharply in the 1970s, reaching a low point of 170,000 in 1983; since then the figures have risen, and by the end of the 1980s ten per cent more children were being born than in 1983 (see De Beer 1989 for a comprehensive account of demographic trends). Marriage rates have moved in similar fashion, falling in the 1970s and with an upturn beginning in 1983, while the number of divorces rose sharply through the 1970s and began to fall back in the mid 1980s. The proportion of one-person households rose from 17 per cent in 1970 to 29 per cent in 1988. Expectation of life at birth has risen steadily since the 1950s; this has happened faster among women than among men, so that the gap in life expectancy between the sexes has widened.

The data on future demographic trends are taken from a study by the Netherlands Interdisciplinary Demographic Institute into likely levels of social-security spending (Van Imhoff *et al.* 1990). The NIDI figures were chosen because they specifically concern private households and are related to household size and composition. NIDI's forecasts indicate the continuation of several major trends. The number of people living in private households will reach a peak of 16.4 million in 2025, when a slow decline will set in. The proportion of old people will reach a maximum in 2035.

NIDI summarizes the main changes in household composition as follows:
- a slight fall in the number of children;
- a sharp fall in the number of couples with children;
- an increase in the number of old people living alone, small in absolute terms but considerable in relative terms;
- a fall in average household size;
- a very sharp increase in the number of people living alone.
(See Van Imhoff *et al.* 1990.)

Our time horizon in this study is the year 2005. Between 1990 and 2005 the number of people living in private households in the Netherlands will increase by around one million to 16.2 million. The trend towards single living will continue: from 12 per cent of the population in 1990 the figure will rise to 16 per cent in 2005. The changing proportions of people living alone in the different age groups in the trend study are shown in table 5.1.

Table 5.1. Percentage of people aged 20+ living alone (private households only), 1990-2005

	Men 1990	1995	2000	2005	Women 1990	1995	2000	2005
20-54	13	14	16	17	10	11	12	13
55-74	13	16	17	19	27	28	28	29
75+	22	23	25	26	62	64	64	63

Source: NIDI.

Over the next fifteen years the number of men aged 20-54 living alone is expected to rise by some 38 per cent (from 500,000 to 700,000); the number of women in the same age group living alone will increase somewhat more, namely by 43 per cent (from 380,000 to 545,000). The number of people in the 55-74 age group living alone will almost double (from 150,000 to 290,000) in the case of men and rise by some 35 per cent in that of women (from 360,000 to 480,000). Among those aged 75 and over the number living alone will also rise: in fifteen years' time around 400,000 women in this age group will be living alone, compared with fewer than 100,000 men.

In addition to these demographic characteristics our population groups are also related to perceived health and educational level, and it is to trends in these that we now turn.

Educational levels have risen sharply over the last fifteen years and are expected to continue rising over the next fifteen. Fewer young people now enter lower vocational education (aimed at the least academic 12-16-year-olds), while the numbers of school-leavers entering higher vocational education or university have increased considerably, particularly among girls (CBS 1989). The databases used in the trend study also show rising educational levels in the 20-54 age group: the proportion of men with some form of post-16 qualification rose from 30 per cent in 1974 to 60 per cent in 1988, the corresponding figures for women being 20 per cent and 50 per cent respectively. As part of the trend study we projected educational levels among adults in the period 1990-2005; our estimates indicate that the proportion of men with post-16 qualifications will rise from 61 per cent in 1990 to 76 per cent in 2005, and that while the proportion will remain smaller among women it will increase more rapidly (from 51 per cent in 1990 to 68 per cent in 2005). The general upward trend in educational levels will also affect those aged 55 and over. The proportion of men in this age group with post-16 qualifications will rise from 42 per cent in 1990 to 54 per cent in 2005; here too there will be a catching-up process, as the lower figures for women show a faster rate of increase (from 18 per cent to 31 per cent) (see Policy Paper 1990).

People's perception of their own health also seems better now than ten or fifteen years ago, notably among the younger old in the 55-74 age group (see table 5.2). The trend cannot be established with any certainty, however, since the survey questions covering perceived health have undergone a number changes over time.

Old people's apparently very favourable perception of their own health in 1974 probably reflects the phrasing of the survey question, which asked not how respondents assessed their health but how satisfied they were with it; it is well established that old people tend to emerge as "very satisfied" (Turksma 1982) in surveys of satisfaction of many kinds. Apart from this exceptional figure the other results show a clearly improving trend among the younger old, while the perceived health of the older old has shown little change.

Table 5.2. Percentages of the 20-54, 55-74 and 75+ age groups satisfied with their own health (1974) or describing their own health as good or very good (1977-88)

	20-54 %	N	55-74 %	N	75+ %	N
1974	81.7	3179	67.8	952	75.4	183
1977	82.4	2681	54.9	859	54.1	185
1980	83.0	1978	58.8	629	57.6	99
1981	82.6	4818	57.6	1685	50.8	455
1982	82.9	4694	55.0	4636	45.3	1588
1983	85.4	7376	61.5	2462	53.5	641
1984	84.4	4855	62.4	1642	50.2	474
1985	85.5	4656	63.9	1599	60.9	455
1986	85.9	4746	65.6	1597	55.3	479
1987	86.8	11305	68.9	3647	62.4	845
1988	86.7	4201	65.5	1378	54.9	428

Using statistical analysis we can determine the correlation between perceived health and the other characteristics used to define our population groups. In the 20-54 age group educational level and household situation (whether or not the respondent lives alone) correlate with perceived health, with the more educated and those with a partner taking a rosier view of their health than do the less educated and those living alone, while men tend to judge their health more favourably than women; these differences are however small. Over the period under consideration there was a slight but significant upward trend. Analysis of the subjective health of people aged 55 and over shows that women in particular have come to take a more favourable view of their health; the trend is most marked among women aged 55-74, but those aged 75 and over have also become more likely to judge their health to be "good" or "very good". A slight improvement in perceived health is also detectable among men aged 55-74; among those aged 75 and over there has been virtually no change. The differing trends in perceived health among men and women correspond generally with the differences in the decline in mortality and increase in life expectancy.

Simultaneous rising trends in life expectancy and subjective health mean that the period of life marked by illness and disability is being pushed back into ever older age; the younger old of the future can thus be expected to feel healthier than those in the same age group today. Educational level emerges from the statistical analysis as a major "determinant" of subjective health, so that rising educational levels can be expected to lead to an improvement in subjective health. At the same time the number of people living alone will increase, and they tend to feel less well than do those who have a partner.

Statistical extrapolation of perceived health into the future indicates an increase in the proportion of the population judging their health to be "good" or "very good". The improvement in perceived health will mainly affect the younger old. The proportion of men aged 55-74 taking a favourable view of their own health will rise from around 65 per cent in 1990 to 75 per cent in 2005; among women the rise will be from 67 per cent to almost 80 per cent. Among men aged 75 and over the proportion with "good" or "very good" subjective health will remain roughly constant at 56 and 60 per cent respectively for those living alone and those with a partner; among women in this age group some improvement is expected, with the proportion with "good" or "very good" subjective health rising from around 55 per cent in 1990 to 60 per cent in 2005.

The four defining characteristics - age, sex, household size and perceived health - can be combined to give many different population groups. Not all are equally relevant to the use made of ambulatory care, however, and several simplifications were therefore made. Among the under-20s the only distinctions made were by age and sex, while among those aged 55 and over we disregarded educational level. This latter simplification was necessary because use of ambulatory care by members of this age group with post-16 educational qualifications is so limited that no statistically sound estimate was possible. Statistical analysis also showed that in the case of persons with a favourable view of their own health there was no need to make distinctions by educational level and household size, since these variables contributed little or nothing to explaining the use of ambulatory care by those with "good" subjective health. The number of population groups was eventually reduced to twenty, and the trends in care use by them were analysed. The groups are shown in table 5.3.

This section's main conclusions are that:
- the number of people living alone will continue to rise over the coming decades, with single living especially common among women aged 75 and over;
- educational levels will continue to rise across the board;
- subjective health has improved over the last fifteen years and is likely to continue improving, notably among the younger old.

Table 5.3. Population groups in the trend study of ambulatory care

Age	Perceived health	Household Size	Education
1 20-54	Good		
2 20-54	'Less than good' or 'not good'	Two (or more) persons	
3 20-54	'Less than good' or 'not good'	One person	Low
4 20-54	'Less than good' or 'not good'	One person	Intermediate or high
5 55-74	Good		
6 55-74	'Less than good' or 'not good'	Two (or more) persons	
7 55-74	'Less than good' or 'not good'	One person	
8 75+	Good		
9 75+	'Less than good' or 'not good'	Two (or more) persons	
10 75+	'Less than good' or 'not good'	One person	

5.3. Past trends in the use of ambulatory care

Since we are concerned in this study with trends relevant to home care, the trend study on the use of ambulant care focuses on those services which are now, or are in future likely to be, most involved in home care. In the first instance these are general practice, community nursing, home help and general social work (classed in the Netherlands as core primary services), but we also looked at physiotherapy and at outpatient care provided by specialists. We give utilization trends for each of these services, setting them against supply trends in each case.

118

The *general practitioner* has a central role in primary care: almost everyone in the Netherlands is registered with a GP, and 70 per cent of people consult their doctor in any given year. As a rule it is also the GP who gives access to more specialized medical and paramedical care. Looking at trends in GP care, it is striking that neither the proportion of the population consulting their doctor nor the number of contacts has increased significantly since 1974. Figure 5.1 shows the proportion of the population consulting their doctor on one or more occasions in each three-month period.

Figure 5.1. Percentage of the population aged 20 + consulting their doctor at least once in each three-month period, 1974-88

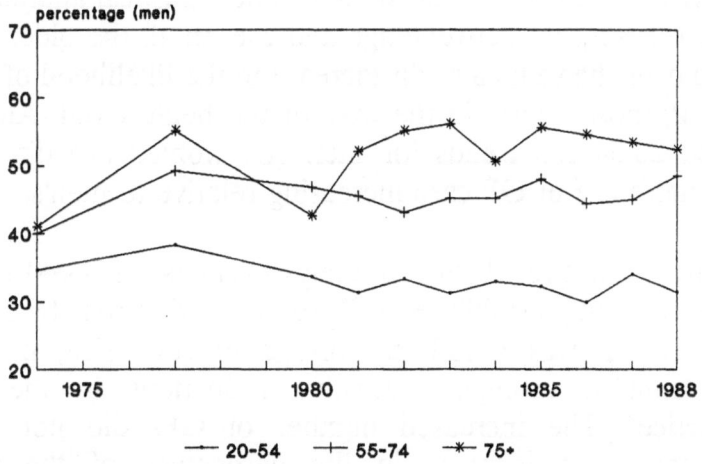

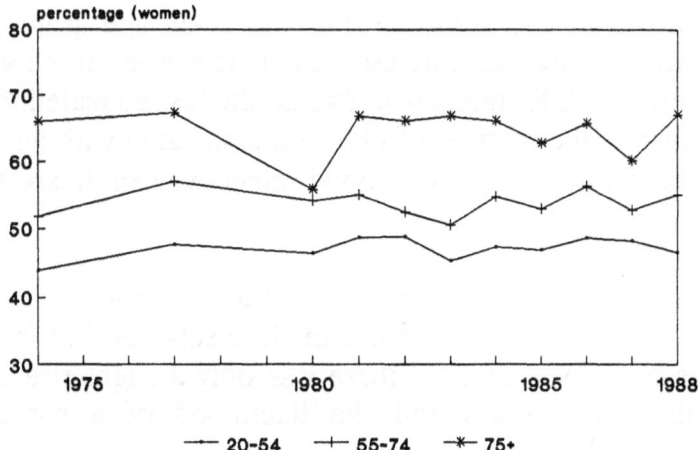

For each population group we made a trend calculation of the use of GP care, expressed as the likelihood of having one or more contacts in a three-month period; analysis showed the main determinant of visits to the doctor to be subjective health, in both the 20-54 and 55+ age groups. The improvement in subjective health noted in the previous section has not led people to visit their doctor less frequently, however; on the contrary, frequency of visits has increased slightly among those with good subjective health relative to those whose subjective health is poor. In the population aged 20 and over men are less likely to consult their GP than women and those with a partner less likely than those living alone; these correlations apply over the whole period 1974-1988. Figure 5.1 shows old people to make more use of GP services than do those aged 20-54, and statistical analysis confirms this relationship between age and use. In all the older groups we find over the years a slight increase in the likelihood of consulting a GP, most clearly in the case of the healthy old. Among those aged 20-54 the trends for men and women are different, with women's use of GP care increasing relative to men's.

In the period to which this analysis relates (1974-88) the ratio of independently established GPs to population rose by 26 per cent. The result was a fall in average practice size, promoted by government through successive reductions in the "standard practice". The increased number of GPs did not produce a proportionate increase in the percentage of the population consulting their doctor; only in the older population groups is a significant influence visible. For the 20-54 age groups increased density of provision was associated with a greater likelihood of consulting a GP among women and the less educated. Finally, the increase in the number of GPs was associated with an increase in the likelihood of those with good subjective health contacting their doctor.

It would not have been surprising if an increase in the number of GPs had led to increased use of their services, but in the fifteen years from 1974 to 1988 there was only a slight rise in both the number of contacts and the likelihood of a contact in any three-month period.

120

There are many plausible explanations for the low correlation between the number of GPs and the consumption of care. A few important ones are given below.

1. The main effect of the increase in the number of GPs and fall in practice size has been longer consultations, reflecting the changing nature of the doctor-patient relationship. Patients are increasingly likely to present with complex care requirements and expect fuller explanations from their GP. The increase in consultation length is observable *inter alia* in the videos of consultations made by NIVEL since 1976.

2. GPs have to devote more time to consultations with other services and to non-patient-related activities. Over the last fifteen or twenty years the number of other providers - specialists, physiotherapists, other paramedical practitioners, social workers - with whom GPs have to deal has risen sharply; there has also been an increase in the number of GPs working in group practices and health centres, and many home teams have been established particularly in rural areas. A National Study by NIVEL has shown doctors in small practices to devote proportionately more time to non-patient-related activities such as administration, in-service training and consultation.

3. There is no financial incentive for GPs to increase the number of contacts. For most of their patients GPs receive a fixed capitation fee, irrespective of the number of consultations or other interventions.

The data used in this trend study do not enable us to identify which of these explanations has most weight. The increase in the number of GPs has anyway not been spectacular: over the same period the number of specialists doubled, while the number of physiotherapists actually quadrupled.

The number of *specialists* has grown and they have come to play an ever larger part in medical care. The care they provide has increasingly become independent of hospital admission, and a decline in average length of stay has been associated with a growth in the number of outpatient contacts. The survey figures used in this study show that among the elderly in particular there was an increase in the numbers examined or treated by specialists on an outpatient basis; among those aged 20-54 there was a fall in the proportion having one or more contact in each three-month period.

Figure 5.2. Percentage of the population aged 20+ having at least one consultation with a specialist in each three-month period, 1974-88

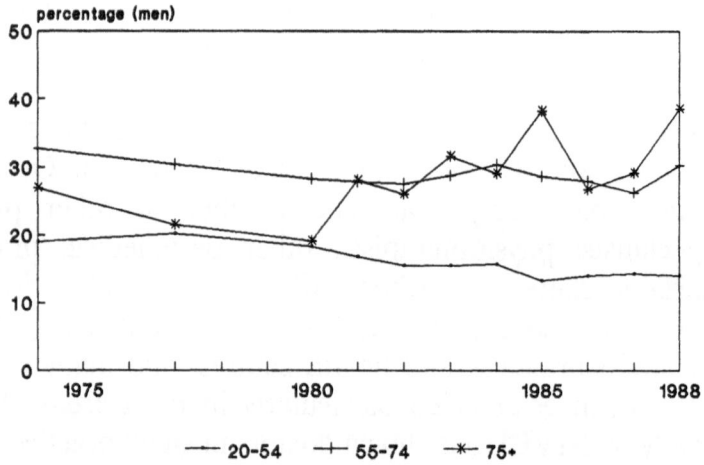

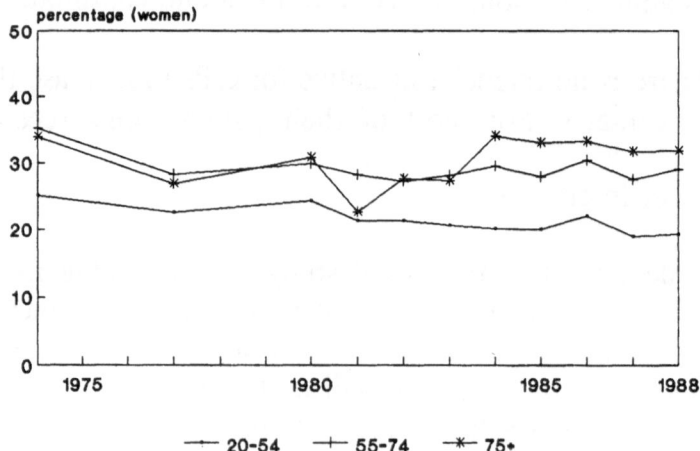

The trends visible in figure 5.2 are confirmed by statistical analysis of the likelihood of contact with a specialist in each three-month period: this shows an increase among older people and a fall in the 20-54 age group. As in the case of GP contacts, the main determinant is subjective health and men and the less educated

122

make less use of specialist outpatient services than women and the higher educated. The rising trend among the elderly is most marked among the over-75s, but over the fifteen-year period as a whole (1974-88) it was the younger old who made greatest use of outpatient care. Among the old there are no significant differences between men and women in the likelihood of contact with a specialist.

We have not attempted any detailed analysis of the relationship between growth in the number of practitioners and increasing outpatient care, since it is impossible to determine how far the increase in outpatient care can be ascribed to the increase in the number of practitioners. Other factors are also involved, such as bed closures and certain social trends (see also chapter 2), which are unconnected with the growth in the number of specialists.

Among primary practitioners growth has been particularly marked in the paramedical professions, the largest of which in numerical terms is *physiotherapy*: the number of physiotherapists rose from some 1,500 in 1972 to 13,000 in 1990, of whom around 9,600 practise in the primary sector. As the number of practitioners has risen, so too has the use made of their services. In 1974 some five per cent of the population consulted a physiotherapist on one or more occasions over a twelve-month period, including both intramural and extramural care; in 1989 it was found that, excluding inpatient treatment, 13 per cent had had physiotherapy in the preceding twelve months (Swinkels 1990). The picture is shown in figure 5.3.

Consultations with physiotherapists increased more rapidly among those with good subjective health than among those whose subjective health is poor, a result which also emerged from statistical analysis of GP contacts. In the 20-54 age group consultations increased more among women and those with a partner than among men and those living alone; there are also differences between the sexes when household size is taken into account, with men who live alone being less likely to consult a physiotherapist than women who live alone. The sexes also differ when educational level is brought into the picture: in men a lower level of education is associated with greater likelihood of consultation, a correlation not found among women.

Figure 5.3. Percentage of the population aged 20+ having at least one consultation with a physiotherapist in each twelve-month period, 1974-88

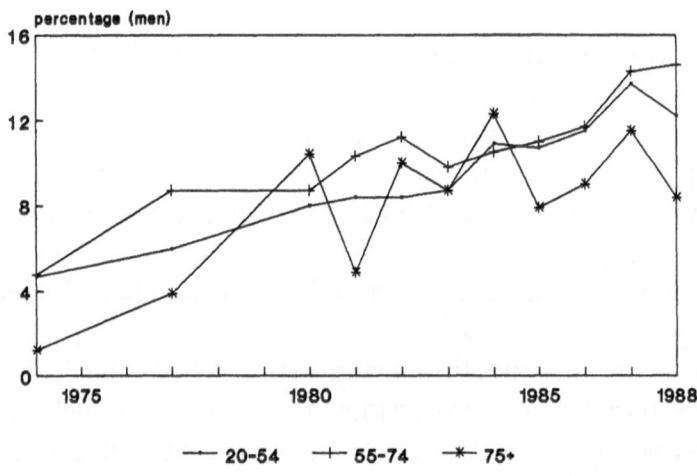

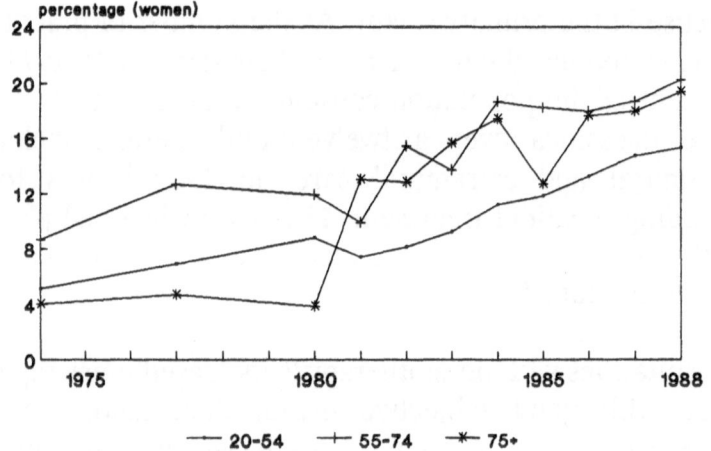

Among those aged 55 and over it is mainly the younger old (55-74) who receive physiotherapy, while women and those living alone are more likely to consult a physiotherapist than men and those with partners. Those with good subjective health who live alone are more likely to consult a physiotherapist than those with good subjective health who have a partner. Finally, the younger old who live alone are less likely to receive physiotherapy than the younger old who have a partner.

We also analysed whether the increase in the proportion of the population receiving physiotherapy in any one year was associated with the rising ratio of physiotherapists to population. A very marked correlation was found - unsurprisingly, given the sharp rise in both supply and use.

For most people contact with primary and outpatient care is limited to the practitioners mentioned above. The other services for which use trends were studied chiefly target particular groups: the main recipients of community nursing and home help are the elderly, while general social work includes among its clients relatively large numbers of benefit recipients and people living alone. In the databases used in this study these target groups account for only a small part of the sample; conclusions as to trends in care consumption are thus based on small numbers of respondents and are therefore somewhat shaky. Moreover the different surveys did not always ask the same kinds of question about the use of these services. In the case of community nursing and social work a time series can be compiled from 1981 to 1988; in the case of home help we have figures for 1974-88, but since the surveys from which they come differ widely our analysis of service use is based on data from the NIVEL National Study of 1987 and 1988.

As noted earlier, it is government policy to strengthen primary care. In the case of *community nursing* this has produced both an increase in practitioner numbers and a process of merger and expansion. Access outside office hours has been improved and evening- and nightcare are now available. The service's functions are both individual (personal health) and collective (public health), but in our trend study we focus only on the number of individual home contacts between nurse and patient. Between 1981 and 1988 around 1.5 per cent of the population aged 20-54 received community-nursing care annually, rising to around two per cent among the 55-74s; the figure is highest among people aged 75 and over, eight per cent of whom are visited by community nurses in the course of a year. The trends in service use since 1981 are shown in figure 5.4.

Figure 5.4. Percentage of the male and female population aged 20+ having contact with a community nurse in each twelve-month period, 1981-88

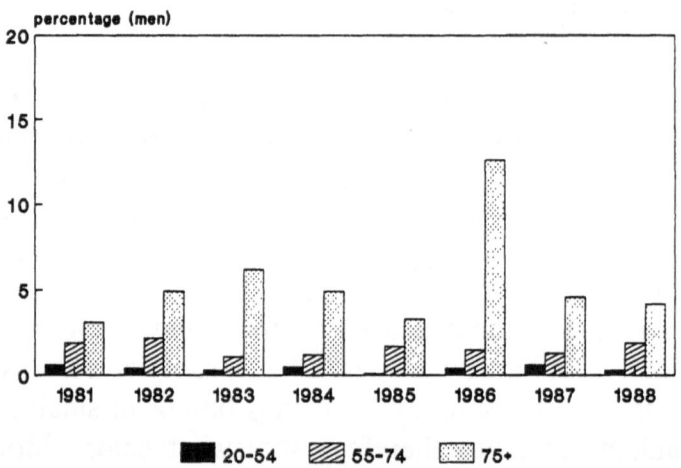

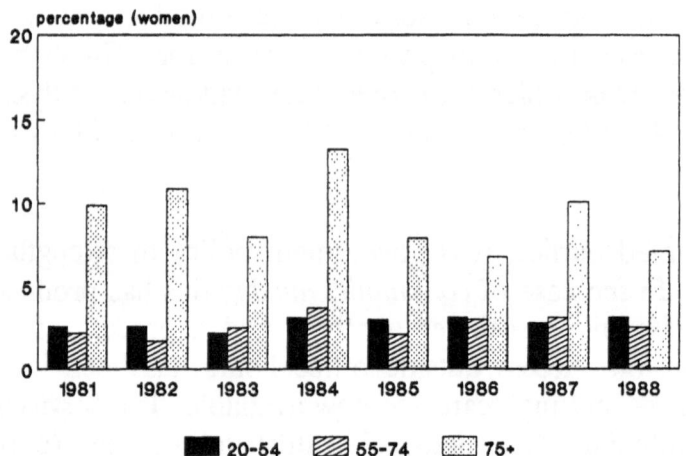

The graphs show marked fluctuations, an effect of the small numbers receiving community-nursing care; even so some conclusions can be drawn. First, we can clearly see that it is above all the very elderly who use the service, and among them chiefly women; second, the proportion of the very elderly receiving care in any on year seems to have fallen since the mid 1980s, despite the growth in the number of community nurses over the whole period 1981-88. These survey findings are confirmed by community-nursing records.

Here again we made a number of statistical analyses to determine which variables had the greatest power to explain differences in the likelihood of having one or more contacts each year. Among people aged 20 and over it is above all those whose subjective health is poor that receive community-nursing care; given the nature of the support to which the analysis relates, namely individual contacts, this is not surprising. The correlation is less strong in the case of women aged 20-54. Women with partners have more contact with the service than do men with partners, reflecting community nurses' role in maternity home care. Among people who live alone those whose educational level is low have more contact with the service than do those with a post-16 qualification; this difference is not found among people with partners.

Among the elderly the main community-nursing clients are people aged 75 and over whose subjective health is poor; in addition those who live alone are more likely to receive care than those with partners, a difference which is more marked in the younger old than in the older old.

Home help is another service much used by the elderly. Figure 5.5 shows use to have increased among old people living alone and decreased among those with partners, a shift which appears mainly related to the need to share out increasingly scarce resources. CBS figures indicate that the number of care hours peaked in 1985, since when it has fallen (Konings 1990). The shortage of home helps currently making itself felt particularly in the cities (Van Tits and Groot 1990) affects the figures for service use; the Social and Cultural Planning Office has found the proportion of the population receiving home help to have fallen, again particularly in the cities (Kwekkeboom 1990).

The same SCP study also shows home-help clients to be concentrated among people on low incomes and with a low level of education, findings confirmed by analysis of the NIVEL data from 1987 and 1988. Among the elderly it is above all the older old who live alone and whose subjective health is poor that receive home help. It is noteworthy that among women aged 55 and over service use correlates particularly with perceived health, rising sharply among those whose subjective health is poor. Among elderly men use is higher among those who live alone.

Figure 5.5. Percentage of the population aged 20+, living alone or with a partner, having received home-help support in each period of one or two years, 1974-88

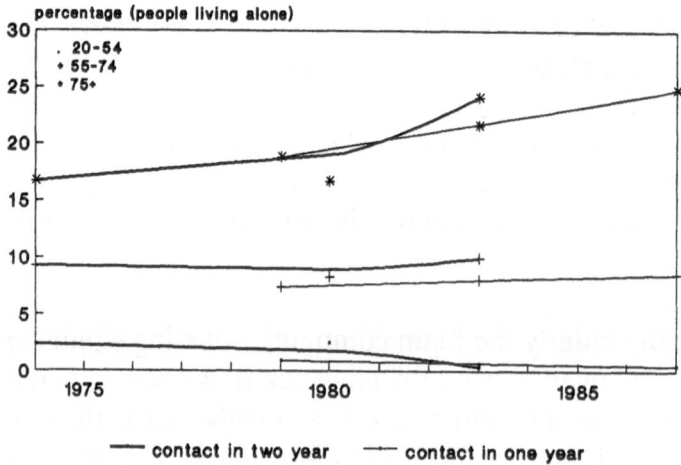

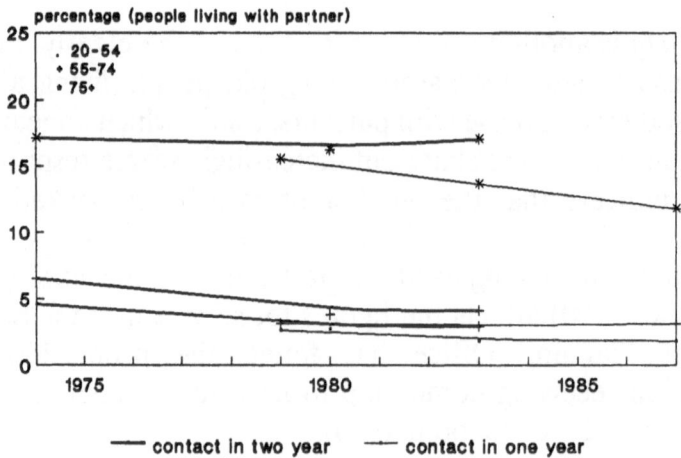

General social work has always numbered society's more vulnerable members among its clients, offering them both material and non-material assistance. From 1,500 in 1970 the number of social workers rose to 2,700 in 1988. Social work is measured and recorded in "client units", i.e. individual clients or client systems receiving support as a unit; what are known as short-term contacts are excluded. Since the mid 1970s the number of client units has risen sharply, paralleling the increase in social-work staff. Contacts completed in the period 1983-88 show support increasing particularly in the case of people living alone and those in the 40-64 age range (CBS 1989).

Figure 5.6. Percentage of the male and female population aged 20+ having contact with general social workers in each twelve-month period, 1981-88

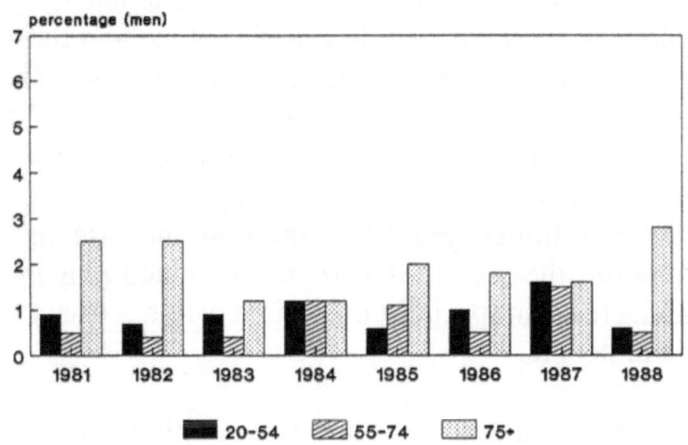

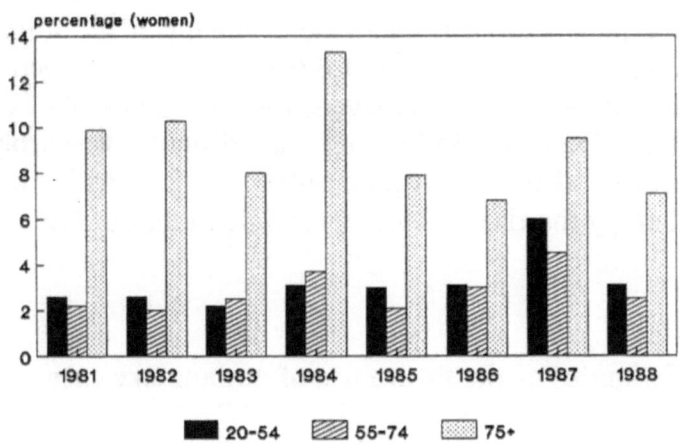

The CBS has combined and analysed health-survey data on the receipt of social-work support over the period 1981-88 (CBS 1988). Such support is sought notably by people whose subjective health is poor; indeed, perceived health is the strongest explanatory factor to emerge from the analysis. Clients are also concentrated among older people, the divorced, those on low incomes and the unemployed, and women are more likely to seek support than men. These are also broadly the results that emerge from the analysis of our combined database: perceived health, sex, educational level and age all affect the likelihood of contact with general social workers. In the 20-54 age group people whose educational level is low have made increasing use of social-work support, while among women aged 75 and over use levels have fallen.

The main patterns and trends in the use of ambulatory care are thus as follows. Women, people who live alone and those aged 55 and over generally make greater use of ambulatory care than do men, people with partners and younger age groups. The younger old are major users of physiotherapy and specialist outpatient care and the older old of GP care, community nursing and home help. Over the last fifteen years the sharpest increase has been in physiotherapy; the use of GP care has remained roughly constant, while an increase in specialist outpatient care has occurred notably among old people.

In section 5.2 we noted that subjective health had improved since the mid 1970s. While statistical analyses of care use show subjective health to be a major determinant of the utilization of the various services, it does not follow that better subjective health necessarily means lower use levels. Indeed, the number of people consulting GPs or physiotherapists has risen more sharply among those with good than with poor subjective health; in the case of physiotherapy the rise was marked, while in that of GP care it was slight.

5.4. Estimates of the future use of ambulatory care

Extrapolating from past trends gives us an indication of future levels of service use, and in this section we give our estimates for the period 1990-2005. Some of the inputs have already been considered: demographic trends, trends in care use by different population groups, and trends in the supply of care. Three different estimates were made using these inputs. We began with a *demographic estimate*. The principle involved is simple: age-specific

130

rates of care consumption are assumed to be constant and demographic forecasts are used to calculate the size of the various age groups in the future, enabling us to calculate age-specific care consumption in the future.

A demographic estimate of this kind has the major drawback of ignoring utilization trends not due to demographic change: as we saw in the last section, the rapid growth in physiotherapy reflects an increase in supply rather than any demographic shift. Nor does it take account of social changes, e.g. in educational level and subjective health, which are not classed as demographic and therefore not included in demographic forecasts. As we have seen, both these variables affect service use and both are changing in ways that can be expected to affect use levels in the future.

These objections can be overcome by introducing additional calculations. We compiled a *trend-based estimate* extrapolating from past trends in care use as well as in the size of the different population groups; this was not possible in the case of community nursing, home help and social work, however, and in these cases we extrapolated from the trends in group size only. We also prepared a *supply-related estimate*, in which group size was extrapolated from past trends but use levels in each group were estimated on the basis of the expected supply of practitioners; this tells us the level of service use given a particular trend in practitioner numbers. Supply-related estimates were compiled for the utilization of GP care and physiotherapy.

The factors taken into account in the demographic estimate were age, sex and household size, with households being divided into those comprising one person and those comprising more than one. Our calculations only cover people living in their own home; those living in nursing homes or homes for the elderly are excluded. The results, shown in index form (1990 = 100) to point up the trends, are given in table 5.4. In the case of GP and specialist care and physiotherapy they relate to *numbers of contacts*, while in that of community nursing, home help and social work they relate to *numbers of persons* having contacts in the course of a year. It should be noted that the figures cannot be interpreted as a straightforward indication of the growth in the volume of care that will be needed.

Table 5.4. Demographic estimate of care use, 1990 - 2005 (1990 = 100)

Service	1990	1995	2000	2005
GP	100	104	107	110
Specialist	100	104	108	113
Physiotherapy	100	105	109	112
Community nursing	100	106	111	116
Home help	100	107	115	123
General social work	100	106	110	114

GP, specialist, physiotherapy: number of contacts.
Community nursing, home help, general social work: number of clients.

The demographic estimate shows which types of provision are most sensitive to population aging. The home-help service will be particularly affected by the increasing numbers of old people and people living alone. In the case of community nursing the expected rise is smaller; here the effect of population aging, though considerable, is partially offset by the fall in the number of young children receiving care. Contacts with GPs, specialists and physiotherapists will not increase much as a result of population aging, with annual growth rates of less than one per cent.

Table 5.4 shows changes affecting the whole population. Calculations for the different age groups show that demographic changes will lead to a fall in the use of ambulant care by children aged 0-4 of some 11 per cent between 1990 and 2005, while use by those in the 5-19 and 20-54 age groups will remain roughly constant; only among people aged 55 and over is an increase expected, amounting in the case of the 55-74 age group to around 25 per cent. The greatest increase will be among those aged 75 and over, amounting to 50 per cent for each of the services mentioned. This shift of emphasis towards the older age groups will cause changes in the pattern of care which are not directly reflected in the percentage figures. Since contacts involving old people are generally more time-consuming, a contact with a young person cannot simply be equated with one with someone of 75 or over, and GP contacts with elderly patients are far more likely to involve home visits. In the case of community nursing and home help we estimated only the increase in the number of people receiving care every year; the available data do not allow us to calculate numbers of contacts. Here too a shift in the pattern of care will probably increase workloads, with more contacts per week, longer periods of dependence and more evening- and nightcare.

In determining the effects of demographic change we have charted only one aspect of future care use. Our demographic estimate assumes constant use per head of population, and in the case of some services - notably physiotherapy and specialist outpatient care - this is unrealistic. Estimates which extrapolate from past trends in care use or take account of future supply levels provide us with a means of refining the demographic estimates in major respects.

In the case of GP and specialist outpatient care we made *trend-based estimates* which extrapolate to the year 2005 from past trends in the average level of care use by each age group as well as from trends in group sizes. Our estimates, for the population as a whole, are in table 5.5.

Table 5.5. Trend-based estimate of the use of GP and specialist outpatient care, 1990-2005 (1990 = 100)

Service	1990	1995	2000	2005
GP care	100	104	107	111
Specialist outpatient care	100	97	94	94

The trend-based estimate of numbers of GP consultations differs little from the demographic estimate, either across the whole population or in the various age groups. When past trends are taken into account we find the number of contacts by men aged 20-54 falling and the number of contacts by women in the same age group rising; the demographic estimate assumed numbers of contacts to remain constant. Among people aged 55-74 contacts will increase slightly more than indicated by the demographic estimate among men while remaining constant among women. Among people aged 75 and over the trend-based estimate indicates a slightly greater increase in the number of contacts.

Taking account of past trends sharply alters the expected pattern of contacts with specialists in outpatient clinics. The trend-based estimate is of a sharp fall (of almost 40 per cent in fifteen years) in the number of outpatient contacts by people aged 20-54 and a doubling in the number involving people aged 75 and over. However, since there are fewer old people than people aged 20-54, this estimate shows a fall in the number of contacts overall.

In the case of general practice and physiotherapy we can estimate future numbers of practitioners and thus make calculations which take future patterns of supply into account. In the case of physiotherapy in particular an estimate which does this is likely to be more realistic than one based only on past use levels and demography, since extrapolation from past use trends implies assuming that the rapid increase in the supply and use of physiotherapy which occurred in 1974-88 will continue into the future. In fact the number of practising physiotherapists is expected to rise little if at all, and consumption is therefore likely to rise less rapidly than in the past. Our supply-related estimates of the future use of GP care and physiotherapy reflect this less rapid growth in supply; the size of the population groups continues to be calculated from past trends. In the case of GP care we assume that by the year 2005 practices will be reduced to no more than 2000 patients, which, with a population of sixteen million, gives some 8,000 independently established practitioners. In the case of physiotherapy our supply-related estimates assume that in 2005 there will be almost 11,000 practitioners working in primary care.

Table 5.6. Supply-related estimate of the use of GP care and physiotherapy, 1990-2005 (1990 = 100)

Service	1990	1995	2000	2005
GP care	100	102	104	105
Physiotherapy	100	101	103	104

Both supply-related estimates show an even smaller growth in the number of contacts than emerges from the demographic estimates. There are two reasons for this. First, both involve assuming that people whose subjective health is good will have fewer contacts with GPs and physiotherapists than those whose subjective health

134

is poor, and that for large sections of the population subjective health will continue to improve over the coming years. (Statistical analysis of the trends in care use shows that the number of people having contacts with GPs or physiotherapists has risen more sharply among those whose subjective health is good than those whose subjective health is poor (see section 5.3). This trend in the likelihood of contact is extrapolated, whereby the number of contacts is assumed to remain the same and is thus smaller for persons with good subjective health than for those with poor subjective health.) Were subjective health not to improve further, the supply-related estimate for physiotherapy would show a growth of twelve per cent between 1990 and 2005. Second, these estimates assume that the growth in the number of practitioners will be much smaller over the next than over the last fifteen years. Taken together these two trends point to a very small growth in the number of contacts.

In the case of community nursing, home help and general social work it proved impossible to compile trend-based or supply-related estimates involving extrapolation from trends in both population-group size and use per head of population. As an alternative to the demographic estimates we give below an estimate in which use (expressed here as numbers of clients) remains at the same level as used in the demographic estimate but changes in the population groups follow the trends.

Table 5.7. Trend-based estimates of the numbers of persons having contact with community nursing, home help or general social work, 1990-2005 (1990=100)

Service	1990	1995	2000	2005
Community nursing	100	103	105	106
Home help	100	105	108	113
General social work	100	102	102	101

The trends in the population groups mean that the expected growth in the numbers of people having contacts is lower than in the demographic estimate. The differences mainly reflect the decline in use by persons aged 20-54 and 55-75, these being the age groups expected to show a rise in educational level and an improvement in perceived health. The increase in use among old people differs little from the demographic estimate. In the case of social work this estimate shows use remaining at its 1990 level; this is noteworthy, since the demographic estimate showed an increase of almost one per cent per year. The difference is entirely due to the model's assumption of a declining need for social-work support associated with rising educational levels and better subjective health. The realism of this assumption is open to question. It may well be that large sections of society will be better educated and enjoy better subjective health in the future and that this will reduce the need for social-work support, as the more highly educated, when faced with psycho-social problems, tend to contact a Regional Institute of Ambulatory Mental Health Care (RIAGG) rather than seek social-work support; higher levels of education may also help ameliorate problems in the area of social competence. What is uncertain is whether all will benefit from these trends. It could be argued that rising educational levels and improving subjective health will further widen social inequalities, given the many laggards who will not share in the improvement, and the widening gap could result in increased need for social-work support.

5.5.   Cost implications

In this chapter we have so far looked at changes in the consumption of different types of primary care and of outpatient specialist care; it is to the cost implications of these changes that we now turn. Our cost estimates for the period to 2005 assume *unchanged policy*, i.e. they make no allowance for moves to intensify home care (see chapter 6) or for possible organizational changes (as described in chapter 7).

As part of the trend study we made two different estimates of the percentage change in the consumption of care. The demographic estimate assumed constant age-specific consumption on the part of men and women and on the part of those living along and those with partners, in all cases in private households only. A variant was the trend-based estimate, in which we extrapolated from trends in care consumption within the various population groups as well as in the groups' size.

The trend-study estimates point to modest volume growth. This ignores certain social developments and increased demand for home care, however, and there is therefore a case for regarding the estimates as minimum likely levels of care use. An upper limit for likely volume growth can be found in a recent report by the National Public Health Council (NRV). In its report relating to the Financial Overview of Care (FOZ) for 1992 a number of provider groups gave an indication of the volume growth they believed to be needed over the next four years (NRV 1991), and it is reasonable to assume that the growth in consumption will not exceed what is regarded as necessary by the various interest groups concerned. This estimate can therefore serve as a ceiling. For the sake of comparability the professional organizations' figures were extended to 2005, with the volume growth they deem necessary being spread over the entire fifteen-year period. A third estimate, finally, was based on the volume increase regarded as necessary in the Financial Overview of Care for 1991, extrapolated through to 2005.

Table 5.8. Percentage change in the use of ambulatory care, 1990-2005

Service	Demographic estimate	Trend-based estimate	FOZ trend	NRV FOZ report
GP care	10	11	16	23
Specialist care	13	-6	16	42
Physiotherapy	12	4	16	27
Community nursing	16	6	12	45
Home help	23	13	20	51
General social work	14	1	8	27

NB In the demographic and trend-based estimates, use is expressed as numbers of contacts in the case of GP and specialist care and physiotherapy and as numbers of persons having contacts in that of community nursing, home help and general social work. The FOZ estimates all relate to volume.

The various estimates of future volume trends differ widely, and extrapolation over the whole fifteen-year period brings out the differences very clearly. The figures shown here must therefore be seen as no more than indications of the upper and lower limits of volume changes, the upper limit being the growth regarded as necessary by the professional groups concerned and the lower the trend-based estimate from the trend study; the demographic estimate and the FOZ trend serve as a sort of middle variant. The figures for volume changes are the starting point for the estimates of percentage changes in costs over the period 1990-2005 given in tables 5.9 and 5.10; the calculations were carried out by the secretariat of the NRV's permanent committee on financial and economic affairs.

Table 5.9. Percentage increase in the nominal cost of ambulatory care, 1990-2005

Service	Demographic estimate	Trend-based estimate	FOZ trend	NRV FOZ report
GP care	84	86	94	106
Specialist care	89	58	94	136
Physiotherapy	88	75	94	112
Community nursing	111	93	104	161
Home help	124	106	118	173
General social work	108	85	97	131

Assumptions:
- general average annual increase in pay	3.2%
- general average annual increase in material costs	2.7%
- additional average annual care-specific pay increase	1.0%
- additional average annual care-specific increase in material costs	1.0%
- average annual inflation	3.0%

Table 5.10. Percentage increase in the cost of ambulatory care, 1990-2005, adjusted for inflation

Service	Demographic estimate	Trend-based estimate	FOZ trend	NRV FOZ report
GP care	18	19	25	32
Specialist care	21	2	25	51
Physiotherapy	20	12	25	36
Community nursing	35	23	31	68
Home help	44	32	40	75
General social work	34	19	27	48

Our estimates indicate that the costs of ambulatory care will at least double over the period 1990-2005; how much higher they are than this will depend on how much extra provision is made for home care in addition to the extra care necessitated by demographic change. The changes implied by the introduction of home care are considered in chapter 8, which compares the various scenarios and looks at their implications for the cost of care.

5.6. Conclusion

An important conclusion might be that population aging is not after all such a problem. Growth in care consumption, in terms of volume of the number of persons having contact with care providers, almost nowhere exceeds one per cent per year; only in the case of community nursing and home help is the estimated increase slightly greater than this, and even here the annual figure drops below one per cent if account is taken of trends in subjective health and educational level.

This conclusion needs qualifying, however. First, both the trend analysis and the estimates look at care through somewhat peculiar spectacles. Our analysis was limited to actual consumption of care and ignored unmet needs (manifested e.g. as waiting lists); moreover the data on care consumption came from surveys, with all the uncertainties that this involves. We can expect social-work clients, community-nursing patients and those receiving specialist outpatient treatment to be underrepresented, a pointer in this direction being the much higher user figures found in these services' records. These too must be treated with caution, however: there is a risk of double counting, in that someone who receives care twice in one year is often registered as a new patient or client on the second occasion. The survey figures are however the only ones which both cover care consumption by different population groups and extend over a series of years.

Second, the mathematical model we used has its limits. It treats as equivalent all contacts with a particular type of practitioner and thus fails to do justice to the reality of the situation, not allowing e.g. for the difference between GP consultations involving older and younger patients. In the case of social work, home help and community nursing the model counts only clients or patients, i.e. it assumes that everyone receives the same amount of care; this too is an oversimplification. Next, the model takes no account of happenings outside the primary sector, even though - for example

- lengthening waiting lists for places in nursing homes and homes for the elderly will increase the demand for ambulatory care by some unknown margin. Finally, no account is taken of new policy, in particular measures to promote home care.

Our analyses and estimates may well indicate the lower limit of the growth in care consumption; an upper limit was mentioned in the previous section. While it is important to recognize certain social trends that *could* lead to much slower volume growth than is currently often envisaged (see e.g. Van der Maas 1990), it is clear that demographic and social trends will produce a situation in which there are many old people with high care needs.

Given our focus on the organization of primary and home care we end with the following proposition: consumption of simple ambulatory care, in the form of a limited number of contacts with one category of care provider, will increase only slightly, while provision for complex care and home care will need to expand to cope with the growing numbers of very elderly people. There will thus be a shift in the pattern of care, with the providers of ambulatory care having increasingly to confront the complex requirements of elderly patients.

6. Complex home care

6.1. Introduction

The previous chapter described trends in care utilization starting from the present situation of Dutch health care, i.e. analysing expected consumption in each care category as currently constituted; moreover the trends were described without reference to their desirability or otherwise. The trends envisaged concerned both what is normally classed as primary care and specialist outpatient care and the more complex forms of home care. Possible developments in home care which both meet a public need and extend the policy of substituting extramural for intramural care are the subject of this chapter.

Our central questions concern the nature and scale of the need for complex home care and the conditions under which it can be delivered. To answer them we carried out a study involving consultations with experts.

Questions as to the nature and scale of care needs - how much care, in what situation, for which patients, under what conditions - are difficult to answer, since so much depends on circumstances: patients' illnesses or disabilities, their personal situation, legislation and regulation, the availability of care providers and so on. To arrive at reasonably general conclusions we elected to focus on a set of patients which in terms of care needs was as homogeneous as possible, restricting consideration to those with chronic or serious conditions likely to make heavy demands on home-care capacity. These are chronic or serious conditions of low incidence and high prevalence which make people dependent on help and support in their daily lives and require a mix of care from several sources. The care of such patients, complex home care, is the area of primary and home care where organizational problems are at their most obvious.

Complex home care, where it serves to replace or prevent admission to hospital or nursing home, has to date been covered by supplementary funding. Regular primary care as currently delivered to or accessible from people's homes is outside the scope of this chapter, whose focus is thus on services which take the place of intramural care.

The nature and scale of the services to be provided as part of complex home care are described in terms of functions, without reference to the practitioners who currently deliver them. We do this because, as the planned reforms of care insurance take effect, it is not established which practitioners will perform what functions in the future organization of health care.

This chapter is built up as follows. We begin by looking at existing functional classifications, concluding that definitions of care in terms of functions are better derived from care needs. In the process we develop a system which, starting from deficits in functioning, generates classes of patients. The range of functions required is then presented for each patient class. Finally, we formulate conditions which need to be met if the various care functions are to be delivered in the home.

6.2. Care functions

An important part of the Dekker Committee's remit was to outline a health care system in which certain processes of change were initiated, with "the supply of care shifted from an unwanted to a wanted location, without loss of quality" (Dekker Committee 1987). The Committee dealt at length with the need for the substitution of extramural for intramural services, regarded as necessary because existing resources could not cope with the consequences of an aging population; it was also seen as an essential means to the end of greater patient independence. A key element of the Committee's proposals was a "reordering of functions": "The basic package should be delivered flexibly and transparently. The definitions used must therefore refer not to the persons or institutions which provide care but to the types of care to which the patient is entitled. Current definitions of care packages in terms of institutions must make way for ones couched in functional terms." Health and social services which perform the same function - e.g. long-term nursing, whether in a nursing home or by community nurses - should be treated as a single whole, with the boundaries between the primary, secondary and tertiary tiers becoming much more fluid. The Committee distinguished thirteen functions which, while between them covering all conceivable forms of care, are too composite in nature for a systematic analysis of care activities; one such function is "the nursing, treatment and personal care of the chronic sick and care-dependent, whether intramurally, on a daycare basis or in the home."

A more systematic classification is that developed by Heydelberg for the Welfare Policy Harmonization Council (Heydelberg 1988). Heydelberg starts from the three principal purposes of health care: to promote and maintain health, to restore health, and to help people cope with illness and disability. Each principal purpose is associated with a coherent set of functions for its achievement:
- health promotion and maintenance (prevention): primary and secondary prevention;
- health restoration (cure): medical diagnosis, medical therapy, rehabilitation, aftercare;
- coping with illness (care): nursing and personal care, support and infrastructure.

This classification has been adopted e.g. by the National Public Health Council (NRV 1989b). While systematic, Heydelberg's approach is not without its shortcomings. It lacks a function encompassing the psychosocial support and minor forms of psychotherapy provided by social workers in addition to concrete assistance. Also lacking is social support, an essential element of care. The "support and infrastructure" function seems excessively composite, encompassing as it does such social services as the provision of meals, adaptations to the home, transport and so on, together with concrete help such as contacts with government bodies, care agencies and so on. The "medical diagnosis" and "medical therapy" functions are perhaps ill chosen; most types of care involve some form of test, investigation or assessment before actual delivery begins, and there is a need for a function reflecting this activity for all service providers. The same applies to "medical therapy" and "information and advice", which practitioners in all services provide in their different ways; in one case information and advice are given on the patient's condition, in another on possible admission to a nursing home or home for the elderly. Finally, patient independence should be a prime concern in both cure-oriented and care-oriented activities; every care provider, from specialist to community nurse, will almost by definition build on what patients can do, on the healthy part. For this reason we need distinguish between activities which involve carrying out tasks on patients' behalf and those which involve helping patients to perform tasks for themselves.

The shortcomings we have discussed make for problems when the abstract functions need to be translated into more concrete activities. An example can be found in the "Discussion paper on home care" (NRV 1989c): the "nursing, care, support" function is divided into the tasks of nursing, personal care and psychosocial support, which are then subdivided into nursing activities (help with activities of daily living, dressing wounds, supervising medication, etc.), caring activities (help with activities of daily living and household tasks, etc.) and support activities (psychosocial and social support, etc.). This produces a very broad function group and moreover it seems strange to bracket help with activities of daily living with both nursing activities and caring activities.

The trouble with these classifications seems to be that groups of functions are virtually entirely based on existing occupational profiles in the various categories of care provider. It is precisely because specialists and GPs, and community nurses and home helps for that matter, undertake activities involving on some occasions social care, on others medical care and on yet others counselling, that the work of the various practitioners needs to be disentangled to bring out the fact. We decided to begin by identifying patterns of need and to work from them to the requisite care activities.

6.3. Deficits in the patient system

Where people have many health problems they cannot function independently in their normal surroundings, and the purpose of care is to promote or restore the capacity for independent living or, where this is impossible, to make dependence as bearable as possible. As noted, a definition of care in terms of functions should be closely geared to the nature of the needs concerned; we must therefore consider for a moment how care needs arise. Illness, disability or problems may produce an objective need for care; how they are perceived will lead to a subjectively felt need. The demand for professional care is determined by this subjective need and by other factors, such as age, socioeconomic status and the availability or otherwise of informal care. In practice there is a weighing-up process, whose outcome is hard to predict and which differs from one patient to another, which leads one client to contact a care provider and another with a similar problem not to. Taking care needs as our starting point implies describing them in such a way as to bring into the picture the elements playing a part in that process.

How the need for care is manifested will reflect subjective experience, the availability or otherwise of informal care and so on, but the need itself arises as a result of illness (hereafter we follow the WHO in using the term "disorder": any absence or abnormality of a psychological, physiological or anatomical structure or function). A disorder may result in pain and distress, immobility, inability to wash or dress, neglect of the home. People differ in their ability to cope with disorders: a condition which crushes one may scarcely touch another. Individuals' care needs also relate of course to the nature of their social networks: access to informal care may make the difference between independent living and admission to a nursing home or home for the elderly, so that the absence of informal care is a third cause of an inability to deal with problems. The nature of the disorder is of less importance here than the deficits in independent functioning to which it leads. It is not so much the illness or psychiatric problem itself that makes care necessary, rather its consequences in the form of inability to perform activities of daily living and household tasks and reduced social competence.

Four types of deficit can be distinguished; they are shown in table 6.1. The first is the disorder itself; the second relates to the individual's response, i.e. difficulties in accepting it psychologically and inadequate social adjustment; the third arises where informal care is unavailable, and the fourth type comprises the handicaps and limitations resulting from the other three. As we are concerned with deficits in both individuals and networks we use the term "patient system", defining dependence as a situation in which the burden of illness exceeds the carrying capacity of the patient system as a whole.

In this approach care is not only indicated in connection with disorders in the narrow sense; moreover it is geared to the patient system as a whole and its purpose is to strengthen the patient system in such a way that capacity for independent living is promoted or restored.

Table 6.1. Four types of deficit

Type 1: Deficits in health.   The disorder in a narrow sense.
Type 2: Deficits in psychosocial competence.   Inability to cope.
Type 3: Deficits in the patient system.   Generally, the absence of informal care.
Type 4: Deficits in functioning.   Deficits in social competence, inability to perform activities of daily living or household tasks[1].

---

[1] Deficits in social competence are manifested in problems in dealing with official bodies, arranging for services, transport etc.
Deficits in the ability to perform activities of daily living mean difficulty with eating and drinking, washing, toileting, sitting down and standing up, getting in and out of bed, moving about in the home, dressing and undressing, moving about outdoors, using stairs and attending to one's feet.
Deficits in the ability to perform household tasks involve difficulty with cleaning, cooking, preparing meals, making beds, washing and ironing, and shopping.

146

6.4. Delphi study

The purpose of this chapter, to determine the pattern of home care needed for patients with complex problems and the conditions under which it can be delivered, can now be specified in more detail: care needs must be defined in terms of functions and may differ depending on the deficits in health and psychosocial competence, in the patient system and in functioning.

Building on the concept of deficits we constructed a set of "paper patients" varying with respect to:
1. health deficits, operationalized as the presence of a specified chronic condition (forms of CNSLD, nl. COPD, cardiovascular disease, arthritis, dementia, diabetes and cancer);
2. deficits in psychosocial competence, operationalized as subjective health;
3. deficits in the patient system, i.e. the absence of informal carers in the patient's household;
4. deficits in functioning, i.e. the frailty of old age, difficulty with activities of daily living and household tasks.

Paper patients varying with respect to these characteristics were submitted to Delphi panels made up of experts representing six professional groups (specialists, GPs, physiotherapists, community nurses, home helps and social workers) who were asked to indicate the types and levels of care required by each; consensus was sought through the successive rounds of the Delphi process. Our experts also arrived at a classification of the paper patients on the basis of their deficits and considered the conditions under which those in each class could be cared for at home. The results of this exercise are summarized in subsequent sections. We look first at how care activities were grouped into functions; we then indicate what classes were constructed on the basis of the deficits, considering the care requirements of each; finally we consider the conditions for care delivery.

6.5. From care activities to functions

Functions are clusters of similar or related care activities considered without reference to the practitioners who currently perform them, so that a function-based approach is highly suited to a scenario study which aims to construct alternative futures not tied to existing structures. We designed a such an approach on the basis of the care activities distinguished for the purposes of the Delphi study. Five criteria were developed for the grouping of care activities into functions.

First, functions are best limited to the activities of the primary process, the relationship between care provider and patient; framework-setting activities such as consultation are excluded completely: where would one draw the line? Primary prevention is excluded for the same reason. *Second*, the importance of a task is not in itself a reason for treating it as a function in its own right. *Third*, we distinguish consistently between doing things for patients (execution) and helping or enabling patients to do things for themselves (support). *Fourth*, a functional classification must cover the work of all relevant practitioner groups and should moreover divide those activities appropriately. This reflects the requirement that a functional classification should not be tied to existing provider categories. The *fifth* requirement is methodological in nature: functions may not overlap, they must be formulated unambiguously and they must be economical (i.e. encompass no more activities than is strictly necessary).

As we saw earlier, paper patients were used in determining what care activities are commonly undertaken; the activities identified were then grouped into functions on the basis of the criteria just outlined. To keep the structure manageable the twelve separate functions were combined into four principal groups, the names of which refer to their principal purposes. The term "medical care" may give rise to confusion; chosen because the primary purpose of the functions shown is medical treatment, it is not intended in any way to suggest that the activities concerned are the preserve of the medical profession. The four principal groups of functions are shown below, followed by descriptions of the twelve activities comprising them.

148

Medical care
- diagnosis, observation and monitoring;
- non-drug treatment;
- drug treatment;
- supervision and support during treatment.

Physical care
- execution of activities of daily living;
- support in connection with activities of daily living.

Domestic care
- execution of household tasks;
- support in connection with household tasks.

Social care
- counselling;
- concrete assistance;
- psychosocial support;
- social support.

The activities shown are by way of examples rather than exhaustive lists.

Diagnosis, observation and monitoring
Tests and history-taking, diagnosis, identification of care needs; observation and monitoring of patients' physical condition and identification of disease-specific factors; monitoring of decline in intellectual faculties; supervision, accident prevention, safety measures; prevention of unnecessary exertion; promotion of good day/night rhythm, daily timetable and daily activities.

Non-drug treatment
Dressing wounds, checking for complications, parenteral feeding, administering enemas; ensuring decent nutrition; care of skin and feet; ensuring adequate mobility; occupational therapy; maintenance of physical condition through therapeutic exercise; remedial exercise, breathing exercises and action to minimize shortness of breath in conditions of the respiratory tract; memory training, maintenance of a daily rhythm.

Drug treatment
Determination of medication regimen, preparation of drugs, administration and dosage adjustment; special forms of administration such as parenteral pain control using epidural catheters, intravenous administration of antibiotics, continuous parenteral administration of cytostatics.

Supervision and support during treatment
Supervision of medication, therapy, diet, compliance with therapist's recommendations; advising on practical ways of minimizing pain; teaching how to prevent complications.

Execution of activities of daily living
Help with physical hygiene; help with feeding, washing, toileting, sitting down and standing up, getting in and out of bed, moving indoors, dressing and undressing, moving outdoors, going up and down stairs, caring for feet and nails.

Support in connection with activities of daily living
Encouragement of self-care through involvement of client in care work; support for activities of daily living undertaken by client; instruction in the use of aids and appliances such as wheelchairs, height-adjustable beds, alarms, assistance with colostomy and incontinence equipment and materials, assistance with parenteral feeding, assistance with administration of oxygen.

Execution of household tasks
All types of domestic help: cleaning, cooking, preparing and providing meals (perhaps including parenteral administration), bedmaking, laundry, shopping.)

Support in connection with household tasks
Supervision and support in connection with household tasks; practical assistance with meal preparation.

Counselling
Information on sickness and changes in social life; information on complications; advice on therapy, lifestyle, nutrition, risks; advice on prostheses and special clothing; information on equipment,

adaptations to the home, transport, alarm systems etc.; information on the availability of primary and specialist care.

Concrete assistance
Identification of sources of help; referral to other agencies; arranging physical and domestic care; organizing adaptations to the home, arranging meals, equipment in the home and special services; organizing suitable transport, holidays, excursions; arranging day treatment and if necessary admission; help in arranging funding for equipment. Contact with other helpers; form-filling, letter-writing. Contact with people who have had similar experiences.

Psychosocial support
Helping patients come to terms with their condition; support in connection with deficits in functioning, help with giving up work and changes in life circumstances; support for the dying; dealing with psychosocial problems, fear and loneliness, disorientation, panic and problem situations; both individual support and discussion groups; promotion of active participation in patients' associations.

Social support
Support for the partner; help in building up and maintaining a network of informal carers; efficient deployment of and support for informal care; ensuring structure and a regular daily rhythm; paying attention and keeping company; prevention of isolation and monitoring informal care through regular visits; help with hobbies and leisure activities.

6.6. Supply and demand brought together

In this section we describe the care requirements of complex home-care patients, the paper patients in the Delphi study, dividing them for this purpose into care classes on the basis of numbers of deficits. The underlying reasoning is as follows. Someone with a serious disorder who is very elderly, does not feel healthy, lives alone and has difficulty with activities of daily living and household tasks is someone with many deficits: their care needs are complex, extending over several fields. Someone else with the same condition but who is relatively young, feels reasonably healthy, has a partner and can still manage activities of daily living and household tasks does not have complex care needs, despite their disorder. The indicators were divided into categories and scored to determine the extent of the deficits. A patient with few deficits (e.g. a serious disorder only) scores higher than one with many (the disorder itself, old age, absence of informal carers, difficulty with activities of daily living and household tasks).

To check our classification of patients, in a subsequent phase of the study paper patients with a specific chronic sickness but with different scores for other deficits were submitted to panels of practitioners (GPs, specialists, community nurses, home helps, physiotherapists and social workers). In the course of the study it became clear that the nature of the disorder was of relatively little importance in relation to care requirements: the fact of having a serious or chronic disorder is of greater weight than the actual nature of the disorder. The eventual outcome of the exercise was a division into four patient classes (the diagnoses are given for guidance).

Class 1
The class with fewest deficits, it excludes all cancer patients; its members are predominantly adults and the younger elderly and they feel healthy. They generally live with a partner and have few difficulties with activities of daily living or household tasks. These are the younger patients (arthritis, COPD, diabetes, dementia).

Class 2
Members of this class, which comprises mainly younger cancer patients and older and very old patients with other conditions, have two deficits; they do not feel healthy, generally live with a partner, have some difficulties with activities of daily living and many with household tasks. These are older and very old patients with arthritis, COPD, cardiovascular disease, diabetes or dementia and younger patients with cancer.

Class 3

Members of this class have three deficits and are in the middle and older age groups. They do not feel healthy, may well live alone, and still have some capacity for activities of daily living but not for household tasks. The main groups are older patients with arthritis, diabetes, COPD or breast or stomach cancer, younger patients with gastric or intestinal cancer and very elderly dementia sufferers.

Class 4

Patients with four deficits are very old, do not feel healthy, live alone, and can manage few activities of daily living and no household tasks. These are the very elderly sufferers from arthritis, cancer, dementia or COPD.

We then considered what functions needed to be available to patients in such classes. This resulted in "function profiles", i.e. packages of functions for the various classes (see tables 6.2-6.5).

Table 6.2. Care requirements of Class 1 patients

CLASS 1
Younger and intermediate age groups; subjective health good; partner; few difficulties with activities of daily living or household tasks
Medical care 6-8 consultations per year; 15-20 sessions of exercise therapy; 0-4 home visits per year for purposes of diagnosis, observation and monitoring, treatment, drug treatment, supervision and support during treatment
Social care 0-2 consultations per year in connection with information and advice (counselling)

The care of Class 1 patients mainly comprises medical consultations, exercise therapy, a few home visits mainly to check physical care and perhaps the occasional talk about available care facilities and the problems associated with illness and adapting to it. By "consultation" is meant a visit by the patient to the care provider; this contrasts with home visits, which tend to be fairly prolonged and to occur *ad hoc* rather than regularly.

Table 6.3. Care requirements of Class 2 patients

CLASS 2 Intermediate and older age groups; subjective health poor; partner; few difficulties with activities of daily living but some with household tasks
Medical care 10-12 consultations per year; 15-20 sessions of exercise therapy; 10-12 home visits per year for purposes of diagnosis, observation and monitoring, treatment, drug treatment, supervision and support during treatment
Physical care 1-2 sessions per week support in connection with activities of daily living
Domestic care 1-2 sessions per week execution of household tasks
Social care 0-2 consultations per year and short-term support in connection with counselling, concrete assistance and social support

Class 2 patients are on the borderline between consultations on providers' premises and home visits. Consultation, both medical and social, is more intensive. Regular home visits are needed for the purpose of physical care, and assistance with physical care is provided several times a week. The heavier domestic tasks are performed by helpers coming in every week. In this situation the patient will need several information sessions and will require help in arranging the necessary care. Short-term social support will occasionally be necessary.

Table 6.4. Care requirements of Class 3 patients

CLASS 3 Intermediate and older age groups; subjective health poor; may well live alone; moderate difficulties with activities of daily living, severe difficulties with household tasks
Medical care 4-6 consultations per year; 1-2 brief home visits per month; 15-20 sessions of exercise therapy per year; 10-12 home visits per year for purposes of diagnosis, observation and monitoring, treatment, drug treatment, supervision and support during treatment
Physical/domestic care Help is needed every day with either activities of daily living or household tasks
Social care 0-6 consultations per year; 6-8 support sessions for purposes of counselling, concrete assistance social support and psychosocial support

In Class 3 the emphasis shifts from consultations on care providers' premises to care at home. Physical or domestic care is needed every day, with care providers both executing tasks and helping patients perform them. Medical care is intensive, with many consultations and regular home visits. There is weekly exercise therapy, albeit probably not throughout the year. Social care is more intensive, with psychosocial support needed as well as counselling, concrete assistance and social support. The complexity of the situation necessitates coordination among care providers. All concerned are also involved in concrete assistance in the area of adaptations, applications for assistance, preparation for admission, involvement of volunteers, and so on.

Table 6.5. Care requirements of Class 4 patients

CLASS 4
Oldest age group; subjective health poor; lives alone; considerable difficulties with activities of daily living and household tasks
Medical care 6-8 consultations per year; 4-6 brief home visits per month; 15-20 sessions of exercise therapy per year; 14-16 home visits per year for purposes of diagnosis, observation and monitoring, treatment, drug treatment, supervision and support during treatment
Physical care 3 sessions per day of help with activities of daily living
Domestic care 4-5 (up to 7) sessions per week of help with household tasks
Social care 2-4 consultations per year and 10-12 support sessions for purposes of counselling, concrete assistance, social support and psychosocial support

Care for Class 4 patients is very intensive: they have so many deficits that the limits to home care appear to have been reached. The situation is different in the case of terminal patients; here home care is possible because it is of limited duration. In the case of non-terminal patients all helpers will be intensively involved in preparing for their admission to hospital or nursing home, caring for them in the period preceding admission.

The potential burden on professional carers is clearly considerable, raising the question of whether the primary sector is capable of taking it on: in what ways do the current organization of care and current legislation need to change to make complex home care possible?

6.7. Conditions for complex home care

In our study we found that seven sets of conditions had to be met if complex home care was to be possible. These were, in order of importance:
- *the patient system must have the necessary carrying capacity*;
- *the home environment must be suitable in physical terms*;
- *organization and coordination must be adequate to the task*;
- *delivery must be flexible and volume must grow*;
- *more types of care are needed*;
- *sufficient aids and appliances must be available*;
- *regulatory and funding arrangements need modification*.

These conditions apply at different levels: the micro-level (carrying capacity of the patient system, suitability of the home situation), the meso-level (organization and coordination, flexible delivery, more types of care, availability of aids and appliances) and the macro-level (regulation and funding). Meeting all seven is no easy matter, since some cannot be influenced at all, others only after improvement of the care system and yet others are out of helpers' reach. Patient-level conditions are obviously hard to alter; how far a patient and his or her social network want home care and possess the necessary carrying capacity will of course vary from case to case, and where the physical environment of the home is unsuitable modifications can rarely be carried out immediately. System-level conditions are within practitioners' and institutions' reach; much will depend on whether better organization and coordination can be achieved than is now possible or customary. The macro-level conditions depend on government and are thus not susceptible to rapid change. We now look at the seven conditions in turn.

Carrying capacity of the patient system
The patient must want to stay at home, be able to be left alone and still have some mobility; he/she must still be able to do some housework. The informal-care network must be up to the job, with carers willing to help at irregular times. Informal care must be backed up by counselling and expert support. Our panel members saw informal care as a vital element in complex home care; this means that home care will often be impossible where people live

alone. What informal carers can do depends on various factors: over short periods people are willing to devote a great deal of time to caring for others, but where the period of dependency is long or unknown the scope for informal care is reduced. The nature of the personal relationship between carer and patient is also important: a person who is liked or with whom the carer has a personal tie will generally be able to count on more informal care than someone else. The potential role of informal care clearly also depends on the number of carers available.

Physical environment
The patient's home must be on one floor or have a lift. In some cases the kitchen will need adapting (seating, safer equipment) and in virtually all cases the bathroom and toilet (handrails). Safety measures may be required (ventilation, fire alarms). In the case particularly of those living alone an alarm system is needed to which care providers can respond and the patient must be reachable by telephone.

Organization and coordination
If care is to be delivered flexibly and in the required amounts, responding to problems without bureaucracy or waiting lists, then radical changes are needed in the area of organization and coordination. More rapid processing of applications would help align supply and demand. Good communications are needed between client, specialist and the carer at home regarding their respective tasks. Wherever possible any given patient should always be visited by the same set of care providers, so that they do not come into contact with too many different people. The centres from which care services are operated should preferably be close to clients' homes. Agreements need to be made on the coordination of care and aids and appliances. It is important that there be one contact point for this purpose, to which clients' alarm systems should be linked; there should also be a regional information unit to respond to all questions about home care. A coordinator is needed whose job will include the compilation of reports. Nursing, care and treatment protocols need to be developed which include criteria for the use of untrained workers. Information material is needed, as is provision for continuing training for carers. Institutional decision-making needs to be

accelerated, including that relating to adaptations to clients' homes, and it must be possible for carers to be reached round the clock; in addition to access the main conditions to emerge from the study were: more rapid processing of applications, consultation on respective tasks, agreements on care coordination and continuing training.

Flexible delivery
The first requirement is the avoidance of waiting lists. The flexible deployment of home help and community nursing and effective use of informal care are a precondition for intensive home care, especially in long-term situations. Where informal care is unavailable supplementary home care must be provided flexibly and without limit, implying 24-hour care, weekendcare, eveningcare and nightcare or sleep-in services. Non-medical services and informal care in particular must be capable of being deployed flexibly, in response to clients' needs and at the times they wish. As compared with the current situation this means visits several times a day outside regular contact hours; this would need to be supplemented with a "care on call" scheme providing for *ad hoc*/immediate care outside normal hours. Of all these requirements our panel considered the flexible deployment of home help and community nursing to be the most important.

More types of care
Home care for patients with complex conditions will necessitate, depending on the condition, the deployment of additional types of care. These may include:
- pastoral care;
- the services of social workers and psychologists;
- rehabilitation;
- exercise therapy;
- orthopaedic care and physiotherapy at home over extended periods for arthritis sufferers and COPD patients (daily "clapping");
- backup by dietician for community nurses, home helps and GPs;
- home visits by practitioners from pain-control clinics;
- specialized (intramural) nursing care;
- specially trained personal carers;
- domestic help for the family;

- laundry services;
- wheels-on-meals for younger clients;
- specialist consultations in the home situation.

Where a patient is unable to obtain all the informal care he or she needs from family and friends, organized voluntary workers must be deployed through the volunteer centre e.g. to provide transport or help with leisure activities. Our panel also stressed the importance of contact with others in a similar position and with self-help groups, preferably starting before the patient leaves hospital. The must be provision for acute hospital admissions, nursing-home admissions where some disaster occurs, and, in the case of dementing patients, temporary admission to the geriatric section of a general hospital or nursing home (e.g. to allow informal carers to take holidays). In some cases, such as rheumatoid arthritis and dementia, facilities are needed for daycare (day nursing geared to clients' needs). Sheltered housing, supervised living, daycare, rehabilitation and day treatment aimed at maintaining patients' functions, also in a sense form part of the home-care package. For some patients, e.g. those with dementia syndromes, wider provision is needed for emergency admissions. Schemes need to be established providing for holiday admissions and overnight stays in nursing homes or homes for the elderly to provide a respite for informal carers. Rapid screening facilities are needed for all chronic patients, with nursing homes, Regional Institutes for Ambulatory Mental Health Care (RIAGGs) and departments of health care of the elderly acting in a consultative capacity. The option must be available of making short-term use of the technical facilities of the secondary, specialist, sector. While our panel did not see any one of these additional care types as indispensable, the possibility of temporary admission to hospital and specialized nursing care were seen as having great importance.

Aids and appliances
Here the first requirement is that patients be aware of the full range of what is available. More nursing aids and medical equipment need to be provided, including intravenous infusion sets, home respirators, humidifiers, oxygen equipment, air extractors, height-adjustable beds with adjustable backrests, and shower stools. Aids to mobility are also required: loan schemes are needed for

160

wheelchairs and specially adapted cars as well as for smaller pieces of equipment. Patients must have greater opportunities to try out and/or borrow beds, chairs and so on. Central stores need to be established for all aids and appliances. Of the various possibilities the panel regarded seven as desirable-to-essential: height-adjustable beds, nursing aids, mobility aids, opportunities to test equipment, short-term loan schemes for wheelchairs and cars, an "equipment on call" scheme and a central store.

Regulation and funding
The regulatory and funding system will have to change if the first six conditions are to be met. As we have seen, home care need not be restricted to the terminal phase of illness and the period over which maximum care is available therefore needs extending; this means more procedures, more staff, reimbursement of transport costs, adequate funding for home adaptations and aids and appliances (including alarm systems); funding must also be available for social activities, including holidays. The regulatory system will need modifying to facilitate multidisciplinary action, e.g. allowing nurses to carry out medical tasks, while the official agencies which have to approve applications must adopt less bureaucratic procedures. The funding system must be tailored to flexible delivery. Home care should be funded under the Exceptional Medical Expenses Act (AWBZ); if this is impossible the separate schemes must be expanded, with extra resources for GPs, community nurses and home helps (additional money for additional hours). A minimum requirement is that the financial division between the community-nursing and home-help services be ended (e.g. dropping the charge scheme and the requirement of membership of a community-nursing association). Voluntary work should be encouraged through payments for sleep-in services and a scheme to meet volunteers' expenses. The expenses of self-help groups and individuals helping on the basis of their own experience should also be met. Our panel further suggested the law be changed to allow domestic helps and cleaners to avoid income tax. Finally, care coordinators will need to be appointed at public expense, and more care workers will certainly be needed. Conditions regarded by our panel as essential are: reduced bureaucracy, regulatory and funding reforms, bringing home care under the Exceptional Medical Expenses Act, funding for home

adaptations and aids and appliances, and better pay for nursing auxiliaries.

The conditions do not all apply with equal force in all situations, as becomes clear when we consider them in relation to each patient class. Our study showed that Class 1 patients can normally always be cared for at home, without any additional conditions having to be met; in the case of Class 2 patients home care is possible provided the regulatory and funding system is improved; Class 3 and 4 patients can only be cared for at home if all the conditions are met. The conditions apply more strongly to Class 4 than to Class 3 patients.

6.8.   Conclusion

The experts consulted as part of our study emphasized that informal care was an essential condition. While there is virtually no limit to the burden that informal carers can bear in the short term, depending always upon the situation, home care becomes extremely problematic should the burden persist. The conclusion should perhaps be that home care for Class 3 patients should be subject to the availability of informal care and time-limited, and that in most cases patients in Class 4 are better served in an intramural setting. The exception is perhaps terminal care, where the desire to die at home weighs more heavily than the technical aspects of care and the situation is clearly time-limited. It is noteworthy that our experts did not exclude seriously ill patients from home care; no less noteworthy is their conclusion that current capacity is probably adequate, with expansion a less urgent need than the better use of existing facilities. What did emerge was that, with the exception of Class 1 patients, the organization of primary care and the legislative and regulatory framework is not yet suited to the delivery of complex care. The number of conditions needing to be met increases with the number of deficits affecting the patient.

The system of provision could conceivably be based on the care profiles for each class. Four different home-care budgets could then be made available, with the right to the services for which the budgets would provide dependent on the number of deficits affecting the patient concerned. Disbursement could be flexible, decided in consultation with patients and their informal carers: less medical and more physical care, for example, with care functions being combined in line with patients' wishes and needs. Such a system of client budgets is attractive, since defining care packages in terms of functions does of itself not guarantee flexible delivery; flexibility can however be achieved by allowing the patient and/or their care manager to determine and alter the content of the care package as they see fit. Such a proposal, albeit couched in cautious terms, has emerged from the National Public Health Council (NRV 1990).

Balanced against the various problems and conditions we have discussed is the desirability of home care. The term implies not so much care that is cheaper or in some technical sense better as care that improves the quality of life. On this point we drew attention in chapter 2 to the notion of the liberated patient, able to receive care at home if they so wish. Home care is concerned not so much with patients' health, narrowly defined, as with their welfare in a broad sense.

7. Towards scenarios for the future organization of primary and home care

7.1. Introduction

Our scenarios, like other parts of this study, are empirically underpinned wherever possible. The temptation to wipe the slate clean and set about the visionary task of designing a new structure will be ignored, for two reasons: the present system has its good points and there is no sense in change for its own sake ("if it ain't bust, don't fix it"); moreover any scenario which took too little account of realities would be rejected as impractical in the final assessment.

The scenarios in which this section culminates draw on three sources of information: an evaluation of the *present care system*, bringing out both obstacles to home care and features worth retaining; an analysis of current *experiments in care-innovation*, practical approaches to continuity of care, the substitution of extramural for intramural care and the concept of customized care; and an examination of elements in *foreign care systems* which can help widen our field of view and stimulate the imagination.

The scenarios are assessed for their likely effectiveness and feasibility in the next chapter. In this chapter we continue in section 7.2 with a description of the general features that care and the care system need to possess, considering a series of questions. Section 7.3 evaluates the functioning of the system of extramural care as presently constituted, pinpointing its strengths and weaknesses. Section 7.4 examines care-innovation projects in the Netherlands with a view to identifying general features of use in the scenarios. Various relevant examples from other countries are discussed in section 7.5. The abundance of information contained in sections 7.3-5 is then evaluated in section 7.6, while in section 7.7 our four scenarios are described with their variants.

7.2.   Care and the care system in the future

This outline of desirable attributes in a future system of primary and home care serves as a point of departure for the rest of the chapter, providing a context in which we can pinpoint the strengths and weaknesses of the present system and useful elements in care-innovation projects and determine the relevance of foreign examples.

Our vision of care and the care system in the future places central importance on *quality* and *continuity*. Basing our thinking mainly on the classification used in the National Public Health Council report on quality, organization and funding, we arrive through a combination of various sources at the following features of care, of its organization, of care providers and of material facilities (Bachrach 1981; Ministry of Welfare, Health and Cultural Affairs 1986; NRV 1990).

Delivery
Services must be genuinely accessible, without unacceptable physical or financial barriers; everyone must be aware of their rights and of the procedures for obtaining care. In the case of non-complex care certain constraints may be acceptable and even desirable with a view to preventing overconsumption.

The range of services must be comprehensive and all functions must be capable of being delivered in combination and at home. They must be tailored to clients' needs: this means that careful assessment is required, not just at the start of a period of care of treatment but also at intervals thereafter, of what care functions are needed, at what times and of what intensity. This ties in with the promotion of patient autonomy. The care delivered must be no more than a necessary complement to the capacities of the patient system, with medicalization being avoided. The theme of continuity has several aspects: different episodes of illness must where necessary be seen in conjunction; patients must not be confronted with too many different care providers; and where care needs change the organizational structure must not impede the transition from one service or function to another. Finally, care must be delivered in an effective and efficient fashion, i.e. it must achieve its objectives with least use of resources.

Organization
The purpose of the machinery of care is to help care providers towards the objectives set with the help of a sensible distribution of tasks, internal and external procedures and a vision of caring. Its primary features must include effectiveness and efficiency: the extent to which goals are being achieved must be kept constantly under review, as must the costs associated with their achievement. Customized care is possible only in the context of a flexible and internally coherent organization, i.e. one in which there are effective procedures for coordinating the work of different individuals and sections and whose outward orientation enables it to respond quickly to changes in care needs and other developments.

The care providers
The attributes needed by care providers relate closely to the nature of the care they provide: their job is to operate a needs-led system which delivers comprehensive and continuing care and respects clients' autonomy. They must possess expertise and a willingness to update and adapt it through continuing training. Suitability depends in part on personal attributes; practitioners must of course also be willing to cooperate with one another.

Material facilities
Modern equipment and techniques will become more important in home care. Complex home care has been made possible in part by technological advances. The more expensive the equipment is, the greater is the cost-awareness required in its use. The fact that it is operated in the home implies a special focus on safety and ease of use.

These features give pointers to the direction in which health care should develop, and we shall return to them explicitly in the next chapter where they will be used in the assessment of our scenarios.

7.3. Evaluation of the current care system

While it is clear from the previous section that the current care system is inadequate in many respects, it must be borne in mind that the features we deemed to be essential very much reflect our concern with complex care. The great majority of care needs will not make such heavy demands on organization and coordination, of course, and in our evaluation of the current system we shall where necessary distinguish between the two categories. In this section we begin by describing current structures and procedures in neutral terms, going on to identify their strengths (to be retained wherever possible) and their weaknesses (both existing shortcomings and those likely to develop as complex home care expands). Finally we look at a problem affecting not the care system itself but rather the potential for shaping it.

Outline of the current system
Characteristic features of Dutch health care are its tiered structure, differentiated funding system and segmented organization, dominated by non-governmental institutions. The tiers divide the system into subsystems each with broadly comparable functional characteristics and a broadly similar orientation. The relationship between tiers is hierarchical in that access to a higher tier requires referral from a lower, and such referral entails the transfer of responsibility for treatment. The primary sector is organized on segmented lines, unlike the secondary, with institutions and independent practitioners enjoying a high degree of autonomy and no one institution having an obvious coordinating role in respect of the whole; any cooperation therefore depends on the voluntary participation of the institutions and individuals concerned.

A comparable situation exists with regard to funding: the system is funded by quasi-public health insurance funds and private insurers, from patient charges, municipal grants and the contributions of members of community-nursing associations, and under the Exceptional Medical Expenses Act. Virement between providers in the primary sector funded from different sources (let alone between providers in different sectors) is impossible, so that shortfalls in one area of care cannot be met from surpluses in another.

Strengths

Where non-complex care is concerned the tiered structure is one of the current system's strengths: the barriers between the tiers prevent the more specialized forms of care being used unnecessarily, while for the patient their existence acts as a brake on medicalization. Moreover the generalist approach of the primary sector gives greater scope for taking mental and social factors into account in consideration of patients' problems, thus helping to prevent any unnecessary assumption of responsibilities by professionals and consequent erosion of patient autonomy. A widely envied feature of the Dutch system is the relative stability of GPs' patient populations: having "one's own" doctor promotes continuity of care in both complex and non-complex cases. To a lesser extent a similar link exists in community nursing, in that in each district a relatively stable team has the job of meeting all care needs. Small-scale decentralized organization helps to ensure that non-complex care is available and accessible. The low level of bureaucracy and the plural nature of care provision can also be seen as strong points.

Weaknesses

Whatever its strengths, the system's compartmentalized nature makes for a rigidity that impedes the delivery of a care mix from different sources. The impact is felt in complex cases, where inadequate coordination and cooperation mean that care cannot be tailored to individual patients' needs. The obstacles to resolving the problem in the primary sector are considerable: the harmonization of catchment areas and target populations is still a long way off, especially in the cities (De Bakker 1987; Boerma and De Veer 1991), while institutional and professional autonomy gets in the way of cooperation and can generate conflicts of interest where community nurses, social workers and home-help managers are attached to health centres. Finally, the current funding system tends to impede rather than promote integration within the primary sector.

Shaping the system

The current structure of primary care, in which non-governmental institutions play a powerful role (see chapter 2), gives little scope for central direction. This is evident e.g. from the results of official policy on health centres: after fifteen years it cannot be said to have borne more than modest fruit. A renewal measure of the 1970s and 1980s, the health centre has not caught on on any great scale: the 160 or so centres set up so far account for only just over eight per cent of GPs, almost eight per cent of community nurses, just over twelve per cent of general social workers, five per cent of community-based physiotherapists and just over 17 per cent of community-based midwives (Hessels 1990; Van Dam and Hingstman 1988). Of significance from our viewpoint is the absence from most centres of home-help services.

Health centres are mainly concentrated in urban areas where circumstances were such that health care had to be set up or reestablished from scratch and where all concerned were willing to participate (Boerma 1989). The prospect of working in a health centre, with the associated loss of autonomy, has proved unattractive particularly to established independent practitioners. In response to the limited scope for central direction, noted with regret in the policy paper *Nota 2000* (Ministry of Welfare, Health and Cultural Affairs 1986), a virtue now appears to have been made of necessity: the state is drawing back, leaving operation of the system largely in the hands of those directly involved, influenced by financial incentives and competition. It is not clear that this will produce the desired result; it also remains to be seen how far the system's users - the demand side - can operate as fully-fledged market participants (Hendriks 1990).

Conclusion
The need for health care reform follows mainly from the requirements of complex home care (see chapter 6); where other types of care are concerned great caution is needed in any moves affecting such features of the system as indirect access to specialist care, the pivotal role of the GP, and the easy accessibility, plural structure and unbureaucratic nature of the service. Provision is currently too fragmented and insufficiently patient-centred for the delivery of complex home care, however; incentives for participants to join together in providing a comprehensive service are lacking, and the government's powers to alter the situation are limited. It is however questionable whether a switch from managing supply to

managing demand and reliance on market forces will ultimately produce better results.

7.4. Care-innovation in the Netherlands

7.4.1. Introduction

Experiments in care-innovation are an obvious source of information for this study; it is taken from project records (cf. Hessels 1991). Care-innovation projects often offer part-solutions to problems which our scenarios must also address. Our classification of the various schemes is intended to give a picture of approaches conceived in the field for the purpose of facilitating complex home care or other forms of care in the community. We are concerned with broad outlines, looking at such general features as the nature of the care provided and the organizational context.

In determining our criteria of classification we focused on the features which relate most closely to the central goal of substituting extramural for intramural care:
- where the care is delivered (i.e. at home or in an institution);
- where the recipient lives (again, at home or in an institution);
- who the providers are (here there are four groups: hospitals, nursing homes, homes for the elderly and primary care providers, i.e. GPs, community nurses and home helps).
Combining "location of care" with "place of residence" gives three main categories, within which projects are classed by provider type (see figure 7.1).

We discuss, for each category and subcategory in turn, the kinds of project that exist, the nature of the renewal, and the role played in implementation by services within and between tiers.

Figure 7.1. Classification of care-innovation projects by place of residence of recipient, location of delivery and provider type

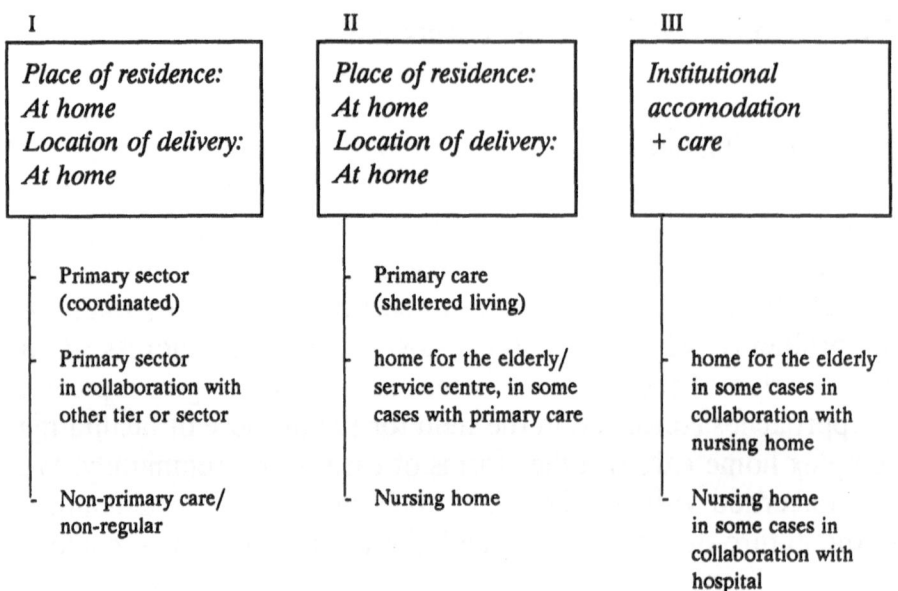

I

Place of residence:
At home
Location of delivery:
At home

- Primary sector
  (coordinated)

- Primary sector
  in collaboration with
  other tier or sector

- Non-primary care/
  non-regular

II

Place of residence:
At home
Location of delivery:
At home

- Primary care
  (sheltered living)

- home for the elderly/
  service centre, in some
  cases with primary care

- Nursing home

III

Institutional
accomodation
+ care

- home for the elderly
  in some cases in
  collaboration with
  nursing home

- Nursing home
  in some cases in
  collaboration with
  hospital

7.4.2. Care at home

Care at home delivered by primary care providers, with coordination
Delivery is in the hands of mainstream primary care providers, with supplementary provision for complex care for terminal patients, old people for whom nursing-home care is indicated, people with type II diabetes, the physically handicapped and patients discharged early following an operation. To this end there is cooperation among primary care providers; in many cases the merger of community nursing and home help is far advanced. Agreements are reached with specialist providers on consultation and the transfer of expertise. The medical axis (GP/specialist) generally operates separately from the nursing/personal care axis. Protocols have been developed for specific patient categories; while these sometimes encompass both primary and specialist care they still deal separately with the medical and non-medical axes. The procedures for determining who receives community-nursing and home-help services are already largely integrated; in some cases

there is a central point providing access to care and operating a form of care coordination.

Care at home delivered by primary care providers jointly with another tier

There is cooperation between primary care providers and practitioners or institutions in another tier, with non-primary inputs varying in scale. Minor crossovers include exercise therapy provided in patients' homes by practitioners based in nursing homes and care given by rehabilitation centre physiotherapists, jointly with primary practitioners, to patients who have been discharged early from hospital. Another type of input comes from hospitals helping with the application of medical technology in the home situation for the benefit of chronic patients for whom admission is indicated. Somewhat more ambitious is a nightcare project involving cooperation between a nursing home and the home-help service; a related scheme involves a nursing home making emergency beds available to a coordination and access point for old people. The next stage is represented by care networks offering a comprehensive package of primary and secondary or tertiary care. Such networks generally exist to serve a particular category of patient, such as the terminally ill, the disabled, the elderly or those who have been discharged early from hospital. Some of the care is delivered at home; in certain cases, as in that of respite care, it is delivered in an institution. Some care networks involve volunteers, who may receive backup from professional care providers.

Non-mainstream care at home

Private home-care agencies, both commercial and non-profit, offer services which mainstream organizations cannot as yet provide, whether for lack of staff with the necessary expertise or because the care concerned falls outside the existing funding system; in many cases such agencies can also operate more cheaply. The category of non-mainstream care also includes volunteer-only projects such as those providing home support for AIDS patients, organizations for practical home help and a sitter service.

7.4.3. Half-way projects

We now come to our second main project category, where patients live at home but receive care elsewhere. The classification by care provider is somewhat less clear, since the location of delivery tends to coincide with the provider of care. As well as concentrated care in an institution patients often also receive formal or informal care at home.

Sheltered living
The location and nature of the care provided depend on the target group; its intensity may increase or decrease as care needs vary over time. A simple form of sheltered living is the residential annexe of institutions of intramural care; divided into flats, its residents receive minor personal care and domestic help from the primary sector. In more complex situations there is greater integration between intramural and extramural functions, with a range of options from the minor (for people for whom a place in a home for the elderly is indicated) to the relatively intensive (for those for whom nursing-home care is indicated).

Daycare in homes for the elderly or service centres
There are also various levels of daycare. Many projects supplement the informal care available to old people, bringing it up to the level provided by homes for the elderly. The emphasis is on social support and a "helping hand" with shopping and the like. The home-help service provides this care or is at least actively involved. Some homes for the elderly offer a fuller service, emphasizing treatment and support; the role of community nursing is greater here.

Daycare in nursing homes
The fuller forms of care already mentioned are comparable with daycare in nursing homes, which also offers a way of alleviating the problem of waiting lists. Since those waiting for a nursing-home bed may live in their own home or in a home for the elderly, this type of daycare can involve cooperation between primary care providers, nursing homes and homes for the elderly; this may take the form of a care centre, offering a combination of daycare, observation, tests, sitter services and telephone helplines.

7.4.4. The role of the intramural sector

For the sake of completeness figure 7.1 includes a category for institutional accommodation and care not involving the primary sector. While the projects concerned fall outside the scope of this study we nevertheless devote brief consideration to them, since they serve similar objectives in a different setting. We then look at hospitals' role in the development of home care.

Care-innovation projects in the "institutional" category are of a similar nature to the half-way projects. Examples include projects involving the delivery of nursing-home care in homes for the elderly; aimed at integrating these two originally quite distinct facilities, they enable residents of homes for the elderly to receive supplementary care up to the level of that available in nursing homes without having to transfer. Elsewhere hospital care is provided within nursing homes to alleviate the problem of blocked beds. These projects are geared to particular categories of patient such those discharged from an orthopaedic or neurological ward. One nursing home collaborates with a hospital in operating a gerontological outpatient unit.

Our descriptions of care-innovation projects have given little attention to the role of intramural institutions. Comprehensive care requires vertical as well as horizontal integration and many projects involve moves in this direction. Without the intramural sector being explicitly mentioned as a partner, over two thirds of the projects in the largest category ("care at home") involve cooperation with one or more such institutions: of the 123 primary-sector projects, 37 per cent involve cooperation with a hospital, 30 per cent with a nursing home and 19 per cent with a home for the elderly.

7.4.5. Conclusion

For all their diversity, the projects all seek to ensure through cooperation and coordination that various types of expertise are deployed effectively in complex care; where primary provision falls short expertise or facilities are borrowed from a hospital or nursing home. Little imagination is needed to take the process a step further. A care network that has to deal with very diverse and complex care requirements and respond to changing needs must be able to combine the necessary functions in a single organizational structure. That we found no example of such a structure indicates a limitation of the care-innovation projects for our purposes, namely that the schemes are generally aimed more at process and content improvements than at organizational innovation unrestricted by existing relationships and interests. Nevertheless the projects are a useful source of inspiration in the development of our scenarios, and the classification shown in figure 7.1 is developed in section 7.6 into several care formats.

7.5. Examples from abroad

The limitation from our viewpoint of the care-innovation projects - that they cannot disengage from the status quo - can be offset by introducing examples from other countries' care systems, of interest because they represent what are for the Netherlands unconventional approaches. We look successively at a wide variety of matters: primary-sector beds, Health Maintenance Organizations as instances of vertical integration, individual care brokerage, the position of medical specialists in Germany, and an example of a non-regulated system (Belgium). Since a care system giving a greater role to market forces is in large part driven by financial incentives we also look at a number of moves under this heading.

Primary-sector beds
While a contradiction in terms in Dutch health care as presently constituted, primary-sector beds could usefully form part of a new organizational structure for complex home care in particular; experience of this arrangement exists in Finland and the United Kingdom (*inter alia* Backman 1988; RCGP 1990). Finnish experience reveals a major problem, namely the length of time (34 days on average) that beds are occupied by patients with chronic or geriatric problems. In Britain's general practitioner community hospitals the length of stay has been kept down (to an average of 17 days) e.g. by applying an age floor (16 years) and a ceiling on planned length of stay (one month) and by excluding psychiatric

patients and those needing specialist care. In both systems an important role is played by nurses, who must possess the necessary expertise.

Vertical integration and coordination: managed care
Health Maintenance Organizations (HMOs) in the United States combine the delivery and funding of care; the organization makes contracts with doctors and hospitals and has a fixed budget. Within a closed structure (with doctors under contract of employment and members using defined services and care providers) efficient internal planning and control are possible. The principle of "managed care" is given effect through a strict system of authorizations, discharge planning, the systematic search for alternatives to operations, continuous checks on the efficient use of resources, and case management (Prince 1987). Systems of this kind depend for their operation on the use of computerized information systems. A number of variants are possible, the commonest being the Prepaid Group Practice. A PGP employs (selected) doctors, who thus have no interest in providing unnecessary care; PGP patients (members) must make use of this closed group of care providers. The closed nature of this arrangement facilitates efficient internal planning and control. Within the PGP direct access to specialists is generally barred by a referral system involving the primary care physician. Since patients cannot always see the doctor of their choice, there is a well developed system of medical records to ensure continuity.

Individual care brokerage
Case managers in the Kent Community Care Project covered very small geographical areas in which they had the job of identifying care needs and arranging the necessary care for old people living at home. The managers, each with an average of some thirty clients, had considerable discretion in the use of their budgets. A standardized needs assessment was conducted not only before delivery began but also at regular intervals thereafter to monitor changes in clients' capacities and deficits. The Kent project ran into a number of problems: the new procedure elicited new demand, clients' rights were not always clear, and the organization was somewhat bureaucratic and unsuited to short-term care. The care manager's job also proved a difficult one, owing in part to

177

their autonomous position *vis à vis* the client and in part to the continuing pressures on their creativity in finding efficient ways of meeting care needs. When the experiment ended there was little enthusiasm among mainstream providers for making this form of care brokerage a permanent feature (Van Lieshout and Heydelberg 1991).

The Social Health Maintenance Organizations set up by the US government to provide long-term care for the elderly put great emphasis on measuring care needs, with various instruments being developed for this purpose. Where a health-status questionnaire (completed annually) revealed a need for care of whatever kind, a trained care manager would visit the person concerned in their own home to determine the nature and extent of their needs; the manager also had the job of ensuring that the services to which the client was entitled were used efficiently. The fact that the experiment was not a success in financial terms reflects the difficulty of controlling acute care.

The boundary between intramural and extramural care
In Germany the dividing line is not so much between generalist and specialist as between intramural and extramural care. While generalists and specialists are to be found in both sectors the boundary between the sectors is sharp: independently practising ambulant specialists are not involved with hospitals and hospitals do not generally have an outpatient department (BASYS 1989; Crombie *et al.* 1990). In principle this offers a way of integrating generalist and specialist care (the medical axis) in extramural care; in Germany this does not happen in practice, however, since GPs and ambulant specialists are both directly accessible and therefore stand in a competitive relationship to one another. The general practitioner with a fixed list of patients was unknown in the Federal Republic, though moves in that direction are planned (Sachverständigenrat 1989).

An unstructured and unregulated system
In Belgium GPs and specialists are freely accessible independent practitioners; competition between them is considerable and their respective tasks are ill defined (many specialists do general work and some GPs have acquired expertise in the diagnosis and

treatment of particular conditions). In this untiered system - non-system, some might say - costs are controlled by a system of financial disincentives in the form of patient charges (De Smet 1983; Crombie *et al.* 1990; Groenewegen *et al.* 1991). Whatever its undesirable effects, the Belgian system shows that acceptable health care can be delivered with a minimum of regulation and at a relatively low cost to the community: as a percentage of national product the cost of health care in Belgium is significantly below the average for OECD countries (OECD 1990). Moreover the system gives full rein to innovatory initiatives and plural provision geared to local circumstances.

Financial incentives
Financial incentives affecting supply and demand can play a large part in determining how health care works. We look first at the remuneration of doctors, then at options for patient charges.

A GP remuneration system combining fee-for-service and capitation elements will promote the substitution of extramural for intramural care only if the services for which fees are payable are carefully chosen. A study in Denmark found curative procedures closely tied to diagnosis to be most effective, i.e. most likely to reduce referrals (Flierman and Groenewegen 1989). There are also more indirect ways of giving doctors an interest in the efficient use of resources. In Prepaid Group Practice schemes in the United States doctors share the organization's risks in that they receive a salary bonus whose amount depends on its financial results (Schut 1986; Weiner and Ferris 1990). In the British National Health Service large group practices manage their own NHS budgets, excluding certain intramural costs and the costs of accident and emergency services, preventive care and screening (Department of Health 1989). It remains to be seen how many risks the providers of care run and whether poor risks tend to be excluded.

Charges to patients tend to depress demand but their impact depends in large measure on their nature: the effect of fixed payments such as flat-rate prescription charges has proved much weaker than that of percentage payments, as levied in Belgium, where there is a closer link with levels of consumption. Services for which charges are made are normally of the kind where the initiative rests with the care-seeker (Van de Ven 1985).

Conclusion
Experience elsewhere with primary-sector beds has some relevance to our scenarios; "own beds" give the primary sector greater opportunities and flexibility than do "borrowed beds". Of less relevance is the experience of HMOs in the United States, closely geared as they are to the situation in that country, though a business-style system offers a valuable model for the organization of complex care. The model also shows that other, less structured, approaches are possible as well as the HMO. There are question marks over individual client budgets and the scope for financial incentives: their introduction in the Netherlands would be no easy matter and their effects could well disappoint. The position of doctors in Germany shows that functions which are almost automatically grouped together in the Netherlands can be separated. Belgian experience, finally, calls into question the need for complex structures and detailed regulation.

7.6. Interim balance sheet

Before going on to describe the scenarios we consider the possible contributions to them from the various matters covered above.

7.6.1. Elements from the current structure

The requirements of complex care may be hard to reconcile with the interests of other care types, making it far from certain that one structure can encompass both. In both cases there is an interest in keeping medicalization and the erosion of patients' responsibility to a minimum; this attitude is more in keeping with primary than with secondary approaches, however, so that scenarios emphasizing the secondary sector's role must focus particular attention on maintaining patients' personal autonomy. Unless catchment areas and target populations coincide effective cooperation will be impossible and patients will find it hard to know what is available and where.

Smallness of scale and organizational simplicity help the delivery of straightforward types of care but are a handicap in complex cases. The stronger organization and larger scale of operation needed for complex intensive care should preferably be accompanied by decentralized delivery to offset the drawbacks of size. Function-based delivery is impossible while there are financial conflicts of interest between providers supposedly offering a comprehensive service; remuneration and funding systems must therefore be better harmonized. The major role played in the Netherlands by non-governmental organizations means that many interests have to be accommodated in the restructuring of health care; the outcome will thus be a plural system. Finally we need to examine whether market forces are a sufficient organizing principle and what still remains to be done by the state.

7.6.2. Models for care-innovation

Building on our classification of care-innovation projects we now stand back a little to get the overall picture. The care formats outlined below, which are in a sense a streamlined summary of section 7.4, are differentiated by the extent to which primary and secondary functions and facilities are involved in complex home care. The four formats we distinguish are: strengthened primary sector; primary sector plus; expanded primary sector; and cross-tier network.

Strengthened primary sector
There is cooperation within care functions; nursing and personal care are very largely integrated. There is provision for care coordination where necessary; generally one of the care providers has this task. While the stress is on a wide-ranging package of generalist care supplementary facilities and services are available for certain categories of patient requiring complex care. There is a close relationship, involving cooperation and referrals, with nearby hospitals.

Organizationally the strengthened primary sector can take the form of a federation, with autonomous institutions and practitioners, or of a stronger structure encompassing most or all functions.

Primary sector plus
This extends the previous format, with the primary sector receiving help from the secondary and tertiary sectors in connection with complex home care. A simple example of such cross-sector assistance would be an exercise therapist from a nursing home continuing treatment in the patient's home; elsewhere a neighbourhood or service centre might supplement the primary sector by providing premises for daycare or a coordination unit; a third form of assistance is that available from volunteers, particularly in the care of the elderly; the last "primary plus" variant involves commercial home-care agencies, which stand outside mainstream care provision but could be used in support.

Extended primary sector
This further move away from the tiered system has two variants, one involving cooperation with a home for the elderly and the other with a nursing home. The link with the home for the elderly is for daycare by home help and community nursing and thus resembles that with the service centre. The home for the elderly can also make beds available for respite or nightcare. The daycare given in cooperation with a nursing home is generally somewhat more intensive, with the emphasis on personal care and support.

Cross-tier care network
This represents more an extension than a reflection of what has been done in care innovation. Little remains of the tiered structure: all health services in a particular region form a coherent whole, linked by agreements, protocols, consultancy services etc. A cross-tier care network probably requires a stronger structure than a federal arrangement.

7.6.3. Inputs from abroad

As the British and Finnish examples show, primary-sector beds are a realistic option; existing facilities could be used to provide this new service. Bed availability alone is not enough, though: outpatient facilities, allowing consultation with specialists, paramedical care and occupational therapy must also be available. Measures may be needed to prevent beds being blocked.

The highly developed internal-management system used in Health Maintenance Organizations, with their business-style approach to care, shows that much development work remains to be done in the Netherlands in the area of information processing in health care.

Individual care budgets and care brokerage have several snags, with reverse substitution (i.e. of intramural for extramural care) and overloading of the system the main dangers. Clearly defined entitlements and effective procedures for determining care needs are essential (see also the care classes in chapter 6).

The German example alerts us to the possibility of integrating extramural generalist and specialist care and to the desirability, within such an integrated system, of not allowing direct access to specialist care.

Finally we looked at other countries' experience of financial incentives. If practitioners are to receive fees for specific extramural services these must be carefully chosen; the most appropriate are those which are diagnosis-specific. Salary bonuses are effective only if they relate to financial results that can be influenced by the individual practitioner. The risk to professional practitioners must not be excessive. In a system relying on financial incentives there is a danger of poor risks being excluded. Experience of patient charges shows that flat-rate payments are not effective in controlling demand; proportional charges work better, but must be levied for services over which the patient has influence.

7.6.4. Conclusion

As the foregoing indicates, our scenarios are not plucked from the air: outlines of a future structure for health care are in part already visible and it is unnecessary, and indeed impossible, to build a new system from scratch. Evaluation of the current system shows there to be little justification for radical reform in non-complex care; to the extent that structural change is necessary the care-innovation projects provide many interesting pointers. It is very much to be hoped that complex home care will be as easily accessible in the future as primary care is now, with as little tendency to medicalize problems unnecessarily.

If we stand back from diverse reality and draw together strands from the different approaches, then scenario outlines become visible. Introducing concepts from other care systems allows us to extend the range of possibilities in ways that the renewal projects cannot, tied as they are to the current structure of health care in the Netherlands. Seen from within the current structure the concepts in question - primary-care beds, business-style home-care organizations offering comprehensive care, the uncoupling of functions which have traditionally been linked, the introduction of financial incentives affecting both supply and demand - thus appear somewhat radical.

7.7. Scenarios for the organization of care

A general requirement that the scenarios must meet is that they be able to deliver both complex and non-complex primary and home care; in addition each must make some provision for coordinating complex care. The scenarios are not detailed blueprints: they do not specify funding methods, legal structure or internal design; nor are they exclusive prescriptions for the care system as a whole, in that different scenarios could coexist and elements from different scenarios be confined.

7.7.1. Classification

The four scenarios described in this chapter represent positions on two dimensions:

- *centralized versus decentralized control*
  Every organization faces the choice between centralized and decentralized control. This feature determines in part how care is coordinated; in a merged model, for example, coordination is an internal matter, while in a federal structure it is a function superior to or at the level of the participating units.

- monopoly versus diversity and competition in primary functions
At present primary functions are the preserve of primary care providers and access to specialist care is indirect. The future of this monopoly - whether it is retained or abandoned - is crucial to the shape of the future care system. A primary monopoly is not quite the same thing as a tiered structure: tiers are concerned not only with regulating access to care but also with the organizational separation of generalist and specialist functions. Here we are concerned only with the monopoly aspect.

Figure 7.2 combines the two dimensions to give the four scenarios described, with their variants, in the rest of this chapter.

Figure 7.2. Two organizational dimensions, four scenarios

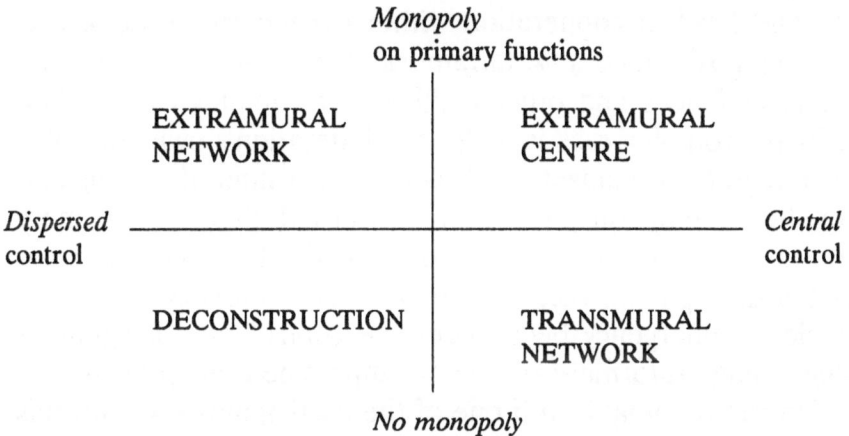

Within each scenario variants can be created by shifting the organizational centre of gravity with respect to the two dimensions or varying the range of care available.

7.7.2. Extramural network

In this scenario the providers of primary care do not belong to a single inclusive organization, but since they depend on one another to provide a comprehensive service they collaborate for the purpose on the basis of an extensive system of agreements and protocols. While such collaboration obviously entails obligations the participating practitioners and institutions retain their autonomy, i.e. can withdraw and enter a different network. This represents a federal approach comparable in some ways with an expanded home team. The coordination of care requires special measures: mutual coordination, particularly in respect of complex care, is secured and adjusted through regular team meetings. In non-complex care the situation remains as now; in complex care, if there is no separate case manager, one of the main care providers is given the extra task of coordinating individual patients' care. That primary and home care are the preserve of the primary sector does not mean that the team has a monopoly on them in its catchment area. Particularly in the more urban areas other organizations may very well be active in home care; their form may be quite different, perhaps more closely resembling other scenarios. In this scenario the link with secondary care depends on the cooperation of the specialized hospital-based functions. The nature and level of cooperation within the federation affects its negotiating position *vis à vis* intramural institutions and hence the availability of beds and other facilities for complex care. If bed capacity for complex care is under the federation's own control it is best integrated organizationally with the extramural nursing and personal-care functions; the unit concerned then has primary responsibility for the day-to-day conduct of affairs. GP access is regulated through contracts. For temporary admissions use could be made of emergency beds under the control of a hospital or nursing home. Informal-care teams supplementing professional provision can be organized if one of the participants takes on this task, ensuring that the team is integrated into the overall supply of care.

We distinguish the following variants on the extramural network.

Many small monodisciplinary units
In this most basic variant services are provided by professionals practising alone or with one partner and by separate monodisciplinary institutions; community nursing and home help are not integrated. Cooperation is needed among a relatively large number of providers; while it would perhaps be welcome in this situation, there is no separate provision for case management.

Larger organizational units
This somewhat more ambitious variant involves clusters of primary providers, with independent practitioners such as GPs and physiotherapists working in monodisciplinary structures with greater facilities for diagnosis, treatment and the employment of support staff. Community nursing and home help are integrated into one organization. These heavier structures provide a basis for links with related specialized functions in hospital; GP groups, for example, may enter into agreements with specialists on the latter's contribution to home care and the promotion of quality and expertise.

Separate provision for care coordination
Taking the previous variant a little further we can imagine a care coordinator working from a central unit where clients' details are processed and decisions are reached on the care indicated. This variant shares many features with the integrated district model in the policy paper *Nota 2000*, certainly if combined with "own beds" e.g. in a nearby home for the elderly (Ministry of Welfare, Health and Cultural Affairs 1986).

7.7.3. Extramural centre

This scenario combines all primary functions in one organization; it might be called a merged model. The power structure within the organization means that care coordination is mainly an internal question: how is coordination of the various sections' activities organized, and how is the care of individual clients coordinated (e.g. by the appointment of a care coordinator)? Such structures are of course limited to complex care; non-complex care normally operates through individual contacts between provider and recipient. Depending on the position of the care centre and local circumstances other providers may be active in the same geographical area; the relationship with them may be marked by coordination and the division of functions or by competition. Where specialized care is needed procedures and agreements exist with local hospitals; such care may be employed at various levels and with varying degrees of intensity in both consultation and treatment. Coordination is the care centre's responsibility where specialist care is delivered at home. The centre has a stronger negotiating position *vis à vis* intramural providers than that does the extramural federation in the previous scenario; it can reach agreements on temporary admissions with a hospital or nursing home or alternatively have beds under its own control, whether in a hospital, nursing home (perhaps with a local annexe) or nearby home for the elderly or in a facility of its own. Such situations closely resemble the two dispersed models in *Nota 2000*, though the internal structure of the primary sector in those models appears looser (Ministry of Welfare, Health and Cultural Affairs 1986). To mobilize and maintain informal care programmes of information and instruction can be developed, delivered by someone appointed for the purpose or by one of the care providers.

The variants on the extramural centre are as follows.

Centre based around enlarged group practice
Here the centre develops from a group of GPs or group practice which has expanded to include practice nurses, home carers, paramedics, a social worker, some general staff and a small technical section. There is a difference between such a group practice operating in an urban area, alongside many others, and one in a rural area with a local monopoly. Doctors can largely retain their autonomy in this structure; relationships somewhat resemble those in a large health centre where the doctors own the premises, jointly or otherwise, and regulate their financial arrangements through a partnership contract.

Centre based around home-care organization
Here the basis for the care centre is a strong organization which has grown out of the merger of community nursing and home help. Independent practitioners such as GPs and physiotherapists are tied to the centre by contracts or may be employed by it (this arrangement already exists in some health centres). The type of relationship will depend on the various services' local degree of organization.

Centre not tied to existing provider categories

Here all functions are combined in an organization not tied to any one category of provider but specially established for the purpose; it may emerge from a local initiative or be set up by an insurer or local authority. The difference between this variant and the preceding ones is that no one provider category is dominant at the outset; this should help promote balanced cooperation.

7.7.4. Transmural network

In this scenario the primary functions are not the exclusive preserve of the traditional primary providers. This does not mean that the primary sector cannot play a part, simply that in a transmural structure primary and home care can also be delivered by the secondary sector. Specialist care may be directly accessible, whether for part of the patient population or across the board; the involvement of the intramural sector, most obviously hospitals and nursing homes, is thus much greater than in the two extramural scenarios and there are beds earmarked for use in complex home care. Generalist care may be organized in different ways, with varying degrees of independence or as part of the intramural organization. An associated question is that of the extent of the primary sector's role in home care; here too several variants are possible. The second feature of this scenario is central control, which may be vested in one of the participating organizations or in a specially created structure. Not all combinations are equally plausible: we shall not, for example, consider the option of a hospital under the control of the primary sector providing outreach services, though a nursing home operating extramurally and under the control of a primary-care organization is a possibility. Cooperation between primary and secondary providers is important here too. Wherever control lies, the transition between generalist and specialist care must be properly regulated by agreements and procedures. The organization of informal care is possible in this scenario, but since intramural institutions have not traditionally been active in this area additional measures may be needed.

Nursing home under primary-sector control
The range of primary care is extended to include both beds in nursing homes and their treatment and care facilities; the whole is under primary-sector control, implying among other things that GPs also work in the nursing home. The structure in the primary sector may be federal or unified in a single organization; the extension of services to include nursing-home facilities does require a considerably more ambitious organization.

Hospital and primary sector together
This network encompasses all specialist and generalist care. Hospitals provide a full range of services for complex and non-complex care, complementing and cooperating on an equal basis with primary-sector organizations in their areas. Though large organizations, hospitals can deliver some services on a small scale outside their own walls, e.g. in external outpatient units. With regard to the organization of the primary sector, here too both federal and unified structures are possible, though hospitals would probably prefer collaboration with a single primary organization rather than a federation. Control is not vested in either of the partners but in a specially created structure. Within the model numerous subvariants are of course possible. This variant on the transmural network has much in common with the network scenario described in the scenario report "The hospital in the twenty-first century", in which hospitals are located in regional networks of mutually complementary facilities alongside other hospitals, nursing homes, homes for the elderly and extramural services (STG 1990).

Hospital-based care only
In this variant the primary sector ceases to exist in its present form: all primary and home-care services are hospital-based, with hospitals providing generalist as well as specialist care. To minimize problems of physical access the delivery of some types of care can be dispersed; hospitals may also place limits on the right of access to certain types. The organizational structure can range from a single large organization employing all care providers to one providing facilities for use by independent practitioners.

7.7.5. Deconstruction

In this pluralist scenario there is neither monopoly nor central control. Many forms of organization exist, depending on local circumstances, and familiar divisions between providers and institutions in both the primary and the secondary sector disappear. New areas are entered and explored in the light of expectations regarding demand and under the banner of product differentiation there is a tendency towards segmented provision. To ensure that comprehensive care is available to patients with complex needs, and indeed to ensure access to suitable care in what is often a confused situation, individual care coordination - the only permanent integrating function in this scenario - is essential. Characteristically, the care coordinator can operate either as a kind of independent broker or attached to an insurer or home-care organization. The coordinator uses clients' individual care budgets to buy the best care at the lowest cost, whether generalist or specialist, provided by a single practitioner or a cooperative structure, conventional or alternative, non-profit or commercial, intramural or extramural, local or distant. Minimal regulation means that the system can adapt easily to local circumstances and changing care needs. This scenario could be complementary to the description of the similar scenario in the study "The hospital in the twenty-first century"; that scenario is largely limited to the care provided by hospitals and small units ("villas") and says nothing about the coordination of care, in our view an essential function (STG 1990). There are almost unlimited variants on this scenario; we shall not discuss any here.

7.8. Conclusion

The scenarios set out in this chapter are based on information from various sources; the inputs from our evaluation of the current care system, analysis of care-innovation projects and consideration of other countries' systems are described in our interim balance sheet (section 7.6). The four scenarios and their variants, the culmination of the chapter, are the subject of the evaluation exercise in the next chapter.

8. The scenarios: assessment and synthesis

8.1. Introduction

When the care insurance reforms are in place insurers and providers will enter into contracts covering the cost and quality of care. If the entitlements of patients needing complex home care are defined in terms of functions (see chapter 6) insurers will be free to conclude contracts with different types of organization as in the scenarios detailed in chapter 7. The advantages and drawbacks of the various organizational approaches as exemplified in the scenarios will clearly need to be weighed one against the other as this occurs.

For the present we can assess our four scenarios for their general usefulness and possible effects on care provision, picking up elements and conclusions from earlier chapters; this chapter thus represents a synthesis of the report.

In the *first* instance we consider the scenarios in the light of the desirable features of care and the care system formulated at the start of chapter 7. In practice this also means taking account of the social developments outlined as an external context in chapter 2, since the features concerned are not plucked from the air but rather reflect social attitudes and developments affecting health care.

Elements for a *second* round of assessment are taken from the results of the Delphi study described in chapter 6. The question we address is whether the scenarios meet certain mainly organizational conditions for the delivery of complex care in the home situation.

The *third* stage is a consideration of the scenarios' intended and unintended effects on the delivery of care and its costs. As well as the effects on health care of demographic and other external developments (see chapter 5) structural changes in the care system also have an impact. Shifts may occur in both the pattern of care use and the performance of tasks by provider groups, and these forms of substitution, which may run counter to the intended effects of the system, imply modification of the general use trends that we have calculated. In this connection we also indicate in general terms the effect on costs of shifts in patterns of care and delivery and take the costs of organizational change into account.

In a *fourth* and last round of assessment we consider factors affecting the feasibility of complex home care and the associated necessary changes; here our focus is not so much on care itself as on those with the job of delivering it. We also examine the scenarios in the light of developments in health care policy, both those already under way and those likely to come. The planned reform of care insurance has considerable implications; the definition of entitlements in terms of functions and the changing position of the health insurers will affect the organization of care and hence the various scenarios' feasibility.

This account of our assessment procedure sets the framework for the rest of the chapter. Having laid down in section 8.2 the various requirements that the scenarios need to meet, we go on to the actual assessment in section 8.3; the results are summarized for each scenario and variant in table 8.1. In section 8.4, finally, we give an overall judgement, looking at feasibility (partly in the light of earlier results), the planned care insurance reforms and other policy developments, and the wishes and capacities that exist in the field.

8.2. Requirements

The scenarios set out in the previous chapter are all intended to deliver both complex home care and normal care for people at home as described in chapter 3. To determine how successfully they do so we assess them in the light of various qualitative and quantitative requirements. The qualitative requirements relate to the nature of the care provided and its organizational context (see chapters 6 and 7); the quantitative requirements derive from estimates of future care consumption (see chapter 5).

Qualitative requirements

As the desired general features of care and the care system in the future have much in common with the conditions for the delivery of complex care they can be combined. The general features as described in chapter 7 are summarized below, together with the corresponding requirements for complex home care which emerged from our Delphi study (see chapter 6).

Features of care delivery
- Availability
- Access   - Delphi: 24-hour access
- Comprehensive package - Delphi: consultation on respective
                                           tasks, agreements on coordination
- Customized care   - Delphi: faster processing of
                                           applications, less bureaucracy
- Promotion of personal
  autonomy
- Continuity
- Efficiency
- Effectiveness   - Delphi: faster processing of
                                           applications, less bureaucracy

Organizational features
- Efficiency
- Effectiveness   - Delphi: faster processing of
                                           applications, less bureaucracy
- Flexibility   - Delphi: as above, more flexible use
                                           of community nursing and home help
- Internal coherence
- Quality control
- Outward orientation   - Delphi: 24-hour access

Features of the care providers
- Expertise   - Delphi: in-service training
- Suitability
- Willingness to   - Delphi: consultation on respective
  cooperate   tasks, agreements on coordination

Features of material resources
- Availability   - Delphi: availability of various aids, alarm systems etc.
- Efficient use
- Effective use
- Safety
- Patient-friendliness, ease of use

Quantitative requirements
The scenarios are assessed for their ability to cope with future care needs and the associated implications for the deployment of professional and non-professional care providers. Estimates of future care use were given in chapter 5; the additional increase implied by intensive home care affects all scenarios equally. We also need to consider how the various scenarios influence the demand for care: each scenario involves modifying the present system in particular ways, and increases in provision - in the form of a coordinating unit, a system of agreements or a new facility intermediate between the primary and secondary sectors - will in all probability affect the demand for and utilization of care. The shifts in question vary from one scenario to another and need to be added to the general trend in care use. Shifts may occur in the desired direction (e.g. if home care reduces waiting lists for nursing-home places, freeing them for patients now blocking hospital beds); unintended and unwanted effects (such as the unnecessary displacement of informal by professional care) are also possible.

Consumption of any one type of care is determined not only by social and demographic trends and scenario-induced shifts but also by the scope offered by each scenario for transferring tasks from one practitioner group to another. Here too shifts may be in the desired direction (e.g. if tasks are transferred from highly qualified personnel to a more appropriate lower level) or not. This opens the way within a scenario to achieving efficiency savings through the transfer and differentiation of tasks; these can then be used to accommodate any rise in care consumption without increasing staff. Our quantitative assessment covers shifts in care consumption and transfers of tasks (with possible efficiency savings), to which we also add the scenarios' effects on cost patterns.

The shifts mentioned are additional to the general trend in care use, which is the same for all scenarios (see chapter 5). Combining the general trend and the scenario-induced shifts gives a broad indication of the consumption of each type of care; we call this the modified trend.

Having indicated changes in the nature and volume of care we then estimate the increase or decrease in total care costs. Cost changes are not all directly care-related, however; they may be associated with organizational changes, such as the construction of new shared premises. Our analysis is limited to additional costs associated with the type of organization for which each scenario provides.

8.3. Assessing the scenarios

We examine quantitative and qualitative aspects of each scenario in the light of the requirements discussed. The *qualitative* aspects are: access and availability; comprehensive care; customized care; clients' personal autonomy; continuity of care; and efficiency and effectiveness. The *quantitative* aspects are: scenario-induced shifts in care use; shifts in the distribution of tasks; and modification of the underlying trend in the volume of care.

In each case our discussion ends with a consideration of likely care and organizational costs.

We ignore conditions which fall outside the scope of the organizational scenarios: access to complex home care clearly depends in all cases on its inclusion in the basic package of care insurance; nor do we deal in this section with the implications of staffing and resource shortfalls for care availability.

8.3.1. Extramural network

Outline

Cooperation through agreements and protocols between autonomous practitioners and institutions in extramural care. Agreements with intramural sector on medical and nursing care normally separate.

Variants - small monodisciplinary units
- larger units (group practices and merged institutions)
- separate coordinating function

Quality
Special measures are needed to ensure *access and availability* in this federal model, given its fragmented structure and the difficulty of harmonizing procedures and ensuring that potential users are aware of what is available and where. This applies particularly to the weaker variant with its small monodisciplinary units. Only smoothly functioning cooperation under appropriate management can overcome the shortcomings of this structure. For non-complex care none of this need be a problem; heterogeneity may even be an advantage, in that if one practitioner is not available another one may well be. Decentralized small-scale delivery promotes access, particularly in everyday care.

Special efforts are also needed to ensure *comprehensive care*, since gaps can easily open up in this loose arrangement and provision is insufficiently structured; the result is a lack of transparency which is undesirable particularly in complex care. Since the various autonomous partners in the federation will each develop their own ways of overcoming shortfalls in provision there is a risk of mismatches. Emergency bed capacity is not under the control of the home-care providers in this scenario; agreements have to be reached with the institutions concerned.

The delivery of *customized care* also depends on the quality of cooperation: many binding agreements will be needed if services across the primary sector and in the secondary are to be tailored to individual care needs. It helps if at the heart of the network

198

there is close cooperation between the community-nursing and home-help services, for example, or a strong GP group; this is then a stronger variant of the scenario. Even then much will depend on funding: there must be no friction over the distribution of care (and hence of resources). Complex care may be funded through individual care budgets or provision may take the form of supplementary resources. In a model involving several relatively autonomous units the care budget is probably a better way of maintaining an optimum service than supplementary funding.

There are no great threats here to the *autonomy of the patient*: the loose structure gives the individual every opportunity to coordinate his or her own care. If there were a threat, it would come from the separate coordinating function in the third variant of the scenario.

The conditions for *continuity of care* are favourable where only one form of care is involved; where several forms are involved continuity can be achieved only through extensive regulation both within the federation and between the primary and secondary sectors. Where the primary sector has its own beds much depends on the agreements and procedures designed to ensure continuity.

Efficiency and effectiveness can be enhanced through a system of individual care budgets, perhaps managed by the care coordinator, in the third variant, or by a care provider. It is important that there be only one flow of funds into the primary sector as a whole to counterbalance the centrifugal forces inherent in this loose structure. In the case of non-complex care restrictions on access, e.g. a referral requirement, must be retained. The federal structure of an extramural network makes it difficult to organize quality control on more than a monodisciplinary basis. The limited organizational superstructure keeps overheads down. Little can be said about the level of direct costs, though poor coordination may generate unnecessary costs through inefficiency. As regards implementation the variants on the extramural network present little difficulty, since they closely resemble the current structure; resistance to introduction would therefore be low, as would its costs.

To what has already been said about *organization* we can add that a flexible structure can respond easily to changing circumstances; the reverse of the coin is a possible low level of internal coherence and client-centredness. The organizational framework and physical facilities needed to ensure the availability of *aids and appliances* are missing from this scenario; aids and appliances will therefore probably be provided for each care category separately.

Quantitative shifts

Care shifts

In the extramural network simple monodisciplinary care is more easily available than complex; overconsumption of simple care is therefore likely, with a risk of informal care being displaced unnecessarily. In the case of complex care it may not be possible to meet demand since care packages must be painstakingly assembled on each occasion. This objection applies more to the less ambitious variant. Where a separate coordinator is attached to the federation there is a risk of waiting lists developing, since the construction of a care programme requires considerable consultation. In the relationship with the secondary sector there are few incentives to alleviate the problem of blocked beds; overconsumption in the secondary sector may therefore continue.

Task shifts

The organizational separation of the primary and secondary sectors is an obstacle to rationalization through the transfer of tasks from specialists to GPs. The variant involving a large GP group in the network is better in this respect, since it creates conditions favourable to the development of cooperation on the medical axis with specialists. The transfer of tasks from specialists to physiotherapists will only occur in the hospital setting. Practice nurses can be employed only in group practices; where appointed, they can relieve GPs of certain routine tasks in the treatment of some chronic patients.

It makes sense where possible to transfer tasks from community nurses to nursing auxiliaries, both of whom belong to the same organization; when the community-nursing and home-help services are integrated home helps can be added to the list. The variant involving larger organizational units offers greater scope for such transfers. Since the mobilization of informal care is not a clear function of any of the institutions or practitioners in the extramural network, the scope for transferring tasks to informal carers is generally limited.

Tasks can be transferred to a coordinator only if one exists, i.e. only in the third variant, and even then the coordinator must respect the autonomy of all participants. The transfer of tasks to social workers is possible, the extent to which it happens depending on the nature of the cooperation within the federation. As was noted earlier, the scope for involving informal carers is limited.

Effect on utilization trends
Since the GP is the most easily accessible practitioner in this scenario the demand for GP care will rise disproportionately in complex cases; the transfer of patients to other practitioners is not assured. In the variant involving group practices part of the extra demand can be met by practice nurses; however, the cooperation between GPs and specialists which this variant favours will tend to transfer more tasks to GPs. The presence of a coordinator will provide some relief in complex cases. On balance we can expect GPs' workload to be in line with or slightly above the trend. Some efficiency savings can be achieved if community nursing and home help are delivered by a single organization, allowing the increase in volume at higher levels of expertise to remain below trend level.

Cost implications
The pattern of costs for the extramural network will not generally differ much from the trend. Efficiency savings from integrating community nursing and home help will mainly go into expanding volume, so that total costs will not fall. We can expect the cost particularly of community nursing and home help to rise owing to shortages on the labour market. The variant involving large monodisciplinary units may allow economies of scale as practice nurses take over certain tasks in the larger general practices. The appointment of care coordinators will probably entail a rise in costs: the coordinators will themselves need to be paid, of course, and as they make primary care more accessible we can expect more people with complex needs to seek care in the primary

sector. The extent to which increased volumes in the primary sector reduce total care costs depends on how easily resources can be switched between sectors.

8.3.2. Extramural centre

Outline

Extramural structure in which all care functions are brought together in one organization (either an employer or a provider of facilities). Care coordination is an internal matter. Links with the intramural sector are governed by agreements and procedures.

Variants - based round enlarged group practice
       - based round home-care organization
       - based round an organization not tied to existing provider
         categories

Quality
The use of shared premises means that *access and availability* are better than in the previous scenario; this is of particular relevance to complex care. On the other hand access may suffer through the coalescence of the primary sector, which could make it harder for patients to identify and contact individual practitioners. The greater scope for policy formation will result in improved procedures and increased clarity for potential clients. There are also scale effects, making it easier e.g. to organized access outside office hours.

Comprehensive care is more easily achieved for the same reason. Conditions are more favourable for reaching agreements e.g. with hospitals, while the larger scale of operations allows functional differentiation and specialization and thus widens the range of care on offer.

Customized care benefits from central control and hence from a closely integrated primary sector - the wider the range of provision, the more easily individual care needs can be met - but in an

202

extramural centre there is some risk of rigidity and bureaucracy which would jeopardize customized care. This model retains the division between the primary and secondary sectors, a potential obstacle to customized delivery in complex home care.

While the *autonomy of the patient* may suffer in this structure, it also gives patients and their representatives greater opportunities of influencing the course of events.

Similar considerations apply to *continuity* as to customized care: here too better results may be achieved in the primary sector but continuity is not assured in transfers between sectors. The system has the advantage that it has one obvious point of entry and that transfers of information are easily organized. The extramural centre can have beds under its control, even under its own roof; these neighbourhood beds can then have a broader function than simply to deal with emergencies and provide respites for informal carers.

The conditions for *efficiency and effectiveness* are more favourable in a tightly structured organization than in a loose federation, albeit heavy demands are made on management and information services. If these work well costs can be tightly controlled, e.g. through budgets for particular types of care or categories of patient. Conditions for quality control are also favourable.

Organizational and overhead costs can easily rise to unacceptable levels in this type of structure, without any corresponding improvement in the quality of care. Where neighbourhood beds are under a centre's control steps are needed to ensure that patients can move on; such facilities can have their own problem of blocked beds, seriously compromising efficiency.

The establishment of extramural centres implies the creation of power centres in primary care able to exercise economic and other pressures on other areas of health care and other sectors. Such countervailing power can have great value in a system relying on market forces.

Attention has already been drawn to the danger of an excessively complex *organization* in which function is subordinated to structure. The advantages of a sound structure, e.g. in maintaining expertise and a decent level of service, can easily become drawbacks; bureaucracy is incompatible with flexibility of response, and if concern with internal coherence comes to predominate this will be at the expense of patient-centredness. The drawbacks of size can be countered by decentralizing delivery to relatively small and independent units; there is no reason why an extramural centre should not work on an outreach basis. As a supplement various incentives could be used to promote effective ways of working.

The supply of *aids and appliances* for use in home care and the related back-up services are easily organized in an extramural centre. A store could develop into a provider of facilities (obtaining, managing and maintaining aids and appliances and giving instruction in their use), which could also serve outsiders.

Quantitative shifts

Care shifts
With access to uncomplex monodisciplinary care more difficult than in the previous scenario overconsumption will not occur; rather the contrary. As all extramural care is provided in one organization the transition from simple to complex care is easily accomplished, increasing consumption of the latter. The secondary sector will make greater use of home care capacity than in the extramural network, reflecting greater availability and the existence of agreements and procedures governing continuity of care, but as the sectoral divide persists the transfer of patients from hospital is not necessarily assured. The fact that hospitals and extramural centres have separate budgets plays a part here.

Task shifts
While the organizational separation of primary and secondary care makes the transfer of tasks from specialist to GP conditional on agreements, the more favourable organizational framework and perhaps clearer policies in respect of specialist care mean that more rationalizing moves of this kind can be than in the previous scenario. If physiotherapists are involved in post-hospital care they

can take over certain tasks from specialists. The size of the extramural centre gives scope for one or more practice nurses who can relieve GPs of certain tasks.

As in the extramural network, conditions are favourable for the transfer of tasks in the area of professional personal and domestic care, since both services operate within the same organization. The greater likelihood of active patient groups developing in this scenario also increases the potential for mobilizing informal care.

On the social side there is also greater potential for mobilizing informal care. Moreover the model includes a strong coordinator to whom tasks can also be transferred. A policy aimed at efficient care delivery, achieved e.g. through the kinds of task transfer mentioned, is also more easily implemented in a centre than a network.

Implications for utilization trends
A developed home-care system will face most services with an increase in consumption, offset to only a very limited extent by the greater difficulty of access to non-complex care, and consumption of extramural care will exceed trend levels despite the efficiency gains in home nursing and personal care and the transfer of tasks to practice nurses and care coordinators. The demand for intramural care may decline if capacity is adjusted.

Cost implications
The Health Insurance Funds Council trials have shown complex home care to be expensive. For there to be an offsetting fall in the cost of intramural care fixed as well as variable costs would have to be reduced, implying cuts in intramural capacity. Moreover the larger scale of the extramural centre implies higher organizational costs than in today's typical health centre.

8.3.3. Transmural network

Outline

Greater involvement of intramural sector in complex home care; possibility of all care being hospital-based. Central control system covering whole range of care.

Variants - nursing home under extramural control
- hospitals working with primary sector on basis of equality
- all care hospital-based

Quality
Availability and access depend on the variant and on the nature of the care required: the more dominant the role of the intramural partner, the more access to complex care becomes easier and access to simple care more difficult. What happens depends on the form of the transmural network, emphasizing in the one case caring and in the other curing functions. Aside from this the involvement of intramural institutions can make it easier for care-seekers to identify and reach the care provider they need. To ensure that physical distance is not an obstacle large organizations could offer certain care programmes on a decentralized basis, e.g. in freestanding outpatient units or community-nursing centres. If extramural capacity is inadequate there is a risk of patients being too readily hospitalized. Access to specialist care therefore needs restricting in some way in the great majority of non-complex cases; in the third variant this could even be achieved through tiered organization within the hospital.

Comprehensive care of a medical nature is easily achieved in this scenario, especially where the network includes a hospital. The advantage of the large hospital with its various departments and services is that by opening itself up it can relatively easily make a wide range of equipment and services available to people living in their own home; this type of function is often underdeveloped in the primary sector. In addition to medical and nursing care, special measures may be needed to ensure the availability of personal care, which risks being squeezed in this scenario.

With regard to *customized care*, the fact that the full range of services is available means that many different needs can be met. There is however some risk of "overcare" or excessive specialist care: customized care implies the right type of care in the right amount, i.e. no less and no more than is needed. The boundary between complex and non-complex care is less sharp in this scenario than elsewhere.

Patients' *personal autonomy* is at risk in this scenario: the greater the degree of organization, the more the individual is likely to be pushed into the background. The possibility of "overcare", and of specialist care being used where generalist care would suffice, opens the way to medicalization and an unnecessary erosion of autonomy.

Continuity of care is relatively easily assured in a secondary-sector institution, even in complex cases, though where comorbidity is likely steps are needed to ensure coordination between specialties. Continuity between primary and secondary care depends in some degree on the structure and position of the primary component of the transmural network. To the extent that the primary sector is a unit in its own right agreements can be reached with the secondary sector. If the division of functions is such that, for example, hospitals provide all complex care and the primary sector what remains, there is a risk of discontinuity at the transition between complex and non-complex care. Home care which is hospital-led may be excessively "clinical", moreover, and while aftercare provided from hospital may be ideal for patients recovering from operations, care at home cannot in general be run as an extension of intramural care.

Efficiency and effectiveness are familiar themes in intramural care; information systems are also relatively well developed. The role in home care which hospitals and nursing homes play in this scenario can be built on existing structures, an advantage from the viewpoint of efficient and systematic delivery. The combination of primary and secondary care in one organization creates conditions favourable to substitution, e.g. because funding which would otherwise be earmarked for the secondary sector can be shifted into primary care. A possible threat to efficiency and effectiveness lies in the fact that transmural networks, particularly the hospital-based variant, will often have a monopoly in their area. In the absence of incentives to counter the adverse consequences there is a danger of care being sucked into the hospital or nursing home. The dangers already mentioned of a rigid and inward-looking bureaucratic organization also apply here.

The availability of a wide range of *aids and appliances* for use in home care is a strong point of the transmural network. Existing hospital and nursing-home facilities in this area can provide the basis.

Quantitative shifts

Care shifts
Since one organization encompasses the whole care cycle there is greater scope for alleviating the problem of blocked beds; indeed, unblocking beds is quite likely to be made a priority, perhaps at the expense of non-complex care, and non-complex needs will tend to manifest themselves as demand for complex care as a result. In the variants which give a dominant position to hospitals there will be a tendency to deliver overspecialized care. Since rather little effort is likely to be made to develop informal care and care networks there is little scope for substituting informal for professional care.

Task shifts
The scope for rationalizing the distribution of medical tasks depends on whether the practitioner groups working in a given organization are such that transfers are possible; variants on the transmural circuit which include a hospital thus offer greater scope for specialist-to-GP transfers than others. Where a hospital forms part of a network, or indeed leads it, the conditions for transferring medical tasks are very favourable.

Provided there is close cooperation or merger between the community-nursing and home-help services, conditions are present for the efficient deployment of professional personal and domestic care. Since the organization of the transmural network will probably not be very attuned to informal care it is unlikely to be mobilized effectively. In the variant involving a nursing home under primary-sector control much will depend on the structure and level of organization of the primary sector. The earlier comment on informal care also applies here. The level of organization in this scenario makes for easy transfers of tasks in the area of social care from GPs and community nurses to social workers and, where they exist, coordinators.

Implications for utilization trends

Since complex care is well developed (perhaps even overdeveloped) in this scenario, GPs and the providers of nursing and personal care and will face additional demand; little of the burden will be borne by informal carers. Integration will allow the transfer of community-nursing tasks to home helps, whose role will therefore expand. GPs and community nurses can transfer social-care functions to social workers, changing the content of the latter's role in health care. The scenario variants involving hospitals will mean extra work for GPs as tasks are transferred from hospital specialists. Most services can therefore expect to face an increase in demand faster than the trend rate, possibly offset by a reduction in intramural care.

Cost implications

The transmural network offers scope for using savings produced by home care to offset the cost of intramural care; it is also more likely than the other scenarios to provide a solution to the problem of blocked beds. These are two cost-saving advantages. On the medical side this scenario offers greater opportunities for transferring tasks to GPs; this too should help hold down costs. A drawback of the scenario is its possible inhibiting effect on informal care and its greater reliance on hospitals and nursing homes. The cost of organizing care will rise, particularly if home care is controlled by both hospitals and the primary sector.

8.3.4. Deconstruction

Outline

No monopoly on home care; no central control; very diverse forms of cooperation; no uniform division of responsibilities; little regulation; coordinators for complex care.

Quality
Access and availability are not restricted by tiering or regulation, at most by financial hurdles. Unless the funding system includes appropriate incentives there is a great risk that insufficient care will be provided for "expensive" patients, i.e. those requiring complex care. With provision so heterogeneous it is difficult for patients to know what is available and where; coordinators are therefore essential for complex home care.

Comprehensive care is not assured. Provision is by definition fragmented; while the different services may well exist this cannot be guaranteed, and in any event they may not be locally available. Without some regulation there is a real risk that only the fortunate few will have access to truly comprehensive care.

Customized care depends very much on local circumstances and on care providers' view of their responsibilities. There is a risk of too much care, and in particularly too much specialist care, being provided, with generalist provision increasingly eroded as a result. Where there are shortages of particular categories of care provider customized care for certain "expensive" patient categories may degenerate to the point that patients lose all freedom of choice.

The *personal autonomy* of the patient is in any event not threatened by excessive organization in this scenario. On the contrary, free rein is given to individuals' creativity in arranging care to suit their own requirements (whether or not such freedom is actually desired).

Continuity is possible where one care provider is involved, provided records are maintained and the patient does not have too many different care contacts. Interdisciplinary continuity is unpredictable and cannot be assured, depending very much on chance groupings of care providers and the system of remuneration. A fee-for-service system is an obstacle to interdisciplinary continuity (since practitioners tend to hold on to their patients rather than refer them on); a capitation system may be an obstacle to continuity with one care provider (since he or she has no incentive to go on providing care). In this scenario there can be no continuity as implied by the notion of the "general practitioner".

More than in the other scenarios *efficiency and effectiveness* depend on the remuneration system and the relationships between providers of care. Overconsumption and medicalization are real dangers, though the effect of patients "voting with their feet" could be to enhance the system's effectiveness.

Aids and appliances etc. for home care are supplied by commercial organizations independent of the delivery of care.

Quantitative shifts

Care shifts
In this scenario there is a risk of care providers selecting on the basis of severity of need, with the more "difficult" patients being quickly referred on. Coordinators will be hard pressed to arrange suitable care for such patients, and in such cases underconsumption is likely. The opposite will be the case with single-category care: with care providers seeking to retain patients longer than necessary there is a likelihood of overconsumption.

Task shifts
In this scenario specialists and GPs normally stand in a competitive relationship to one another, so that the present overlap of tasks is unlikely to change much, but since GPs will seek to link up with colleagues or representatives of other professions the competition is between larger units. In arrangements involving specialists and GPs the transfer of tasks is highly likely, while in group general practice tasks can be transferred to practice nurses; where insurers

establish a broadly based multidisciplinary structure there is scope for rationalization of both kinds. Much therefore depends on the arrangements that evolve.

Given that both are in the same organization there are likely to be transfers of tasks between community nurses and nursing auxiliaries. The home-help service may well not be involved; this will leave the existing overlap between the work of home helps and nursing auxiliaries in place, giving rise to boundary conflicts rather than rationalization. The chances of mobilizing informal care are slight.

The scope for rationalizing the distribution of tasks in social care is generally also limited. It is enhanced by the formation of monodisciplinary or multidisciplinary structures of sufficient size to allow the appointment of a coordinator; an efficient transfer of tasks to the coordinator is then possible, in conjunction with some task differentiation and specialization among the practitioners concerned. The structure has few ties with the world of informal care, so that its potential will remain largely unexploited.

Implications for utilization trends
Such are the obstacles to obtaining complex care in this scenario that the increase in the demand for such care will be limited to what is essential. The result is that people will make more use of services outside the mainstream professional circuit; GPs in particular, but also specialists, will face increasing demand as a result. In part this can be covered by the use of support staff such as practice nurses. In this scenario a large proportion of home care is delivered by commercial agencies. The general drive for efficiency results in many forms of vertical and horizontal integration, producing efficiency savings both on the medical side and in nursing and care. On balance the demand for care will rise faster than the trend in the case of GPs, home helps and, to a lesser extent, community nurses.

Cost implications
The deconstruction scenario implies cost increases in a number of areas. The cost of specialist and intramural care will rise, since patients can go directly to a specialist without referral by a GP and

those with complex conditions are likely to remain in hospital for longer than in the other scenarios. Home-care costs may fall as a result of the use of commercial agencies. Organizational costs are generally low. Where a coordinator is appointed to supervise complex home care then both organizational costs and the volume of care (and the associated costs) will rise.

8.3.5. The assessment summarized

The assessment of the scenarios in respect of quality and quantitative shifts is summarized in table 8.1. Each variant is scored in relation to simple and complex care for the various aspects of quality, shifts in care and in tasks, and cost implications. Caution is needed in interpreting the table. The temptation to read it vertically, counting the pluses and minuses to arrive at an overall score for each variant, is to be resisted: the criteria are dissimilar, and in any event a single mark for each scenario would not do justice to the complexity of the comparison.

Overall, on the criteria applied both the extramural centre and the extramural network with coordinator show many improvements on the present position. The transmural-network variants involving hospitals also score well; the variant involving nursing homes under primary-sector control scores less well. The two extramural-network variants without coordinators and the deconstruction scenario show too few improvements on the points considered.

Table 8.1. Qualitative aspects, care shifts, task shifts: the assessment summarized

	Extramural network						Extramural centre						Transmural network						Decon-struc-tion	
	Small units		Large units		Coordi-nator		GP-led		Centred on home-care		New org.		Nursing home under prim. sector control		Prima-ry/hos-pital coope-ration		Hospi-tal based			
	S	C	S	C	S	C	S	C	S	C	S	C	S	C	S	C	S	C	S	C
Accessibility/availability	+	-	-/+	-/+	+	+	+	+	+	+	+	+	-	-/+	-/+	-/+	-	-/+	+	-
Comprehensive care	-	-	-	+	-	+	+	+	+	+	+	+	+	+	+	+	+	+	-	-
Customized care	+	+	+	+	-/+	-/+	+	-	+	-	+	-	-	-	-	-	+	+	+	+
Patient autonomy	+	+	+	-	-/+	-/+	+	-	+	+	+	+	+	-/+	+	-/+	+	-/+	+	+
Continuity	+	-	+	-/+	-/+	+	+	+	+	+	+	+	-/+	-/+	-/+	-/+	-/+	-/+	-/+	-/+
Efficiency/effectiveness	-	-	-/+	-/+	+	+	-/+	-/+	-/+	-/+	-/+	-/+	-/+	-/+	-/+	-/+	-/+	-/+	-/+	-/+
Organization	+	-	+	-	+	+	-/+	-/+	-/+	-/+	-/+	-/+	+	+	+	+	+	+	-/+	-/+
Aids and appliances	-	-	-	-	-	-	+	+	+	+	+	+	+	+	+	+	+	+	-	-
Care shifts	+	-	+	-/+	-/+	+	+	+	+	-	+	+	+	-/+	+	-/+	+	-/+	+	-
Task shifts	-	-	-/+	-/+	+	+	+	+	+	+	+	+	-/+	+	+	+	+	+	-	-

S   = simple care
C   = complex care
+   = improvement as compared with present position
-   = deterioration as compared with present position
-/+ = improvement on some points, deterioration on others

8.4. Final assessment

As we summarize our assessment of the scenarios it will become apparent that some are more suited than others to delivering a combination of complex and non-complex care. These selected scenarios will then be assessed for feasibility, taking account of the staffing implications of the expected levels of care consumption and the pattern of shifts in care and tasks.

8.4.1. General suitability

The *extramural network* probably does not provide adequate access to complex care, particularly in its weak variant, since the level of coordination required among the different parts of the network may well not be achievable in a federal structure; putting together appropriate care packages requires too much consultation and is too dependent on agreements that cannot be effectively enforced. It is not clear that coordinators can solve this problem, since in this loose structure their powers are limited. Nor is the infrastructure especially suited to the deployment of aids and appliances in home care. The organizational division into relatively autonomous units and the lack of an effective feedback system make it difficult to guarantee the quality of complex home care. A rational distribution of tasks and functions too may be impeded by the divisions between providers. These problems are less serious where the organizational unit is large and a coordinator is in place. The combination of a federal structure for non-complex care with separately organized complex care could be worth considering; this could however create new problems of coordination.

The stronger organization of the *extramural centre*, with its greater scope for quality management and stronger position *vis à vis* the secondary sector, favours the delivery of complex home care. The centre's size enables it to offer a comprehensive range of services and forms of task differentiation and specialization promote efficient delivery geared to needs. Premises could include a department supplying aids and appliances, along with the necessary training and maintenance services. There is however a risk of rigidity and bureaucracy and of a sharp rise in overheads. Where the organization is large the delivery of care is best decentralized. Increasing demand can be met in part by support workers, such as general staff and practice nurses, though this brings with it the danger of too many care providers being concerned with any one patient. The structure, particularly the variant involving an independent organization, lends itself to forms of patient participation and hence to the mobilization of informal care, and this may result in tasks being transferred from professionals to informal carers. Close links with the secondary sector are not guaranteed; the organizational division means that task transfers and continuity are not assured, though they are likely to be facilitated by the fact of a more heavyweight and balanced organization.

Summing up, all three variants on the extramural centre must be deemed capable of delivering complex home care; the third variant, involving an independent organization, appears most balanced, since it is not dominated from the outset by one particular category of provider.

The advantage over the previous scenario of the *transmural network* lies in the range of services offered, with both intramural and extramural care combined in one framework. The variant involving nursing homes under primary-sector control suffers in this regard, as the more specialized hospital care falls outside the system and must be organized separately. Conditions are favourable in the other two variants for continuing and comprehensive care. In the hospital-based variant there is a risk that continuity may suffer through the underdevelopment of non-complex care in the home situation. Organizational unity facilitates shifts towards primary care, helping to reduce pressures on intramural care. Growing demand for primary care can be met by existing and new services at various levels of expertise. There is some risk that the transmural network may overemphasize curing functions, leaving caring functions underdeveloped and offering specialist care unnecessarily; this applies particularly to the hospital-based variant. This tendency is an obstacle to the transfer of tasks to the primary sector.

While none is incapable of doing what is required, our preference goes to the variant in which hospitals and the primary sector cooperate in one organizational framework.

Finally we come to the *deconstruction scenario*. While access is good in principle, selection of patients is likely in practice, especially in complex cases. The independent coordinator directing care flows is not in a position to improve matters very much. Continuity and comprehensiveness are not assured, since what does not exist cannot be bought in. The more different services have to be involved, the more difficult it becomes to construct a care package and ensure the necessary coordination; the likelihood of gaps and overlaps is considerable. The coordinator is probably not an adequate safeguard for complex home care of an adequate standard. Our conclusion must be that this scenario would have difficulty in delivering complex home care.

8.4.2. Implications of current policies and proposals

The general policy context was outlined in chapter one, where the desirability of home care, the substitution of extramural for intramural care and deregulation were discussed. Here we look in more concrete terms at relevant policy developments initiated in the recent past. Since trends in health care policy can only be identified with hindsight (see also chapter 4) our treatment can be no more than rudimentary. The question we address is whether current policy directions tend to assist or obstruct the development of new care forms as discussed in this report.

Deregulation
Central government has a general policy of cutting back its regulatory role, as witness the abolition of the obligation on care insurers to offer contracts to established GPs, the withdrawal of statutory controls on where GPs may practice, reduced certification and licensing, and the repeal or relaxation of the Hospital Services Act (WZV) and the Health Charges Act (WTG). General social work is already run by local government. This policy direction is in keeping with the scenarios involving a light organizational structure, notably the deconstruction scenario but also the

extramural network. It is questionable whether the organizationally heavier scenarios are achievable in a time of reducing government regulation, whatever their potential for delivering complex home care; in this respect deregulation is rather a hindrance than a help.

Care insurance reform

At the heart of the new care insurance scheme is the principle that entitlements are defined as clusters of care functions rather than in terms of providers; within these clusters care from one provider may be substituted for care from another, the delivery of a package of care functions no longer being tied to particular professional groups, care providers or institutions. Under the scheme insurers are free in principle to enter into contracts with the providers of care and can therefore influence its organization: this may have implications for the implementation of certain scenarios, in that, for example, insurers may prefer arrangements in which an integrated home care package can be guaranteed by a single organization. Insurers' influence on the organization of delivery will depend in part on whether they operate nationally in open competition or primarily in "their own" regions. Regional operation gives greater opportunities for monopoly and hence for influencing organizational structures, thereby generating obstacles to the intended pluralist organization of care and the operation of market forces, and more lightly structured organizations could then be at a disadvantage. If insurers operate nationally, however, it is more likely that contracts will be concluded at national level with the existing monodisciplinary umbrella organizations. Models on the lines of the extramural network are more likely to develop in such a situation. If the reform of care insurance has little structural impact then the deconstruction scenario is also a possibility.

These variants are of course possible only if complex home care is included in the basic insurance package; if it is not, a two-tier system may develop with better-off patients more likely to take out supplementary cover.

Links with welfare services

The decentralization of responsibility for general social work to local government at a time of organizational changes in health care resulting from the care insurance reforms brings with it the danger

218

of the two sectors growing apart. Social workers have hitherto played an important part in the care of people at home, e.g. through involvement in home teams and health centres, and we must therefore ask which scenario is most likely to preserve or create the most productive relationship between health and welfare services. It is reasonable to assume that the best route is through agreements e.g. with local authorities or specific welfare agencies, with home care being delivered from within a single organizational framework.

Quality legislation
The need for legislation concerned with the quality of care flows from the ending of supply-side regulation (the current system of recognition under the Exceptional Medical Expenses Act and the Health Insurance Act). There are statutory quality criteria for care provided by institutions; independent practitioners will be covered by the Practitioners in Individual Health Care Act (BIG), which will provide among other things for the protection of certain professional titles and quality requirements. Organizations of care providers have a role in maintaining quality, e.g. through the development of quality care profiles, standards and so on. The loss of autonomy by independent practitioners that is inevitably associated with any form of compulsory appraisal may be a problem in the deconstruction and extramural network scenarios. Resistance to loss of autonomy would also be a factor in the more strongly organized scenarios but would make itself felt mainly at the point when the structures concerned were set up; once in place, they would fit in well with current thinking on quality legislation.

Patients' rights
The legal position of patients or users is likely to be further strengthened. Patients' organizations at national and regional level will play a greater role than at present in consultations with insurers and providers. The right of consent, the right of access to medical records and rules for the protection of privacy will gain in importance. Institutions will have to introduce complaints procedures. Patients will increasingly seek to enforce their rights through the law, promoting the growth of defensive medicine.

Privacy-related obstacles to communications between the providers of services and the managers of institutions (e.g. in modern telecommunications and health care information systems) may cause problems not only in the more strongly organized scenarios but also elsewhere, to the extent that they affect the position of case managers.

Integration of home help and community nursing
Initiated partly by the incorporation of home help into the range of services covered by the Exceptional Medical Expenses Act and now proceeding through mergers and concentration, the process may lead to regional home care undertakings or the formation of chains. This will reduce overhead costs. The system of charges and criteria of eligibility are being harmonized and integrated. Greater flexibility results from improved access and availability and transfers of tasks both within and between the two services (involving both specialization and task differentiation). This development fits in well with the extramural network variant involving cooperation in large units. Home care organizations as in the extramural centre scenario can provide a sound foundation for the organization of complex home care.

Health centres
Health centres will need to find their place in the new and more open structure of health care. Existing grants to health centres are to be withdrawn, starting in the near future; this does not favour the extramural centre scenario, in which existing health centres are among the cores for the new form of organization. The position of general social work may also be jeopardized (see above).

Summing up, it is clear that the policies considered are by no means all conducive to the realization of the scenarios, with the possible exception of the deconstruction scenario. Deregulation plans sit uneasily with the organizational requirements of complex home care, for example, while the Care Insurance Act does not make it more likely that a comprehensive care package would be offered in the weakly structured scenarios. Imminent quality legislation sits more easily with the more strongly structured forms of organization; practitioner autonomy would be a greater obstacle to quality assessment in the more weakly structured variants.

Finally, friction can be envisaged between patients' interests and privacy and the growing information and communication needs of extramural health care.

8.4.3. Feasibility

Having considered the scenarios' ability to meet future care needs we now address the question of feasibility. The first point to be made is that the various scenarios imply clear organizational changes in health care and that these changes depend on structural reform. It should be stressed that there would be no value in indicating without qualification how each scenario and variant could be implemented: just as individual care needs to be tailored to the patient's needs, so too can the care system be expected to adapt to needs and circumstances, which may vary with the nature of the care to be delivered, the characteristics of a region and existing local care facilities. This is one of the reasons why we emphasized earlier on that the scenario outlines should not be taken as prescriptions for the organization of a future care system.

In considering feasibility we must recognize at the outset that change is more likely to succeed if it is limited to what is essential. In concrete terms this means that not much needs to change in relation to non-complex care; the problems are mainly in the area of complex care. More generally the watchword should be: no new structures where they are not needed. In practice this amounts to advocating a certain division between complex and non-complex care, perhaps with lightly structured collaborative arrangements for non-complex care and more heavily structured cooperation, in whatever form, for complex cases. The benefits of large and small scale can also be combined, in that many services can be encompassed by the same organizational framework but delivery as far as possible decentralized.

A further distinction is worth making within the field of complex care, namely between acute care e.g. for post-operative patients and chronic care as provided for arthritis sufferers. In acute home care the patient returns home following early discharge from hospital and needs intensive care over a limited period; this is an extension of the care received in hospital and thus tends to be physical and specifically medical in nature, and its limited duration makes mobilizing informal care easier. In chronic cases the accent tends to be on personal care and activation and the time period is much longer. Patients' needs vary accordingly. The need within a scenario for specifically medical complex home care differs as between acute and chronic patients: where the emphasis is on acute care a transmural scenario is more appropriate, while in the case of chronic patients extramural arrangements, perhaps in combination with nursing homes, fit the bill.

In the light of the "organize only as required" principle a third distinction needs to be made, namely between regions. In rural areas with limited and transparent provision there is no need for strong structures; certainly if there is no hospital in an area, complex care can be delivered satisfactorily through a home team working within an extramural network. In urban areas with a wide range of sometimes ill matched services variants on the extramural centre or transmural network are probably more appropriate, with monodisciplinary or multidisciplinary provider groups operating within them. The weight of the superstructure will depend on the nature of the substructure: where there are health centres covering defined geographical areas little additional organization is required for the creation of an extramural centre, but where a centre grows up around one or more GP groups consideration could be given to drawing in other services to achieve the necessary coordination. Transmural networks make most sense in areas where a hospital has a homogeneous and reasonably small catchment area which matches, or can easily be made to match, the areas covered by extramural care agencies. Expanding primary provision with "primary beds" makes most sense where there is no nearby hospital and transmural arrangements are therefore impossible but cooperation among providers is such that the new facility can be used effectively.

Our preliminary conclusion is that the most feasible structure is the one that best fits the nature of the care required and the needs (e.g. for cooperation) of local institutions and practitioners. No one scenario can therefore be given absolute preference. In chapter 6, with the requirements of plural provision in mind, we defined care needs in terms of functions; this reflected the planned reform of social insurance.

In deciding a strategy for change we must not only look at the organizational level of health care: the main factor determining the success or otherwise of reform is the cooperation of the care providers themselves. An initial lesson from the care-innovation projects is that change is effective only if it is understood and supported by those who have to deliver the service. The imposition of coordinators or coordinating centres and the introduction of care protocols ignores the social psychology of organizations: unless ignorance, lack of confidence, conflicts of interest and ingrained habits are tackled discontinuity and defective coordination will persist. The new organization's sense and value must be recognized and it must meet the needs that are felt at the sharp end, and the chances of achieving this are greater if organization is kept to the minimum needed for the delivery of decent care.

In the case of independent practitioners financial factors are also at work: where change threatens their income cooperation is unlikely to be forthcoming. Remuneration systems should serve purposes bound up with the content of care rather than, as often happens at present, frustrating them. Where financial incentives are given they should create frameworks rather than lay down requirements.

The feasibility of complex home care also depends on factors outside health care. We are concerned at the shortage of nursing and care staff; even setting aside issues of image and remuneration it is evident that the pool on which care services can draw is shrinking. Lower birth rates mean fewer youngsters and hence fewer potential nurses and carers to tend the elderly and infirm. Improving the image of these groups will cost money (promised but not yet provided in the case of community nurses and home helps). Staff shortages can also be tackled through measures in such areas as holiday arrangements and child care, though here too additional resources are a precondition for getting complex home care off the ground.

This leads on to the next problem, the declining availability of informal care, notably within the family, as a result of demographic, social and cultural change. Complex home care depends crucially on informal care; six hours of professional care represents the maximum per 24-hour period, leaving the remaining 18 hours to be covered by self-care and informal care, so that unless current trends are reversed complex home care is very much at risk. The only ray of light in this gloomy picture is the growing number of fit elderly people in the younger age groups. We cannot take it for granted that they will come forward as informal carers, however; informal care will also need to be made more attractive.

Last but not least the scope for complex home care is determined by the patients themselves and those around them, who must have confidence in it and be motivated to make the effort needed. This will involve their weighing the expected quality of care against the quality of life that it makes possible: if home care is seen as second-best it is not a genuine option.

8.5. Conclusion

As we have seen, the scenarios can be considered and assessed from numerous viewpoints and on numerous criteria; readers can form their own picture and reach their own conclusion. The users of care, patients or clients, will tend to emphasize freedom of choice and autonomy, perhaps opting for the scenario or variant - such as the extramural network - most likely to provide them. If complex home care is not covered by basic care insurance a two-tier system may evolve, with only the better-off taking out the necessary supplementary cover.

Depending on their current position in the system the providers of care may tend to prefer the scenario which most strengthens it. In this case of GPs this could be a variant which fits in with the development, already initiated, of GP groups, while community nurses and home helps may prefer an extramural centre based around a strong home care organization; for specialists the transmural network fits in best with the present position. In the hospitals sector other scenarios are also circulating, of which the "network scenario for hospitals" fits in with our extramural network for primary and home care; there is also a deconstruction scenario which closely parallels ours.

Such preferences are not absolute. The choice of a particular organizational type may also be prompted by local circumstances and existing preferences for a given form of cooperation. Where primary care is dominated by strong GP groups delivery will be organized differently than where community nursing and home help form the strongest organization or where a hospital is dominant.

Insurers, like users and providers, may prefer particular ways of organizing care; the impact of their preferences will depend on their position. If insurers concentrate on regional markets, then in the absence of local competition their influence may be considerable; the result may be marked regional variations in the nature and quality of home care provision.

From the viewpoint of the government some scenarios are more in keeping with recent policy developments than others. Deregulation sits uneasily with scenarios involving a strong organization, for example, as does the blurring of tier boundaries with both extramural scenarios.

In this situation, where political and normative ideas and local circumstances play such a large part in the assessment of alternative futures, it is both unwise and impossible to come down in favour of one or other at the end of this report. To do so would tend to focus debate on the reasons for our choice rather than on the real issue, namely the various scenarios' respective merits. The question for us to address as a society concerns the direction we wish to take in primary and home care; the debate needs to be an informed one and the material brought together in this report will hopefully be a useful contribution to it.

Bibliography

Adriaansen, H.P.M.
De participatiestaat. Een nieuw verband van arbeid en welzijn (The participation state. A new framework of work and welfare).
The Hague, VUGA, 1990.

Andersen, R. and J.F. Newman
Societal and individual determinants of medical care utilization in the United States.
Milbank Memorial Fund Quarterly, 51, 1973, 95-124.

Aquina, H.J.
Politiek-bestuurlijke en maatschappelijke veranderingen in de Nederlandse samenleving (Politico-administrative and social changes in the Netherlands). In: Dekker, E. and E. Elsinga (eds.), *Mensen en machten (People and powers).*
Houten, Bohn Stafleu Van Loghum, 1990.

Austin, C.D.
Case management in long-term care: options and opportunities.
Health Care and Social Work, 8, 1983, 1, 16-31.

Bachrach, L.L.
Continuity of Care for Chronic Mental Patients: A Conceptual Analysis.
American Journal of Psychiatry, 138, 1981, 1449-1456.

Bachrach, L.L.
Case Management: Toward a Shared Definition.
Hospital and Community Psychiatry, 40, 1989, 9, 883-884.

Bäckman, G.
Health policy in Finland.
International Journal of Technology Assessment in Health Care, 4, 1988, 375-384.

Bakker, D.H. de
*Afstemming van werkgebieden in Rotterdam: een analyse met
ziekenfondsgegevens (Harmonization of catchment areas in Rotterdam: an
analysis using health insurance fund data).*
Utrecht, NIVEL, 1987.

Bakker, D.H. de
The district concept for primary health care planning: attempts at
implementation in the Netherlands.
Health Policy, 1989, 13, 1, 15-64.

BASYS GmbH
*Gesuntheitssysteme im internationalem Vergleich; Forschungsbericht
(International comparison of health systems; research report).*
Augsburg, BASYS, 1989.

Beer, J. de
Jaren tachtig: ombuiging of voortzetting van demografische trends? (1980s:
reversal or continuation of demographic trends?).
Maandstatistiek Bevolking (CBS), 1989, no. 12, 16-35.

Bensing, J.M.
*Wie wil in Nederland primary health care? (Who wants primary health care
in the Netherlands?)*
Utrecht, NHI, 1983.

Bensing, J.M., M. Foets, J. van der Velden and J. van der Zee
De Nationale Studie van ziekten en verrichtingen in de huisartspraktijk:
achtergronden en methoden (Dutch National Survey of General Practice:
backgrounds and methods).
Huisarts en Wetenschap, 34, 1991, 2, 51-61.

BIZ
Statement on the Budget for Interdepartmental Welfare Policy 1986.
Lower House of Parliament, 1985-86 session.

Boerma, W.G.W.
Local housing scheme and political preference as conditions for the results
of a health centres-stimulating policy in the Netherlands.
Health Policy, 13, 1989, 225-237.

Boerma, W.G.W. and A. de Veer
*Afstemming van doelpopulaties en samenwerking: een studie bij
wijkverpleegkundige teams in de stad (Harmonization of target populations
and cooperation: a study of urban community-nursing teams.*
Utrecht, NIVEL, 1991 (in preparation).

228

Bos, G.A.M. van den, J. Mohrs, J.D.F. Habbema, P.J. van der Maas,
J.G.C. Verhey, J.F. Wendte and S.J. Huisman
*Chronische aandoeningen, hulpbehoevendheid en zorggebruik (Chronic
conditions, dependence and utilization of care).*
Amsterdam, Intitute of Social Medicine, 1986.

Bos, G.A.M. van den
*Zorgen van en voor chronische zieken (The chronic sick, their concerns and
their care).*
Utrecht, Bohn, Scheltema and Holkema, 1989.

Brekel, E.J.G. van den
Fysiotherapie in Nederland 1974-1983 (Physiotherapy in the Netherlands,
1974-1983).
Maandbericht Gezondheid (CBS), 1985, no. 2, 5-16.

Brouns, G. and T. Dassen
Case management. Een taak voor psychiatrisch verpleegkundigen? (Case
management. A job for psychiatric nurses?).
Tijdschrift voor Ziekenverpleging, December 1988, 815-818.

CBS (Central Bureau of Statistics)
*De leefsituatie van de Nederlandse bevolking van 55 jaar en ouder, 1982 (The
life situation of Dutch people aged 55 and over, 1982).*
The Hague, Staatsuitgerij, 1984.

CBS (Central Bureau of Statistics)
Cliëntenonderzoek gezinsverzorging, 1980 (Study of home-help clients, 1980).
The Hague, Staatsuitgeverij/CBS Publications, 1985.

CBS (Central Bureau of Statistics)
Uitkomsten bevolkingsprognose, 1987 (Population forecast results, 1987).
Maandstatistiek van de bevolking, 36, 1, 1988.

CBS (Central Bureau of Statistics)
Gezondheidsenquêtes. Algemeen maatschappelijk werk 1981-1987 (Health
surveys. General social work 1981-1987).
Maandbericht gezondheid, 1988, no. 5.

CBS (Central Bureau of Statistics)
Algemeen maatschappelijk werk tijdreeksen 1983-1988 (General social
work time series 1983-1988).
Sociaal-culturele berichten, 1989, no. 18.

CBS (Central Bureau of Statistics)
Zakboek onderwijsstatistieken 1989 (Handbook of educational statistics 1989).
The Hague, SDU, 1989.

CBS (Central Bureau of Statistics)
Uitkomsten Bevolkingsprognose 1990 (Results Population Forecast 1990).
Maandstatistiek Bevolking (CBS), 1990, No. 12.

CBS (Central Bureau of Statistics)
Maatschappelijk welzijn kerncijfers 1990 (Social welfare - key figures, 1990).
Sociaal-culturele berichten, 1990, no. 14.

CBS (Central Bureau of Statistics)
Statistical Yearbook 1992.
The Hague, SDU Uitgeverij, CBS Publications 1992.

CRG (Central Home Help Council)
Handleiding LIER-systeem (Guide to the LIER national indication and registration system).
Driebergen, Centrale Raad voor de Gezinsverzorging, 1986.

Crebolder, H.F.J.M
Gebruik en gebruikers van fysiotherapeutische behandelingen (Use and users of physiotherapeutic treatments).
Huisarts en Wetenschap, 26, 1983, 42-48.

Crombie, D.L., J. van der Zee and P. Backer
The Interface Study.
London, RCGP, 1990.

Dahrendorf, R.
Meer spelen in een spel met minder nieten (More play in a game with fewer nots).
Report of the Sixth Van der Leeuw Lecture, 4 November 1988, Groningen.
Volkskrant, 5 November 1988.

Dam, F. van and L. Hingstman
Cijfers uit de registratie van beroepen in de eerstelijnsgezondheidszorg 1988 (Data from professional registers in primary health care 1988).
Utrecht, NIVEL, 1988.

Dekker Committee (Committee on the Structure and Funding of Health Care)
Nota Bereidheid tot verandering (Readiness to change).
The Hague, 1987.

Department of Health
Working for patients.
London, HMSO, 1989.

Duijn, J.
Thuiszorg: een inventarisatie (Home care: an inventory).
Rijswijk, Uitgeverij voor Gezondheidsbevordering, 1989.

Dunning, A.J.
Technologie en medicalisering in de gezondheidszorg. Van voor de wieg tot over het graf (Technology and medicalization in health care, pre-cradle to post-grave). In: Dekker, E. and E. Elsinga (eds.), *Mensen en machten (People and powers).*
Houten, Bohn Stafleu Van Loghum, 1990.

FOZ (Financial Overview of Care)
Lower House of Parliament, 21 812, nos. 1-2.
Rijswijk, SDU Publishing, 1990.

Flierman, H.A. and P.P. Groenewegen
Het Deense voorbeeld; een gemengd systeem van honorering per verrichting en abonnement (The Danish example; a mixed system of fee-for-service and capitation payments).
Huisarts en Wetenschap, 32, 1989, 6, 212-218.

Foets, M. and J. van der Velden
Nationale Studie van ziekten en verrichtingen in de huisartspraktijk. Basisrapport: Meetinstrumenten en procedures (Dutch National Survey of General Practice. Base report: measuring instruments and procedures).
Utrecht, NIVEL, 1991.

Foets, M. and H. Sixma
Nationale Studie van ziekten en verrichtingen in de huisartspraktijk. Basisrapport: Gezondheid en gezondheidsgedrag in de praktijkpopulatie (Dutch National Survey of General Practice. Base report: Health and health behaviour in the practice population).
Utrecht, NIVEL, 1991.

Fortuyn, W.S.P.
Ordening door ontvlechting: een advies over de adviesstructuur in de volkgezondheid (Order through deconstruction: an advisory report on the advisory structure for health).
Rijswijk, Ministry of Welfare, Health and Cultural Affairs, 1990.

Friele, R.D. and P.F.M. Verhaak
Vragen om problemen; een onderzoek onder de volwassen clienten van RIAGG en AMW (Asking for problems: a study of adult clients of Regional Institutes of Ambulatory Mental Health Care and General Social Work).
Utrecht, NIVEL, 1991 (draft).

Gerritsen, J.C., C.P. van Linschoten and W.J.A. van den Heuvel
Individuele determinanten van het gebruik van professionele zorg door ouderen (Individual determinants of the use of professional care by older people).
Groningen State University, Department of Health Sciences, 1988.

Gloerich, A.B.M. and J. van der Zee
Verwijzen door de huisarts naar de tweede lijn (GP referrals to specialists).
Utrecht, NIVEL, 1991 (in preparation).

Goldberg, D.
The detection of psychiatric illness by questionnaire.
Maudsley Monographs no. 21, London, Oxford University Press, 1972.

Goudriaan, G.
Thuiszorg tussen de lijnen (Home care between generalist and specialist).
The Hague, HRWB, 1988.

Groenewegen, P.P.
Primary health care in the Netherlands: from imperfect planning to an imperfect market?
Invited lecture given at the conference "Changing roles of government and the market in health care" held Jerusalem, December 1991.

Groenewegen, P.P., J.J. Kerssens and E.C. Curfs
Physiotherapy and the care for disabled and chronically ill people in the community.
Paper presented at the WHO consultation meeting on the care of disabled people in the community, Edinburgh, 1991.

Groenewegen, P.P., J. van der Zee and R. van Haaften
Remunerating General Practitioners in Western Europe.
Avebury, Aldershot, 1991.

Haes, W.F.M. de
Leefwijzen (Lifestyles). In: Dekker, E. and E. Elsinga (eds.), *Mensen en machten (People and powers).*
Houten, Bohn Stafleu Van Loghum, 1990.

Hattinga Verschure, J.C.M.
Het verschijnsel zorg (The phenomenon of care).
Lochem, De Tijdstroom, 1982.

Heerdink, H. and M. Knapen
Kan het een beetje meer zijn? Een oriënterende studie naar het zorgvermogen in de samenleving (More, please! An initial study of society's capacity for care).
Nijmegen, ITS, 1986.

Hendriks, J.P.M.
Twintig jaar hervorming van de gezondheidszorg (Twenty years of health-care reform).
Economisch Statistische Berichten, 1990, 637-644.

Henselmans, H.
Case management in de sociale psychiatrie (Case management in social psychiatrie).
Maandblad Geestelijke Volksgezondheid, 45, 1990, 5, 494-506.

Hessels, E.M.A.
Gezondheidscentra en groepspraktijken per 1 januari 1990 (Health centres and group practices as at 1 January 1990).
Utrecht, NIVEL, 1990.

Hessels, E.M.A.
Innovatie in de zorgsector (Innovation in the care sector).
The Hague, VUGA, 1991.

Hesterman, J.
Thuiszorg-experiment: helft van de subsidie komt bij de client terecht (Home-care experiment: half of the grant reaches the client).
Welzijnsweekblad, 18 November 1988, 9-11.

Heydelberg, E.
Thuiszorg in functies, een onderzoek naar motieven en practische mogelijkheden (Home care in functions, an investigation into themes and practical options).
The Hague, HRWB, 1988.

Heydelberg, E. and B. van den Meydenberg
De wijkverpleegkundige handhaaft zich in de thuiszorg (The community nurse's continuing role in home care).
Tijdschrift voor Gezondheid en Politiek, 1988, 97-101.

Huisman, H. and E. Schadé
Voorlichting over huidkanker (Information and education on skin cancer).
Huisarts en Wetenschap, 30, 1987, 4, 114-115.

Huijsmans, F. et al. (eds.)
Gezondheidszorg in Nederland (Health care in the Netherlands).
Nijmegen, Socialistische Uitgeverij Nijmegen (SUN), 1973.

Imhoff, E. van, N. Keilman and S. Wolf
Huishoudens en uitkeringen in de 21e eeuw (Households and social benefits in the twenty-first century).
The Hague, NIDI, 1990.

Intagliata, J.
Improving the Quality of Community Care for the Chronically Mentally Disabled: the role of case management.
Schizophrenia Bulletin, 1982, 8, 4, 655-675.

Joint
Joint/general social work record system
's-Hertogenbosch, Joint, 1988.

Kam, C.A. de
Op weg naar een open einde (Towards an open end).
Economisch Statistische Berichten, 75, 1990, 3765, 640-644.

Kerssens, J.J., P.P. Groenewegen and E.C. Curfs
Fysiotherapie in de Nederlandse gezondheidszorg: de hulpverleners huisarts en physiotherapeut (Physiotherapy in Dutch health care: the providers, GP and physiotherapist).
Utrecht, NIVEL, 1986.

Kerssens, J.J., E.C. Curfs and P.P. Groenewegen
Fysiotherapie in de Nederlandse gezondheidszorg: klachten van patiënten, indicatiestelling van (huis)artsen en fysiotherapeutische behandeling (Physiotherapy in Dutch health care: patients' problems, GPs' decisions on indicated treatments and physiotherapeutic treatment).
Utrecht, NIVEL, 1986.

Kersten D. and Hackenitz, E.
How to bridge the gap between hospital and home.
Journal of Advanced Nursing, 16, 1991, 1, 4-14.

KISG Jaarboek 1985 (KISG Yearbook 1985).
Stichting KLOZ Informatiesysteem Gezondheidszorg, Houten, 1985.

KLOZ
Thuiszorg, een zorg meer of minder (Home care, a care more or less).
Houten, KLOZ, 1989.

Knapen, M.
Coordinatie in de thuiszorg: Kanttekeningen bij onderzoeksresultaten
(Coordination in home care: reservations regarding research results).
In: *Congresbundel van de studieconferentie 'Coördinatie in de thuiszorg'*
(Papers from the study conference on coordination in home care).
Rotterdam, Nederlands Studie Centrum, 1988.

Konings, M.J.M.
Maatschappelijk Welzijn; kerncijfers 1990 (Social Welfare: key figures,
1990).
Sociaal-culturele berichten, 1990, 14.

Koot, T. and N. Stegerhoek
Zorgzame samenleving tussen recht en ruil (Caring society between right and
barter).
The Hague, HRWB, 1986.

Koster-Dreese, Y.
Met de blik op oneindig (With eyes on eternity). In: Dekker, E. and
E. Elsinga (eds.), *Mensen en machten (People and powers).*
Houten, Bohn Stafleu Van Loghum, 1990.

Kwekkeboom, M.H.
Het licht onder de korenmaat: informele zorgverlening in Nederland (The
light under the bushel: informal care in the Netherlands).
The Hague, VUGA, 1990.

Laeyendecker, L.
Gezondheidsstreven: spiegel der cultuur (The drive for health: a mirror of
the culture). In: Dekker, E. and E. Elsinga (eds.), *Mensen en machten*
(People and powers).
Houten, Bohn Stafleu Van Loghum, 1990.

Lamb, H.R.
Therapist-Case managers: More Than Brokers Of Services.
Hospital and Community Psychiatry, 31, 1980, 11, 762-764.

Langeveld, H.M.
Binding in vrijheid (Commitment in freedom).
The Hague, SCP, Staatsuitgeverij, 1985.

LBO (National Forum for Administrative Consultation)
Het huidige hulpaanbod van de vier kernvoorzieningen binnen de thuiszorg (The current range of services of the four key providers in home care).
LBO, 1987.

Lerman, P.
Deinstitutionalization and Welfare politics. In: Hasenfeld, Y. and M.N. Zald (eds.), *Annals of the American Academy of Political and Social Science*, May 1985.

LHV (National Association of General Practitioners)
De huisarts en de thuiszorg; een handreiking (The GP and home care; a helping hand).
Utrecht, LHV, 1988.

LHV (National Association of General Practitioners)
Thuiszorg uw zorg (Home care, your concern).
Utrecht, LHV, 1990.

Lieshout, P. van, and E. Heydelberg
Casemanagement, De ervaringen van het Kent Community Care Project. Brochure bij de Conferentie 'Zorgvernieuwing in de thuiszorg' (Case management, the experience of the Kent Community Care Project. Booklet for the conference 'Care renewal in home care').
Rijswijk, Ministry of Welfare, Health and Cultural Affairs, 1990.

Lieshout, P. van, and E. Heydelberg
Case Management, lessen uit het Kent Community Care Project (Case management, lessons from the Kent Community Care Project).
Medisch Contact, 46, 1991, 4, 118-122.

Linden, B.A. van der, and A.J.P. Schrijvers
Zorg binnen de perken; leerpunten uit de Amerikaanse SHMO's (Care within bounds; lessons from the American SHMOs).
Medisch Contact, 46, 1991, 9, 269-271.

Linstone, H.A. and M. Turoff (eds.)
The Delphi Method.
Reading, Ma, Addison-Wesley Publishing Company, 1975.

Londen, J. van
Thuiszorg; huiswerk voor allen vóór het jaar 2000 (Home care; homework for everyone before the year 2000).
Inaugural lecture, Utrecht State University, 198787.

LSV (National Association of Specialists)
De specialist van morgen (The specialist of tomorrow).
Medisch Contact, 43, 1988, 11, 327-328.

Maas, P.J. van der
Lang zullen we leven? Over volksgezondheid, vergrijzing en vervuiling (Long live who? Health, aging and pollution).
Rotterdam, Erasmus University, 1989.

Maessen, P.J.J.
Bezuinigingen in de gezinsverzorging: besluitvorming in de verzorgingsstaat (Retrenching on home help: decision-making in the welfare state).
Leiden, Leiden State University, 1989.

McWhinney, I.R.
Disability indicator for measuring wellbeing. The OECD social indicators development programme.
Paris, OECD, Special Studies 5, 1979.

Michels, J.J.M.
Eerstelijn: thuis - tweedelijn: opgenomen (Primary - at home, secondary - in hospital).
Het Ziekenhuis, 1987, 6, 226-227.

Ministry of Education and Science
Werkverband Periodiek Rapportage Bevolkingsvraagstukken, Aspecten van het bevolkingsvraagstuk anno 1987 (Periodic reports on population questions, Aspects of the population question in 1987).
The Hague, Staatsuitgeverij, 1974.

Ministry of Health and Environmental Protection
Structuurnota gezondheidszorg (The structure of health care).
The Hague, Staatsuitgeverij, 1974.

Ministry of Social Affairs and Health
Volksgezondheidsnota (Public Health).
The Hague, Staatsuitgeverij, 1966.

Ministry of Welfare, Health and Cultural Affairs
Nota Volksgezondheid bij beperkte middelen (Health services in circumstances of limited resources).
Rijswijk, Ministry of Welfare, Health and Cultural Affairs, 1983.

Ministry of Welfare, Health and Cultural Affairs
Nota 2000.
The Hague, Staatsuitgeverij, 1986.

Ministry of Welfare, Health and Cultural Affairs
Ontwerp kerndocument gezondheidsbeleid (Draft key document on health policy).
Rijswijk, 1989.

Ministry of Welfare, Health and Cultural Affairs
Basisdocument bij het Ontwerp kerndocument gezondheidsbeleid (Base document for the Draft key document on health policy).
Rijswijk, 1989.

Ministry of Welfare, Health and Cultural Affairs
Werken aan zorgvernieuwing (Working on care renewal).
The Hague, Staatsuitgeverij, 1990.

Mootz, M.
De patiënt en zijn naasten (Patients and their nearest).
The Hague, Pasman b.v., 1981.

Mur-Veeman, I. and I. Thijssen
Thuiszorg in beweging: een veranderingsproces in organisatiekundig perspectief (Home care in flux: a process of change in an organizational perspective).
Mens en Onderneming, 1990, 3, 263-273.

NRV (National Public Health Council)
Nota's zorgverlening en structuur van de eerste lijn (Primary care and structures).
Zoetermeer, NRV, 1987.

NRV (National Public Health Council)
Discussienota Substitutie in de gezondheidszorg (Discussion paper on substitution in health care).
Zoetermeer, NRV, 1989a.

NRV (National Public Health Council)
Advies functies GGZ, deel 2: de organisatie (Functions in mental health care, part 2: organization).
Zoetermeer, NRV, 1989b.

NRV (National Public Health Council)
Discussienota Thuiszorg (Discussion paper on home care).
Zoetermeer, NRV, 1989c.

NRV (National Public Health Council)
Advies kwaliteit, organisatie en financiering thuiszorg (Quality, organization and funding of home care).
Zoetermeer, NRV, 1990.

NRV (National Public Health Council)
Advies inzake de opstelling van het financieel overzicht zorg 1992 (Compilation of the Financial Overview of Care 1992).
Zoetermeer, NRV, 1991.

NK (National Community Nursing Association)
Dienst informatieverzorging. Wijkadministratiesysteem, verpleegkundig methodisch handelen (Information service. District clerical system, methodical nursing action).
Bunnik, NK, 1980.

NK (National Community Nursing Association)
Kruiswerk: voor zorg en voorzorg. Meerjarenraming kruiswerk tot 1996. Verantwoording vanaf 1984 (Community nursing: care and safeguard. Ramification community nursing till 1996. Accounted from 1984).
Bunnik, NK, 1990.

NZR (National Hospitals Council)
Het ziekenhuis aan bod. Beleidsnota Sectie Ziekenhuizen (The hospital's turn. Hospitals Section Policy Paper).
Utrecht, NZR, 1989.

OECD
Health care systems in transition; the search for efficiency.
Paris, OECD, 1990.

Oetomo, B.
Van asyl tot revalidatiecentrum (From asylum to rehabilitation centre).
Groningen, Wolters-Noordhof, 1970.

Philipsen, H.
Strategische functie van het begrip. Beweging in de relatie tussen vraag en aanbod in de thuiszorg. Thuiszorg: emancipatie of nieuwe markt? (The strategic function of the concept. Changes in the relation between demand and supply in home care. Home care: emancipation or a new market?).
Bunnik, ATIS, 1988.

Philipsen, H.
Coördinatie in de thuiszorg, ieders plicht, niemands voorrecht, voor sommigen een taak (Coordination in home care, everyone's duty, no-one's privilege, a job for some). In: *Verslag van het symposium 'Integraal Regionaal' (Report on the 'Comprehensive, Regional' symposium).*
Sittard, Het Limburgse Groene Kruis Provincial Community Nursing Association, 1989a.

Philipsen, H.
Vragen en problemen bij de toepassing van casemanagement in de zorgsector (Questions and problems in the use of case management in the care sector). In: *Verslag van het conferentie 'Case management (Report on Case Management conference).*
The Hague, EvC organisatiebureau/Stichting TMW, 1989b.

Pineau, C.
Adapted from: Roussel, L., L'avenir de la famille (CNR, Unesco seminar, Rome, 1988).
Demos, 6, 1, 1990.

Policy Paper 'Ouderen in Tel'
Policy and position relating to the elderly, 1990-1994. Sub-report 5: data on the elderly.
The Hague, Staatsuitgeverij, 1990.

Pool J.B.
Home teams 1990.
Utrecht, NIVEL, 1992.

Pool J.B. and Hingstman L.
Statistische gegevens per 1 januari over huisartsen en verloskundigen (Statistical information as at 1 January on family doctors and obstetricians).
Utrecht, NIVEL, 1992.

Postma, T.J.B.M. and G.R. Eyzinga
Een perspectief voor toekomstonderzoek in Nederland (An outlook for futures research in the Netherlands).
Maandblad voor accountancy en bedrijfshuishoudkunde, 1978, 108-115.

Prince, A.J.
Nieuwe gezondheidszorg in de V.S.: kostenbeheersing en kwaliteitsebewaking via 'managed care' (New health care in the US: cost and quality control through managed care).
Medisch Contact, 42, 1987, 8, 239-242.

Querido, A.
Godshuizen en gasthuizen; een geschiedenis van de ziekenverpleging in West-Europa (Hospices and almshouses; a history of nursing in Western Europe).
Lochum, De Tijdstroom, 1974.

Riteco, J. and L. Hingstman
Evaluatie invoering verloskundige indicatielijst (Evaluation of the introduction of the list of indications for obstetric care).
Utrecht, NIVEL, 1991 (in preparation).

RCGP (Royal College of General Practitioners)
Community Hospitals - preparing for the future.
London, RCGP, 1990.

Runia, E. and R. van Herk
De verwezenlijking van de beroepsopleiding tot huisarts (Implementing GP training).
Huisarts en Wetenschap, 34, 1991, 3, 117-23.

Sachverständigenrat fur die Konzertierte Aktion im Gesuntheitswesen
Qualität, Wirtschaftlichkeit und Perspektiven der Gesuntheitsversorgung (Health care: quality, economy and prospects).
Jahresgutachten, 1989.

Schadé, E.
De huisarts een zorg (A job for the doctor).
Utrecht/Antwerp, Bohn, Scheltema and Holkema, 1989.

Schadé, E.
Van ziekenhuiszorg naar thuiszorg (From hospital care to home care).
Acta Hospitalia, 1990, 1, 19-31.

Schnaars, S.P.
How to develop and use scenarios.
Long Range Planning, 20, 1987, 1, 105-114.

Schnabel, P.
De zin van de zorg voor ziel en zaligheid. De geestelijke gezondheidszorg in verandering (The sense of caring for mind and happiness. Mental health care in flux).
Gezondheid en Samenleving, 6, 1985, 3, 152-160.

Schrijvers, A.J.P.
Van alle markten thuis: thuiszorg beproefd (A bit of everything: home care tested).
Lecture, Utrecht State University, 1987.

Schrijvers, A.J.P.
Zorgen in de toekomst (Caring in the future). In: Schrijvers, A.J.P. and I. Mur-Veeman (eds.), *Beleid en beheer in de gezondheidszorg (Policy and management in health care)*.
Assen/Maastricht, Van Gorcum, 1990a.

Schrijvers, A.J.P.
Zorg en Schaarste (Care and scarcity).
Economisch Statistische Berichten, 75, 1990b, 3765, 645-648.

Schrijvers, A.J.P.
The Netherlands introduces some competition into the health services.
JAMA, 1991, 266, 16, 2215-2217.

Schrijvers, A.J.P. and J. van Londen
Ontwikkelingen in de thuiszorg. 1. Begripsomschrijvingen (Developments in home care. 1. Defining terms).
Medisch Contact, 45, 1990a, 22, 707-713.

Schrijvers, A.J.P. and J. van Londen
2. Vraag en aanbod (Supply and demand).
Medisch Contact, 45, 1990b, 23, 745-747.

Schrijvers, A.J.P. and J. van Londen
3. Slot: de toekomst (Conclusion: the future).
Medisch Contact, 45, 1990c, 24, 768-772.

Schut, F.T.
Health Maintenance Organizations: een geïntegreerde wijze van verstrekken en verzekeren van gezondheidszorg (HMOs: integrating delivery and insurance).
Lochem/Gent, De Tijdstroom, 1986.

Seidl, F.W. and R. Applebaum
Delivering in-home services to the aged and disabled: the Wisconsin experiment.
Lexington (Mass), Lexington Books, 1983.

Sluijs, E.M.
Huisarts (The family doctor). In: Sluijs, E.M., J.P. Dopheide and J. van der Zee (eds.), *Overzichtstudie onderzoek eerstelijn (Review of research on primary care)*.
Utrecht, NIVEL, 1985.

Smet, R. de
Gezondheidszorg in België (Health care in Belgium).
Medisch Contact, 35, 1983, 1089-1092.

SCP (Social and Cultural Planning Office)
Social and Cultural Report, 1988.
Rijswijk, SCP, 1988.

SCP (Social and Cultural Planning Office)
Social and Cultural Report, 1990.
Rijswijk, SCP, 1990.

Spreeuwenberg, C.
Thuiszorg (Home care). In: *Congresbundel van de studieconferentie
'Coordinatie in de thuiszorg' (Papers from the study conference on
coordination in home care).*
Rotterdam, Nederlands Studie Centrum, 1988a.

Spreeuwenberg, C.
Knelpunten in de thuiszorg (Problems in home care).
Medisch Contact, 43, 1988b, 19, 579.

Stevens, P.G.J.J.
Over veranderingen in opvattingen en structuren (Changing views and
structures). In: Schrijvers, A.J.P. et al. (eds.), *Handboek thuiszorg
(Home-care handbook).*
The Hague, VUGA, 1990.

Stikker, A.J.
Case management.
The Hague, NIMAWO, 1989.

STG (Steering Committee on Future Health Scenarios)
*Ouder worden in de toekomst. Scenario's over gezondheid en vergrijzing
1984-2000 (Growing old in the future. Scenarios on health and aging
1984-2000).*
Utrecht, Jan Van Arkel, 1985.

STG (Steering Committee on Future Health Scenarios)
*Het hart van de toekomst/De toekomst van het hart (The heart of the
future/The future of the heart).*
Rijswijk, STG, 1986.

STG (Steering Committee on Future Health Scenarios)
Anticipating and assessing health care technology, volume 1.
Dordrecht/Boston/Lancaster, Martinus Nijhoff Publishers, 1987a.

STG (Steering Committee on Future Health Scenarios)
Kanker in Nederland. Deel 1: Scenariorapport (Cancer in the Netherlands.
Part 1: Scenario report).
Utrecht/Antwerp, Bohn, Scheltema and Holkema, 1987b.

STG (Steering Committee on Future Health Scenarios)
Toekomstverkenning en beoordeling van medische technologie (Anticipating
and assessing health care technology).
Utrecht/Antwerpen, Bohn, Scheltema and Holkema, 1988.

STG (Steering Committee on Future Health Scenarios)
Scenario's in de volksgezondheid: inleiding in de methodiek van de STG
(Health scenarios: an introduction to STG methodology).
Rijswijk, STG, 1989.

STG (Steering Committee on Future Health Scenarios)
Het ziekenhuis in de 21e eeuw (Hospitals in the twenty-first century).
Rijswijk, STG, 1990a.

STG (Steering Committee on Future Health Scenarios)
Leefomstandigheden, Leefwijzen en Gezondheid. Een aanzet voor scenario's
(Life circumstances, lifestyles and health. Starting points for scenarios).
Rijswijk, STG, 1990b.

STG (Steering Committee on Future Health Scenarios)
Zorgen voor geestelijke gezondheid in de toekomst (Caring for mental health
in the future).
Utrecht/Antwerpen, Bohn, Scheltema and Holkema, 1990c.

STG (Steering Committee on Future Health Scenarios)
Chronische ziekten in het jaar 2005, deel 1, scenario's over diabetes mellitus
(Chronic diseases in the year 2005, part 1, scenarios on diabetes mellitus).
Utrecht/Antwerpen, Bohn, Scheltema and Holkema, 1990d.

STG (Steering Committee on Future Health Scenarios)
Chronische ziekten in het jaar 2005, deel 2, scenario's over CARA (Chronic
diseases in the year 2005, part 2, scenarios on CNSLD).
Utrecht/Antwerpen, Bohn, Scheltema and Holkema, 1990e.

Swaan, A. de
De mens is de mens een zorg (People, care, concern).
Amsterdam, Meulenhof, 1982.

Swaan, A. de
Zorg en staat; welzijn, onderwijs en gezondheidszorg in Europa en de Verenigde Staten in de nieuwe tijd (Care and the state; welfare, education and health care in Europe and the United States today).
Amsterdam, Uitgeverij Bert Bakker, 1989.

Swinkels, H.
Trendcijfers gezondheidsenquête, 1981-1989 (Health survey trend figures, 1981-1989).
Maandbericht gezondheid, 1990, no. 9, 5-25.

Tits, M. van and W. Groot
Zorgen om kruiswerk en verzorging (Concern for community nursing and personal care).
Tijdschrift voor Ziekenverpleging, 1991, 2, 56-59.

Tjadens, F.L.J. and C. Woldring
Informele zorg in Nederland (Informal care in the Netherlands).
Nijmegen, ITS, 1989.

Turksma, L.
Senioren in de samenleving: sociale problematiek van bejaarden (Senior citizens: social problems of the elderly).
Utrecht, Het Spectrum, 1982.

Vandenbroucke, J.P. and A. Hofman
Grondslagen der epidemiologie (Foundations of epidemiology).
Utrecht, Wetenschappelijke Uitgeverij Bunge, 1988.

Velde, F.J. van, and A. van der Zee
De positie van het ziekenhuis uit extern perspectief (The position of the hospital, an external perspective).
Medisch Contact, 45, 1990a, 14, 449-450.

Velde, F.J. van, and A. van der Zee
De positie van het ziekenhuis in intern perspectief (The position of the hospital, an internal perspective).
Medisch Contact, 45, 1990b, 15, 483-485.

Velde, F.J. van, and A. van der Zee
Het functioneren van het ziekenhuis (How hospitals work).
Medisch Contact, 45, 1990c, 16, 525-527.

Velden, J. van der
De rol van de huisartspraktijk in Nederland (The role of general practice in the Netherlands).
Medisch Contact, 19, 1990, 19, 605-608.

Velden, J. van der, D.H. de Bakker, A.A.M.C. Claessens and F.G. Schellevis
Nationale studie van ziekten en verrichtingen in de huisartspraktijk. Basisrapport: Morbiditeit in de huisartspraktijk (Dutch National Survey of General Practice. Base report: Morbidity in general practice).
Utrecht, NIVEL, 1991.

Ven, W.P.M.M. van de
De invloed van de financiering op het gebruik van gezondheidszorg-voorzieningen (The impact of funding systems on the use of health services).
Tijdschrift voor Sociale Gezondheidszorg, 63, 1985, 1, 20-30.

Verhey R. and Kerkstra A.
International comparative study on community nursing.
Aldershot, Avebury, 1992.

VIVAM (Association of General Social Work Institutions)
Het AMW in beeld 1989 (General social work in 1989).
Bunnik, VIVAM, 1990.

Vorst-Thijssen, T., A. van de Brink-Muinen and A. Kerkstra
Het werk van wijkverpleegkundigen en wijkziekenverzorgenden in Nederland (The work of community nurses and nursing auxiliaries in the Netherlands).
Utrecht, NIVEL, 1990.

Vries, M.W. de
Culture and case management: impediments to providing care from the point of view of the patient. In: *Report on 'Case Management' study day.*
Rotterdam, RIAGG RNO, 1988.

Vries, H. de
Planning, toekomstonderzoek en scenario's (Planning, futures research and scenarios).
Beleid en Maatschappij, 12, 1985, 4, 94-101.

Waal, S.P.M. de
Coördinatie van de thuiszorg (Coordinating home care). In: *Congresbundel van de studieconferentie 'Coördinatie in de thuiszorg' (Papers from the study conference on coordination in home care).*
Rotterdam, Nederlands Studie Centrum, 1988.

Weiner, J.P. and D.M. Ferris
GP Budget Holding in the UK: Lessons from America.
London, King's Fund Institute, 1990.

Wennink, H.J. and G. Goudriaan
De eerste lijn en thuiszorg, de verwarring (Primary care and home care, the confusion).
Medisch Contact, 45, 1990a, 37, 1081-1085.

Wennink, H.J. and G. Goudriaan
De eerste lijn en thuiszorg, de zorgvraag (Primary care and home care, the demand for care).
Medisch Contact, 45, 1990b, 38, 1119-1124.

Wennink, H.J. and G. Goudriaan
De eerste lijn en thuiszorg, slot (Primary care and home care, conclusion).
Medisch Contact, 45, 1990c, 39, 1161-1164.

Wennink, H.J. and G. Goudriaan
Substitutie (Substitution). In: Schrijvers, A.J.P. et al. (eds.), *Handboek thuiszorg (Home-care handbook).*
The Hague, VUGA, 1990.

Wennink, H.J. and G. Goudriaan
Case management in de thuiszorg (Case management in home care).
In: D. Graaf, H. (ed.), *Case management, een zorg minder? (Case management, one less worry?).*
Utrecht, Uitgeverij SWP, 1991.

Wennink, H.J. and S.E. Kooiker
Ontwerpvoorstel voor en thuiszorgscenario (Draft proposal for a home-care scenario).
Utrecht, NIVEL, 1988.

Wennink, H.J. and S.E. Kooiker
Een scenario voor de eerste lijn: methodologische overwegingen (A scenario for primary care: methodological considerations).
Tijdschrift Sociale Gezondheidszorg, 68, 1990, 3, 110-116.

Wijkel, D.
Onderzoeksvoorstel scenarioproject 'eerstelijnsgezondheidszorg' (Primary care scenario project: research proposal).
Utrecht, NIVEL, 1987.

Wijkel, D. and A. Morenc
  Vooronderzoek scenario-project 'eerstelijnsgezondheidszorg' (Primary care scenario project: preliminary research).
  Utrecht, NIVEL, 1987.

Wilk, J. van der
  Thuishulp vanuit het patiëntenperspectief bezien (Home care from the patient's viewpoint). In: *Congresbundel van de studieconferentie 'Coördinatie in de thuiszorg' (Papers from the study conference on coordination in home care).*
  Rotterdam, Nederlands Studie Centrum, 1988.

Willems, D.
  Coördinatie van zorg, niet opeisen maar aanpakken (Coordinating care: don't ask, act).
  Bunnik, ATIS, 1988.

Zandt, A.M.C. van de
  Thuiszorg nader bekeken (Home care reexamined).
  Medisch Contact, 42, 1987, 33, 1016.

Zawadski, R.T. and C. Eng
  Case Management in Capitated Long Term Care.
  Health Care Financing Review, 1988, Annual Supplement, 75-81.

Zee, J. van der
  De vraag naar diensten van de huisarts (Demand for GP services).
  Utrecht, NHI, 1982.

Zee, J. van der
  Over de grenzen van de eerste lijn (Across the boundaries of primary care).
  Inaugural lecture, Limburg State University, Maastricht, 1989.

Het Ziekenhuis (The Hospital, Journal)
  Hef lijnenspel op en kom tot geïntegreerde gezondheidszorg (End sectoral divisions and integrate health care).
  Het Ziekenhuis, 1987, 23-24, 1020-1023.

Het Ziekenhuis
  Over twintig jaar is één van de drie ziekenhuizen weg; Greve's visie op planning en bouw (In twenty years one in three hospitals will have gone; Greve's view of planning and construction).
  Het Ziekenhuis, 1988, 17, 744-747.

Het Ziekenhuis

Intramurale gezondheidszorg staat voor breekpunt in de geschiedenis
(Intramural health care at historic turning point).
Het Ziekenhuis, 1990, 16, 669-671.

Index